Strumpets & Ninnycocks

'A devil and no man' otherwise known as Sir Francis Drake,
engraved in c1745.

Strumpets & Ninnycocks

Name-calling in Devon, 1540–1640

TODD GRAY

THE
MINT
PRESS

To Paul Pickering

my former tutor in London, whose encouragement
kept me studying in England as an undergraduate
and who has been a cherished friend ever since

The Mint Press

© The Mint Press & Todd Gray 2016
First published 2016, revised edition 2025

ISBN 978-1-903-35684-5

Cover illustration: *Brothel* by Joachim Beuckelaer, 1562,
courtesy of Walters Art Museum

Cover designed by Topics – The Creative Partnership

The Mint Press, Taddyforde House South, Taddyforde Estate,
New North Road, Exeter EX4 4AT

Distribution: Stevensbooks either at www.stevensbooks.co.uk,
sales@themintpress.co.uk or 01392 459760

Designed, typeset, printed and bound in Great Britain by
Short Run Press Ltd, Exeter

CONTENTS

ACKNOWLEDGEMENTS

I owe a debt to three individuals who organised the Exeter diocesan collection in the twentieth century: Reverend J. F. Chanter, Olive Moger and Rosemary Dunhill made it possible for these documents to be used today. I am not aware that any historian has systematically examined these papers although I have benefitted from the work of Jonathan Vage,[1] Professor Mark Stoyle and Dr Robert Whiting, in his *The Blind Devotion of the People*, who have each assessed or used considerable parts of the collection. These documents have been extensively used for this study alongside depositions from borough courts held in Dartmouth, Exeter, Okehampton and Plymouth (held by the Devon Heritage Centre and Plymouth & West Devon Record Office) and others held in Exeter Cathedral Library & Archive. I am grateful to all the staff who have cheerfully brought out box after box of manuscripts. Staff at the Hampshire Archives & Local Studies Service as well as those at Durham University Library Special Collections have also been very helpful. One word 'greingoomber' has an uncertain transcription and I am indebted to Professor Jonathan Barry, John Booker, Dr Helen Bradley, Ren Jackaman and Tim Wormleighton, amongst others, for their advice. Lady Violet de Vere has continued to be a great support. I would also like to thank Professor Maryanne Kowaleski for her discussion on Exeter's scolds and Professor Richard Hitchcock, Dr Susan North, Richard O'Neill, Professor Mark Stoyle and Dr Andrew Thrush for their help in various stages of research, interpretation and writing. Finally, I would to express my thanks to the members of my Tuesday morning class who stoically endured subject material that might have overwhelmed other audiences.

Preface

Insults, like death and taxes, have been a constant part of the human experience. They continue to pepper everyday conversation as reflections of interpersonal relationships, tensions and rivalries. During the years 1540 to 1640, as now, comments were made in passing, sometimes in great anger and occasionally with considerable inventiveness and humour. The language was rich and the terms were varied. Words were mostly intended to mock, ridicule, scorn or embarrass and the upshot was a mixture of concern, humiliation, fury and a desire for redress. When wit and humour were expressed it sometimes demonstrated a jocular nature, particularly of male conversation, that was rarely recorded elsewhere. The confrontations also provide incidental information about a wide-ranging number of other topics such as vernacular architecture, midwifery and lace making. Insults reveal much about society. Yet, this has been an unexplored topic of enquiry for Devon despite considerable research having been conducted nationally.

It is possible to understand this century of name-calling because of the survival of hundreds of depositions given in several civil courts and in Exeter's Diocesan Court. The latter are among the most fascinating documents held in a Devon archive although as yet few historians have explored the richness of the material. Defamation cases are one of the most prevalent classes and through them can be discovered what was then considered an insult. It has to be understood that the witness statements were concerned with *alleged* name-calling and behaviour; in some or even many of the cases it may be that slander was not actually spoken but it remains significant that the charges were important enough to be declared and denied.

I first came across the church court collection in the mid 1980s while working towards my doctoral thesis and have returned to it in what has felt like hasty if not opportunistic 'snatch and grab' forays. But over the last two years I have reread those papers which cover the years from the Reformation to the Revolution. The extent of the material (it comprises thousands of sheets of paper), a confusing organization, intermittent illegibility and an occasional poor state has made this a daunting exercise. Some papers have been damaged by worm, mould, soot and 'water' particularly that left behind by mice or rats. A portion has been declared unfit for consultation and has awaited conservation for generations. Sections are without individual reference numbers and I have supplied (with permission) page numbers to several deposition volumes and many individual sheets. Frustratingly, parts of some cases can be found scattered across the collection. But the research has been at times exhilarating and always fascinating. Moreover, the papers provide details of Devon's history that cannot otherwise be discovered including what then comprised an insult.

I concluded in the 1980s that sections of the general public would find many words and some subject material not just coarse but probably offensive. I also had my doubts whether journal editors would welcome the breadth of language. It was at this time that the image I had chosen for the cover of my first book was rejected. To my dismay I was informed that a bare-breasted woman was not a suitable subject: the image was a cartouche of a mermaid from a map of the early 1600s but it was still considered risqué. It was then unclear what could be reasonably done with the slander evidence in published form or as a lecture: I envisioned rejected publication proposals or stacks of unsold books let alone deserted lecture halls. Sixteen years later, in 2001, I edited the testimonies relating to the seventeenth-century sexual misconduct of Reverend

John Prince who was, ironically, the author of *The Worthies of Devon*. I was warned that it might be considered inappropriate research and sully any reputation I had gained. *The Curious Sexual Adventure of the Reverend John Prince* went on to become one of my most popular books. However, some words and phrases in this volume are on another level altogether and I hope that on paper the language will not prove entirely shocking. There is no censoring of quotations and all terms and uses of language have hopefully been noted; I hope that contemporary historical debate and interest has sufficiently developed. However, in one respect society has gone backwards. Thirty years ago I freely discussed these documents with archival staff but modern sensibilities have changed regarding what is now considered appropriate language in the workplace. The occasional moments of surprise, disbelief and amazement in various record offices have had to be internalised, until now.

TG
Taddyforde, Exeter
August 2016

INTRODUCTION

Name-Calling, Slander and a Good Reputation

Insults during the 1500s and early 1600s differed greatly from those uttered today. Whereas modern name-calling often refers to one of three parts of the body, those of 400 to 500 years ago were more likely to denigrate incorrect behaviour, mock low intelligence or criticize physical characteristics. Much of the ridicule was about sex and not only was the language colourful but it is also highly informative about sexual practices. A second form of abuse was not verbalised: men and women ridiculed others by making gestures that intentionally broke social protocols. Backsides were shown, hats were worn inappropriately, tongues were stuck out and legs were cocked. Other men and women spat, gurned, urinated or farted. There were many different ways to give offence and being called a strumpet or ninnycock were merely two of them. This study is concerned with the ways in which men and women in Devon chose to name-call. Voices were raised in anger, ridicule or jest, and to not listen to them would be willful deafness.[2] Anyone who refuses to consider insulting gestures is, as an Elizabethan Devonian would have said, a blinkard.

Insults, slander and Devon

The most offensive insults were those given to God; words or oaths considered profane and blasphemous. These commonly referred to Christ's crucifixion such as God's Blood, God's Wounds and God's Heart but there were others including God's Nails. In this period there were constant prosecutions for blasphemy, including for these four terms, in the mayor's court for Exeter as well as those at Barnstaple and Dartmouth.[3] A ballad printed in 1614 itemised swearing:

> 'Much swearing many a one doth use,
>   and so the name of God abuse.
> Some swear by wounds, blood and heart,
>   by foot and sides, and every part;
> By mass, by cross, by light, by fire,
>   by bread, and all they can desire;
> By faith and troth, though they have none;
>   by saints, and angels, and many a one.
> Some swear by this, some swear by that;
>   and some do swear *they know not what.*'

Parliament passed a statute against profanity in 1623.[4]

Until there is another county study it will not be known whether Devonian insults in general greatly differed from those in the rest of England but Sir Walter Raleigh was no doubt representative of general sensibilities when he wrote about the need to keep a cautious tongue. He advised his son 'all quarrels, mischief, hatred and destruction ariseth from unadvised speech, and in much speech there are many errors, out of which thy enemies shall ever take the most dangerous advantage.' Young Walter was urged to avoid public disputes and to remember that 'the tongue of a man causeth him to fall'. The advice of Robert Furse, a gentleman of Dean Prior, was to 'have no delight to keep company with liars, cozeners, whisperers, flatterers, tale-tellers, rowlers, scolders or malicious and vicious persons but keep company with the best,

1. *Medieval carving of a man with his tongue out, one of many throughout Devon which possibly shows disdain or contempt, in the Church of St John the Baptist, Kennerleigh.*

wise and honest company, for the proverb is, the like will to the like'. He also cautioned 'let your mind rule your tongue. First hear, and then speak'.[5]

There are few relevant comments from other Devonians although in 1643 Henry Bourchier, 5th Earl of Bath, characterized Devonians as 'crafty clowns' and Robert Herrick, the poet who was famously discontented in his rectory at Dean Prior, also thought poorly of his parishioners ('rude – almost – as rudest savages').[6] William Cotton, who was consecrated bishop in 1598, complained of the 'western and turbulent people' who had amongst them 'many clamorous and malicious rattleheads'.[7] In contrast, a generation earlier John Hooker, who praised Devon in all things, famously boasted 'it is a common proverb, let a Devonshire man come but once to the court and he will be a courtier at the first'.

Hooker's friend Richard Carew noted his Cornish countrymen's common curses (*ten thousand mischiefs in your guts* and *a thousand vengeances take thee*) but neither have been found recorded in Devon. He also cited three insults (*stinking head, devil head* and *great head*) which have not been identified on this side of the river Tamar. Other Cornish examples are cited in the following pages because the county was part of the diocese of Exeter until 1876 and its slander cases form part of the church court records. Carew claimed the Cornish preferred the word 'boobish' to the English 'lubber'. He may have been unaware that in Exeter at least, and perhaps across Devon, this term was used as the adjective 'boobily': in 1565 a man was called a 'boobily knave', which came from 'booby', a stupid man.[8]

Every element of society in Devon, as elsewhere, endured verbal abuse. Throughout Elizabeth I's reign, and before, her sexual behaviour was subject to national and international speculation, gossip and abuse. A chaste reputation was integral to her pers-onification as the Virgin Queen and no doubt the experiences of her mother Anne Boleyn and sister Mary, as well as the reputation her father gained through his six marriages, made Elizabeth aware of the consequences rumour and chatter could have on her rule. Devonians with high profiles were correspondingly subject to gossip and name-calling. Raleigh was called an atheist, a dangerous epithet in the sixteenth century, and Sir Francis Drake was termed 'a devil and no man' by Spanish sailors after the defeat of their Armada. Sir John Hawkins had significant difficulties with his reputation after he offered his services to Spain but it has suffered much more so with his recent reinterpretation as England's first slaver.[9]

It could be expected that famous men were smeared given their lives were observed and commented upon to a greater degree than those of ordinary people. Men with a higher social position were also perhaps more sensitive to feeling their dignity was compromised. Hooker noted one instance. As the county's first historian he recounted 'the great controversy' between a Devon earl and the city council of Exeter. It originated with insufficient market supplies of fish. This nobleman felt personally insulted when sales to his household were restricted and the earl's argument with the mayor became so heated that his fellow councillors had to rescue him. But Hooker commented that the earl 'could never after brook the city nor any citizen' and later his aristocratic anger turned into malice.[10] As interesting as this vein of history is, this study is concerned with other insults and name-calling, and the upset it caused, among those who had more ordinary lives.

Hundreds of commonplace arguments were recorded in Devon's manuscripts particularly those of the church and civic courts. These were derogatory words, like many thousands of others which were said across Devon, which had advanced from a verbal exchange between two or more people to language which was identified as the basis of a legal prosecution. In effect, name-calling which was seen as ridiculing, mocking, scornful or insulting became legally defined as slanderous.

One such disagreement took place in 1619 at Exeter where wounding words passed between John Newcombe, a cloth maker, and John Harrison, a joiner, and progressed to the guild-hall where justices were told that these men and their wives had engaged in extensive and colourful name-calling. Harrison had called Newcombe a 'cod's head'. By this he probably meant that Newcombe was stupid but he was possibly also referring to a cod in the sense that it was another word for a scrotum. Harrison's wife was told that she had the pox, that she was balding because of disease and it was suggested her backside needed a plaster to cover the pustules. She was also called a drunkard who had been so overcome at the home of Marian Atkins that she had 'pissed where she sat'. Harrison himself was compared with a man named Chollacomb who had been dragged on a hurdle through the streets. These boards were used to bring traitors to their execution. Harrison was also called Doctor Lupus, presumably in relation to the ulcerous disease of the skin. These sharp words hint at more complicated histories but there is a lack of supporting information which makes the insults difficult to fully interpret.[11]

Equally uncertain, and yet more intriguing, is the invective thrown at Joseph Baker in Barnstaple. In 1635 he was called a rogue, a base cuckoldly rogue, a whoremaster, a base whoremaster rogue, a runagate rogue and a beggarly rogue. These terms, as will be seen, were in common usage. It was slightly more unusual that Baker accused his adversary, Richard Harris, of going 'from inn to alehouse and from alehouse to taverns and whorehouses'. But the most extraordinary phrase of all was that Harris told Baker to 'go [again] into Spain and dance with the niggers with bells about thy heels'. No further explanation was made of this comment except one observer interpreted it as meaning that Baker 'had lived incontinently with niggers in Spain'. 'Incontinency' was the inability to restrain sexual passions.[12] The specific reference to bells suggests it was a recognizable form of Spanish dance, perhaps a version of what is now known as Morris dancing. Baker would have had the opportunity of visiting Spain through the commercial ties this North Devon port then had with the Iberian Peninsula. Barnstaple was one of the most ethnically diverse places in Devon and home to some seven 'Negro' or 'Nigger' servants. These two terms were used in the town's parish register to describe men, women and infants. The two terms derive from the Latin adjective *niger* for black and the Spanish and Portuguese derivatives *negro* and the modern hostile use of 'nigger' was first in print in 1775. Another word was also then used to describe Africans: a few miles

2. *Smoking and drinking, two vices of the late 1500s, which were occasionally associated with angry words, by Dirk (Theodorus) Helmbreker, of about 1650.*

away at Tawstock the household accounts of Henry Bourchier, 5th Earl of Bath, record salary payments to 'James Blackamore' who was also referred to as 'James the Blackamoor'.[13] This term was also recorded elsewhere in Devon as having been descriptive rather than necessarily derogatory.[14]

Harris' reference to Spain is a reminder of Devon's then prominence in privateering, exploration and empire. The county remains best known for the establishment of Newfoundland's fishery in the early 1500s, Sir Francis Drake's circumnavigation of the globe from 1577 to 1580, the Lost Colony of Roanoke in Virginia in the 1580s, the defeat of the Armada in 1588 and the sailing of the Pilgrims on the *Mayflower* in 1620. But not one of these events is referred to in the court cases. Instead, the name-calling took place in the settings of everyday life in Devon. Not surprisingly, it occurred in private homes as well as in such places as the market stalls in Exeter, under the arches of Barnstaple Guildhall, at a well in Revelstoke, at a smithy in Tavistock, on Pilton Bridge, in a mill at Rattery and in a weaver's workshop in Paignton.[15] Individuals heard abuse while drying oats in a Littleham malt house, reaping the harvest in Kingskerswell, buying tin at Belstone, coming home from an ale in St Marychurch, ploughing in Poughill, on the way to a harvest dinner at Clayhidon, in the midst of giving birth in Coldridge, hacking of ground in Rewe, on horseback from Rackenford to Sandford, while spinning in Shebbear, weeding in Crediton, at a hurling match at Pyworthy and in the midst of washing clothes in Dawlish.[16] Other insults were doled out while men were drinking or playing cards and other games.[17]

Alice Doddridge was an ordinary Devon woman whose resentment of insults brought her to court but in her case witnesses provided a fuller background than that of the alleged dancer Joseph Baker. The events took place in 1616 in Exeter which was then bustling and would remain Devon's most populous urban area until overtaken by Devonport in the 1700s. Exeter was the centre of the county's woollen cloth trade and had yet to reach its commercial height. That summer Mrs Joan Edmonds, who lived at the lower end of the city in the parish of All Hallows on the Walls, secured Doddridge's services as a midwife. Three other women assisted with the birth. Some fifteen minutes before the delivery a messenger arrived asking Doddridge to leave Mrs Edmonds and attend to a neighbour's dog that was about to give birth. Doddridge prepared to depart but was prevented by the other women. She then asked for the canine to be sent to her but one woman said 'if there was a bitch brought thither this deponent would take it and throw it over the town walls whereunto she [Doddridge] said, *No, by God, not so. Many a body loveth a dog and so do I, and many one will not give his dog for an angel* [a gold coin] & this deponent swore again that if it were brought thither she would throw it over the town walls.' Doddridge attended to the dog after the baby was delivered.[18]

Several lawsuits emanated from this episode. Richard Edmonds cited her for attempting to leave during his child's birth and noted that 'every woman that shall take upon her to be a midwife ought to be a woman of good and honest behaviour and of good name and fame and that every midwife is bound at all times and places especially at the time and place when she doth attend or help any woman that is in travail with child to behave and carry herself honestly and soberly and ought not to leave or forsake or to offer herself to leave or forsake any woman travailing with child before she be delivered, without some extraordinary urgent and necessary occasion'. Doddridge agreed but she found that rumours of her behaviour had circulated. In May 1617 Andrew Stabback met her in Friernhay and called her an old whore, old bawd and old ratted whore. He also said she was unfit to deliver any woman's child and to 'deliver a bitch again'. Stabback instructed her to go to the sign of The Three Pigeons, presumably an alehouse with a poor reputation, and said he would 'buy a plot for her'.[19] A year later Stabback was forced to apologise in church. He approached the minister, showed him the prescribed apology and said to Doddridge 'I am enjoined by the court to ask thee forgiveness but I care not whether thou forgive me or not, the witnesses have sworn that I call thee whore and old whore and old bawd and bid thee go to The Three Pigeons but I never said so but they have sworn it. I care not whether thou forgive me or no.' It did not end there. Stabback once again called Doddridge an old whore as well as a thief.[20] Doddridge won her initial case but her reputation may not have remained intact.

Doddridge's case is unusual in that background information helps construct a narrative for why she was abused but having been called a whore, old whore or old bawd was not uncommon. At least one justice, as will be seen, tried to eradicate swearing in Exeter in the early 1600s and it could be assumed that such language was widespread if not prevalent. Even so, it is unlikely many individuals freely admitted to having an uncontrollable swearing habit. One exception, who lived on the western edge of Dartmoor, claimed she was trying to stop. In 1566 Margaret Worth confessed 'that about

7 or 8 years ago this respondent dwelt with one Mrs Kake of Mary Tavy who was a great swearer and there this respondent learned of her to swear and [it] is now grown into a custom by reason thereof to swear by the Mass, God's Blood and God's Bones when this respondent is angered with her neighbours, and her husband hath beaten her 40 times for it but yet she cannot leave it and is sorry for it and will leave it so soon as God will give her leave.'[21] Her offensive language appears to have been blasphemous rather than in the nature of the personal insults which not just caused offence but ruined reputations.

In the years from 1540 to 1640 religious and political changes gave rise, as will be seen, to the uttering of many insults. An argument in Exeter Cathedral during the Christmas holidays in 1641, in the last few months before civil war erupted, shows how sharp words reflected the increasing tensions between factions. Two young men pushed into the quire, kept their hats on and spoke loudly. One worshipper asked them to display better manners but the intruders escalated the friction by questioning the legitimacy of the service and then ridiculed the music: they offered to find tinkerly rogues whose horns and pipes would provide better music. The two men finally suggested dancing in the cathedral before telling the dean to 'go shit'. Eight months later the city took up arms for war and such verbal disputes were being decided on the battlefield.[22]

Insults took unusual forms with even inappropriate clothing being considered offensive such as when in 1561 Thomas Goodale, an Exeter servant, had showed presumption and disrespect to his betters by his 'unseemly apparel'. The affront given by wearing great hose, great ruffs and a silk hat earned Goodale a fine of 3s 4d.[23] As already noted, there were both verbal and gestural insults. Some could be made by both word and action such as calling men a cuckold, which meant that his wife was unfaithful, or suggesting it by exhibiting animal horns or crooking fingers to 'make horns'. Some implied gestures were also scatalogical including many men, notably, being told by other men to kiss their backsides. This extended into references to farting and excrement.

3. *In the midst of everyday life words were said which caused upset. This scene depicts a Dutch peasant festival, by Adriaen van Ostade, c1674.*

Anyone could be so insulted: in 1567 a Silverton woman was told she was a whore of whom no man 'would set a turd by her within ten miles'.[24]

Both men and women were abused by allegations of sexual activity outside marriage, for having illegitimate children and for being diseased. Sexual misconduct formed the basis of nearly every insult hurled at women and a considerable portion of those against men. Both sexes were called drunkards, beggars and witches. In addition, men were also insulted regarding their honesty and intelligence while women were nearly exclusively ridiculed in being called gossips or scolds.[25] Men and women were also taunted about their physical appearances. A husband's arched description of his wife in *A Peerless Paragon*, a contemporary ballad, matched similar mocking in Devon.

> 'Her squinting, staring, goggle eyes
>   Poor children do affright;
> Her nose is of the Saracen's size;
>   Oh, she's a matchless wight.

11

4. A couple 'playing' on a bed, in a contemporary engraving.

Her ears so hound-like, that they fall
  Upon her shoulder bone;
I know not truly how to call
  Her, she's such a worthy one.

Her oven-mouth wide open stands,
  Her teeth like rotten peas;
Her blabber-lips my heart commands,
  Her neck all bit with fleas;
Her tawny dugs, like two great hills,
  Hang sow-like to her waist;
Her body's round as a windmill,
  And yet I hold her chaste.

Her belly tun-like to behold,
  No more shall be expressed,
But if the truth were plainly told,
  I'm sure they are the best:

Her brawny blind-cheeks plump and round,
    As any horse of war;
Her speckled thighs they are not sound,
    Her knees like hogs' heads are.

Her shoulders are so camel-like,
    She'd make an excellent porter;
I vow I never knew her like,
    If any man consort her.
No shoulder of mutton like her hand
    For thickness, breadth and fat;
With a scurvy mange upon her wrist,
    Oh Jove! how I love that!'[26]

Hundreds of Devonians felt so aggrieved at a perceived insult that they took advantage of an opportunity open to them by law: they went to the church court. Others reported intemperate words to the civil courts. These two sources form the principal evidence for this study.

Court cases, witnesses and their evidence

Unbecoming language featured in the civil court records for Exeter, Okehampton and, to a lesser extent, Plymouth. Some speakers were prosecuted for using uncivil words with fellow citizens or council employees but other profanities or ridicule were recorded in investigations into other alleged misbehaviour. In some instances these words and terms differed, as will be seen, from those noted in the church court.

Indifference, if not contempt, for both courts was occasionally shown. In 1557 a Kenton parishioner dismissed the consequences of losing a case when he said 'the extremity of the law is no more but to go in a white sheet and it is but a sheet'. It was only, he added, a slight matter.[27] In 1620 an Exeter man scorned his potential punishment in saying 'I could but be hanged' and this was also said by another Exeter man who then 'put his hand to his throat saying it would be but a halter and a knot'.[28] In the Cornish town of Bodmin another slanderer said 'if I do not prove it I will give up my head'.[29] William Harrison in his *Description of England* echoed these sentiments in 1587. He felt punishments were widely disregarded and wrote 'this is counted with some either as no punishment at all to speak of or but smally regarded of the offenders'. He asked 'what great smart is it to be turned out of a hot sheet into a cold, or after a little washing in the water to be let loose again unto their former trades?'[30]

The church court was particularly unpopular among reformers but also with Catholics. In the early 1600s a parishioner of South Hill in East Cornwall dismissed being cited as he 'cared not the wagging of a dog's tail'.[31] If the local 'bawdy court' had become detested by then, the national Court of High Commission was even less popular. It enforced national conformity in religion but those who lost a case had no right of appeal. It was compared at the time with the Spanish Inquisition and by 1589 it was claimed that not one person brought before it had been found innocent.[32]

An individual who felt an insult had impaired his or her reputation could seek justice in their diocesan church court. It had jurisdiction over a range of offences although, as will be shown later, there was some overlap with civil courts. Tithes, non-payment of some taxes, rights over pews, medical licenses, probate, and accusations against the clergy were just some of the business which was conducted. The legal foundation for prosecuting defamation originated as early as 1222.[33] Those men and women found guilty would be charged costs, made to do penance or ultimately excommunicated.

Witnesses made statements and were identified with the place in which he or she lived although this was not always as straightforward as it might appear. It was explained in one dispute that the accused shared his name with three other Cullompton men also named John Maye.[34] While it had to be shown there was a public scandal with a consequential loss of reputation, many insults also alleged that crimes had taken place such as theft, sex outside marriage, illegitimate children or murder. In making a defamation accusation, the accused became the accuser.

Statements were verbatim accounts; they were meant to record the exact words that were allegedly spoken. It is of less importance to this study whether the slander was true than in that these were insults that were complained about. There is no certainty in the honesty of witnesses given all depositions concerned allegations of misbehaviour. It could be assumed that in many instances abusive words were actually spoken but some witnesses protested that they were not accurately recorded. Some words were clearly spoken with malice or spite; it is evident that some individuals had long histories of enmity. Evidence could not always have been impartial. Witnesses claimed that antagonists were capital, deadly or professed enemies and some protagonists admitted that they had been unfriendly for a stated period of time. The most vivid description of this was given in Creacombe in 1572. Richard Parkhouse said that when he and James Dodge got together they 'did agree like two butcher dogs'. Moreover, Parkhouse did not want to be interred in the same churchyard as Dodge. He feared they would not rest but rise up and 'would scratch and claw like caterwauling cats.'[35] In other instances it was made clear there were years of 'divers strifes and contentions' or 'rises and contentions' between parties.[36] Some witnesses explained their ongoing dispute. For instance, in Crediton one woman blamed another for her father's financial losses; her anger triggered the subsequent verbal abuse.[37] Likewise, Thomas Badge of South Tawton felt aggrieved when a neighbour complained that his dog had killed a sheep and he subsequently called her a bobtailed whore amongst other insults.[38]

Witnesses had to have heard slander spoken openly in public. Hence in Kingsteignton in 1575 a parishioner thought the 'open speaking' of the words 'must needs be a diminishing of the good name' of the slandered. A Sheldon parishioner recalled that an insult had been whispered in her ear so she repeated it aloud in order for another to witness it. Another slanderer said, in Newton Tracey church, that the vicar's wife had a reputation so filthy that it was unrepeatable. Even those words were slanderous.[39]

15

In some instances a single individual spoke scandalous words but in other cases witnesses heard a mutual exchange of abuse. For instance, in Exeter in 1582 Judith Boyes called John Brook a cuckold and he castigated her as a whore, a 'towncast' curtal and a tallow-faced whore.[40] In 1617 William Isaac prosecuted Elizabeth Butt for calling him a drunkard and a drunken rogue while she accused him of calling her a strumpet and John Evan's whore.[41] Likewise, in 1623 Julian Wood told Jane Castle she was John Biddicombe's whore and Castle told Wood that not only had she been occupied behind a door but she had bought an observer's silence with a jug of beer.[42]

Some cases were halted before sentencing. One of these took place in Dartmouth, then one of Devon's most prosperous ports. During the autumn of 1634 John Bagwell heard chiding and angry words in the street and he looked out of his window to see his neighbours, Joan Penny and John Tailor, in the midst of an argument. The following July he testified that he had heard

Tailor say 'Oh Joan, Joan, remember the butcher that dressed four quarters with one prick? There was one which came out of Exeter which might have been carted out'. Two other witnesses added that he called Penny a dunghill slut. The two parties reconciled nearly three years later: they had a drink and 'pledged' to one another, that is made a promise of good will. Moreover, Penny acquitted Tailor of any court costs, undertook never to molest or trouble him and instructed her legal representative to clear him of further action. Several days later they met once more over breakfast and Penny confirmed all necessary actions had been concluded. It may have been a false allegation given that at least two witnesses had close personal ties with Penny.[43]

Another Dartmouth woman, Elizabeth Hill, also terminated her case with a neighbour, Joan Blackaller, who had called her a whore. Hill received a financial payment from Blackaller.[44] When Elizabeth Braddon lay dying at Alverdiscott in 1612 she sought to end a dispute with Susan Barwick who had said Braddon had illicit sex under a furse bush in the snow. Braddon expressed the hope that God would forgive Barwick as she did. Barwick visited Braddon and said 'you are offended with me for words that I should speak by you, which were made a great deal worse than I did speak them, but seeing that they are offensive unto you I am come to ask your forgiveness for them'.[45] In another instance, two Exeter men ended their dispute by drinking a cup of ale and pledging their friendship. Ironically, one had called the other a drunkard.[46]

An attempt to settle a dispute between two men in Uplyme, on the border with Dorset, resulted in a second complaint. Margery Tidbury protested that when in 1623 Mary Gates had asked her husband John if he had managed to smooth relations with John Tidbury, Mrs Gates had added that it would have been concluded earlier if Mrs Tidbury had not been 'thy whore these seven years'.[47]

◀ 5. *A cottage in Kingsteignton painted by Samuel Prout in about 1819. In this village Richard Benner was allegedly called a knave, false knave and an old fornicator in 1575.*

17

Overlap between the church and civil courts

In 1570 the bishop expressed concern to Exeter's mayor that his court was infringing upon his own church court's jurisdiction in punishing Exonians for sexual misbehaviour.[48] In 1558 Thomas Ware was one such man who had been prosecuted in both courts. Ware had said that Grace Griffiths had stolen two loaves of brown bread but later admitted that he had no justification for saying so. He was imprisoned for five days at the guildhall and then was brought up before the church court.[49] The overlap was separate from a long-standing dispute between Exeter's church and civic authorities over jurisdiction of the cathedral environs. This may have been settled by 1639 when a successive bishop, Joseph Hall, suspected a servant of Archdeacon Helliar had been stealing his pigeons and used the mayor's court to prosecute him for a civil crime.[50]

The dispute over an apparent overlap between the two courts ran through the 1620s. On 4 October 1622 John Medland, an Exeter musician, testified before the church court that he could not have fathered Peter, an illegitimate child of Jane Hobbs, because he 'was an impotent and broken man and therefore could not beget her with child but yet said & confessed that he could not deny or at least not swear that he had never had the carnal knowledge of the body of the said Jane Hobbs'.[51] John Tilly, another Exeter man, also used this excuse regarding another woman: he claimed 'neither did he ever entice or solicit her to have his pleasure of her, for he is impotent and unable to commit any such act with any woman'.[52] However, in Medland's case three months later, on 1 January 1623, the mayor noted that Hobbs had named Medland as the father and ordered him to pay the baby's maintenance.[53]

Occasionally different cases in the two courts fill out the background. For example, in July 1620 an Exeter constable reported to the mayor that he observed William Austin, an innkeeper, climb a widow's stairs. He watched Thomasine Westcott, another widow, follow him and then saw:

'Thomasine Westcott sat down upon the chest, then the said Austin came to her where she sat and thrust his hands under her coats 3 or

6. *Spitting, as shown on this sixteenth-century carving on a bench end in St George's Church at Monkleigh, has been a long-standing act of derision.*

7. *Outside the South Gate as drawn by Thomas Rowlandson. It was here that William Morrell was imprisoned in the early 1600s. The gate was demolished two hundred years later.*

4 times. Then the said Thomasine had gotten his yard into her hand, chastening of it and then the said Austin would strike it upon her hand, saying *where is she gone?* Presently afterwards one Anne Crutchard, daughter to the said Thomasine, came up and the said Austin did likewise thrust his hand into her placket [a slit in a garment] using some words unto her (what they were he this informant knoweth not) but the said Anne replied *This man is as hasty as though he were ready to die for want*, whereupon the said Austin took her by the arm and drew her into the midst of the room and as this examinant thinketh they went into another room where they continued by the space of one quarter of an hour or near thereabouts'.

Westcott was later prosecuted for procuring her daughter Anne who was also convicted of leading an idle and uncivil life. Both were imprisoned. Two years later Austin appeared in the church court complaining that he had been called a cuckold.[54]

Two different court cases hint at the elusive character of Mrs Rebecca Roberts. In a case before the mayor Roberts complained she was called a 'Puritan Whore' because she had requested a neighbour be less noisy late at night. At about the same time the church court forced another neighbour to ask for Roberts' forgiveness in Holy Trinity Church because she too had called Roberts a whore.[55] Much more certain is the nature of William Morrell which was expressed in a series of church and civil court cases. He called one neighbour 'a cuckold, a cuckoldly knave and a cuckoldly roastmeat', another he termed a witwol,[56] he said a couple were unfaithful to one another and he insulted Nicholas Vingwell by calling him a cuckold. When Morrell was reproved for the latter remark he said 'I will prove him to be a cuckold for I saw one Tothill, a papist, in the high gaol occupy her the said Margaret Vingwell'.[57] Four neighbours, two of whom brought defamation cases against Morrell, called him a drunkard, a drunken rogue, a whoremaster, a whoremonger and a base whoremongering rogue. There was also a subsequent appearance in the mayor's court which confirmed that Morrell had been imprisoned at the South Gate. He threatened to kill Nicholas Vingwell and further insulted him by asking if Vingwell could supply him with ram's mutton or bull beef.[58] By the first term he may have implied a cuckold's wife who was available for sex and the latter could have been a cuckold's penis.[59] These terms were also referred to in the ballad 'The Merry Cuckold' of 1629 in which a cuckold states:

> 'Many a time
> upbraided I am,
> Some say I must dine,
> at the Bull or the Rams.'

Another contemporary ballad noted that the tavern for cuckolds was the Ram.[60]

Reputations

At the heart of many prosecutions was maintaining a good reputation. For some, a consequence of rumours associating them with sexual misbehaviour was a subsequent legal prosecution for fornication.[61] This happened when a woman told her Winkleigh neighbours that Nicholas Raleigh had had illicit sex: Raleigh then faced a charge of fornication. However, once he cleared his name Raleigh sued his neighbour for defamation. In 1557 a Plymouth man argued that he was slandered by being called a thief and villain but, more importantly, he said his life was imperiled when he was named a traitor. It also clearly worried two Exeter people when they were called murderers.[62]

Poor reputations could damage the ability to earn a living. This was the case with Alice Maunder, a baker in Bow. In 1576 a rumour spread that she had syphilis and she became 'so feared of her neighbours for that disease that nobody will almost buy any bread of her.' An East Devon midwife, described as 'true and trusty', found it difficult to be employed after she was wrongly accused of stealing. A poor reputation could also threaten housing: the trustees of Axminster's almshouse had the right from 1621 to evict residents defamed with the crimes of drunkenness, adultery, fornication, theft or brawling.[63]

Name-calling could also damage marital prospects. A Dartmouth woman allegedly had her engagement suspended by her fiancée until she proved her innocence. She was one of many such women: in 1576 Joan Savery of Totnes was allegedly unfaithful and the consequence was, a neighbour claimed, 'by reason of these words her husband doth much mislike with the said Joan Savery and is gone from her until she can clear herself of the said reports'.[64] Joan Gibbons, a married woman of Plymouth, had a similar experience: after she was called a whore in 1540 it was claimed 'her husband is like to turn her out at the door for the same'.[65] Likewise, at Dunsford in 1586 a slandered woman was 'hurted by the said speeches and by report her husband to put her from him by reason thereof' and of the rumours regarding a Plymouth wife in 1597 it was claimed 'her husband taketh them in such evil part that he sayeth he will put her from him unless she can clear herself'.[66] Ann Carwithy did not fare any better. In 1616 her husband allegedly believed rumours she was unfaithful and not only had he left her but made her wear old clothes in court to defend herself. He allegedly told her 'they were good enough to go unto the devil in'.[67] The difficulties that a woman could find herself in was expressed in the circumstances of an Exeter woman who 'had brought in men into her house to play the knaves with her and now her husband hearing of it sayeth that he will turn her out of doors and will not live with her except she prove herself an honest woman and she hath 2 young children and knoweth not what to do'.[68] In 1558 the sullied reputation of a Colyton woman caused her to marry. She had been suspected of having illicit sex and decided 'that it should be better for her to marry with him than any other man because she is slandered with him'.[69]

One witness observed the power that slander could have. Robert Cole of Cullompton said 'if any evil name be brought up upon any person it will not be easily put away' while of a Winkleigh widow it was alleged in 1561 that 'men have her in less estimation for this rumour and talk that is had of her'. In 1577 a Stockleigh Pomeroy neighbour warned Florence Bond that she was earning herself an ill reputation because she kept company with young people and attended village revels. He advised her 'to behave herself better that the people might speak better of her'.[70]

Margaret Fox is a striking example of a victim of rumour and the consequence of having a poor reputation; she was repeatedly forced to relocate across the South Hams. Fox explained in 1558 that for 18 years she had lived in Malborough then moved to Modbury, Cornwood and finally to Townstal outside Dartmouth. Gossip circulated that Fox's mother-in-law had taught her witchcraft and the slander, spread by one woman, 'followed her in every place where she came'. Fox explained she had tried, but failed, to be 'out of the speech of folks'.[71] In 1630 Joan Winter, originally of Holbeton, moved more than 3,000 miles from Plymouth to a fishing plantation in New England but her slander as the most drunken whore in Plymouth followed her across the Atlantic and it was there used against her. Mrs Winter also had to defend herself from reports that she had ill-treated her servant girl, Priscilla Bickford. Letters sent across the ocean, and probably tales from scores of Devon fishermen, reported that the maid had been beaten. John Winter, the manager of the island station in Maine, admitted that she had been punished but stressed that the girl went 'meeching' [missing] in the woods and was 'so fat and soggy' that she could hardly work and that the fishermen did not want her to boil the kettle because 'she is so sluttish'.[72] This Devonian's use of the word 'meeching' is interesting in that it is now largely only used in New England.

A poor reputation, such as for being a scandalmonger, could undermine credibility as a court witness. Agnes Heddon, of an un-identified parish, was dismissed in 1626 for being 'a poor beggarly woman, one that goeth from door to door, or at least one that goeth often to the house of the said Jane Rice for relief and there hath it, a common tale teller and a runagate and such a one as for a piece of bread or for some small piece of money will say or swear anything upon her oath'.[73] Another witness was witheringly described in 1622 as 'a man of base and lewd condition, of ill behaviour, an alehouse haunter, and one that hath been often times drunk, and is given to tippling and base company, a very beggar and one that doth profess the black art or a kind of conjuring and doth take money to give notice of things that be stolen or lost, and for a base companion and such a one to whom no credit upon his oath is to be given, one that will say or swear anything for a pot of ale'.[74] The lack of a good reputation was stressed in 1631 when describing John Bartlett of an unknown East Devon parish. He was supposedly 'a base, dishonest, beggarly, poor fellow of no credit or reputation, one that liveth by serving and executing processes, a common bailiff, and was the reputed father of a base child unlawfully begotten on the body of Alice Sweetland of

Axminster who accused him for the same. A filching, thievish and peeking fellow and did steal or was questioned for stealing one John Hand's geese of Dalwood and was whipped at the castle of Exeter for his thievery'.[75] In 1640 the testimony of a witness for Agnes Pratt of Exeter was undermined when it was claimed that Pratt had loaned Grace Grosse clothes 'in regard her own were so ragged and torn as the said Agnes Pratt was ashamed to produce her as a witness and the said Agnes Pratt was so distrustful that the said Grace Grosse would run away with the clothes that she had lent or procured for her that she stripped them off her back ere her return home'.[76]

Credibility was regularly questioned in suggesting that witnesses were unable to be truthful. Hence, in 1585 a Bradworthy woman was described as a common liar and her neighbours' slanderer. This contrasts with a Combe Martin parishioner who was said not to be a liar, harlot, drunkard or in poverty and therefore could not be pressured to tell anything in court but the truth.[77]

The slandered had to prove that their reputations were impaired by the insults. Hence, in 1612 Mary Cowte claimed that her good name had been 'taken away' when she was called a whore and a bottle-arsed jade.[78] Likewise, in 1572 a number of Moretonhampstead parishioners testified that Martin Gross's reputation had been tarnished by Elizabeth Laskey calling him a bulged knave. One explained the 'bulged knave are slanderous words and they do signify that he which is so called is a man of evil life and one that is burnt with a whore according to the opinion and interpretation of this deponent and as he hath heard it often and sundry times so to be accounted and taken in those parts whereas this deponent doth now dwell and that among honest persons his good name and fame is hindered greatly which is so spoken of and so common people do take the same'.[79] Likewise, an Exeter woman was said to have given birth to an illegitimate child in Wales in 1634 and this had a 'great impairing of her credit and reputation amongst those who did bear good will unto her and affected her'.[80]

Witnesses occasionally stressed that reputations were unharmed.

William Maunder's reputation in Rackenford was allegedly un-changed after being called a whoremonger because it was already known he had fathered an illegitimate child. Likewise, in 1618 a witness stressed that two Halberton slanderers had probably ruined each other's reputation equally.[81]

Penance acknowledged the harm. In 1636 damaging insults were flung at Judith Scorch of Shobrooke: she was called a base whore, a thievish whore and a long-nosed whore. For his penance James Dally was ordered to come to church and there say 'in a humble manner':

> 'Whereas I have spoken slanderous words of you Judith Scorch tend-ing to the disgrace and the impairing of your good name, I do here acknowledge that I have offended the law and defamed you there, and am heartily sorry for the same and do desire you to forgive me and I do promise never to offend you in the like manner hereafter'.[82]

Name-calling then, as now, could redefine public perceptions of an individual. This happened in Topsham in 1560. Francis Gale was called a knave and he acknowledged his slanderer by thanking him for 'the new coat that you gave me'. He also referred to it as his new livery.[83]

Disseminating rumours

The low literacy rate in this period made verbal communication the principal means of disseminating news, rumour and gossip. The small population size of Devon's towns and villages accelerated this. In 1600 Exeter had the highest population with some 10,000 people, comparable to modern Honiton or Ilfracombe, while many villages had only a few hundred people. The courts heard that details of private lives were quickly circulated and reputations ruined. Hence, a tale of illicit sex in 1568 in Marldon had become 'the voice of the people'; it was said that 'Nicholas Prowse doth resort unto Margaret Jane at suspect hours'.[84] Nine years before an exchange between two men in the same Torbay village shows how gossip could spread. Richard Pulsford testified that he met another parishioner, Richard Skerne, in a field during the Christmas holidays. Skerne asked:

'What news about Marldon?'

'None at all.'

'Do not you hear that Welthian Hassard is with child?'

'I do hear so indeed.'

'When did you hear so?'

'A fortnight agone.'

'That is almost as soon as I did hear of it. Doest not thou hear that it is mine?'

Puslford admitted he had.[85] At another time Skerne also asked another man while they were hedge-making 'What news at Brixham?' to which a similar exchange followed:

'None'.

'I am sure that you do.'

'The truth is my wife told me Easter night of some. That was you should beget Welthian Hassard with child but I do not believe it.'[86]

At Topsham the same phrase was recorded in 1583 when William Bagwell asked Margery Martin 'What news at Topsham?'

'There is some good and some bad'.

'What bad news is there?'

'Mary, Robert Frie and his wife are fallen out.'

Demanding the cause she answered 'He found Mr Smith's man with her.'[87]

The question 'What news?' was also asked in the village green at Horwood in 1541 and one parishioner replied that in Exeter 'I heard say that you should speak slanderous words by Fishley's wife.' At Alphington in 1585 the same question was also used in regard to a local woman, Joan Michael, and one man forbid his servants from repeating a scandalous story although he said that his field could 'tell tales if it were able to speak'.[88]

Slander was reported as being news in Shebbear in 1615 ('that arrant hollow-mouthed whore Alice James hath brought this news here'), at Kenton in 1617 ('did then and there hear Ann Scadlake say and report that the news was full in the town that a mare was skinned [had sex] down in Mr Hobbs his broom close') and in the same parish in 1604 ('Gossip, I can tell you news – I do hear say that Richard Frost hath a bastard or two at Porlock').[89] Other commonly used terms used was that it was 'spread abroad in the parish', the 'common report', 'the common cry' or 'the common speech'. At Newton Poppleford the behaviour of a woman and her brother-in-law was 'a talk and a bruit'. At Bradninch one witness claimed 'the world did know she did amiss'.[90] But, as already noted, idle talk was not necessarily repeated and believed: a woman heating her father's oven in Colebrooke heard another woman was pregnant 'but said she would not be the author of it nor report thereof before she heard more talk of it'.[91]

Slanderers were sometimes disparaged on the grounds they were merely railers, brabblers, common scolds, scandlers or common taletellers. An unusual insult was given to a Broadclyst woman in 1565: she was told 'she was a slanderous woman of tongue and that she were better to be a whore of her tail rather than of her tongue'. In contrast, a supporter of one Exeter woman who was slandered (she was called 'a jade, a runagate jade, a rogue, a runagate rogue, beggarly rogue and art not worth a quart pot or a groat') was claimed to be 'of far better life and conversation & far better rank & quality than the said Mary Cholwill, meek and lowly, peaceable amongst her neighbours and such a one as is no way given to scolding nor would speak a disgraceful word of any one unless mightily thereunto provoked'.[92]

Non-verbal insults and rough justice

Some insults were not vocalized such as at Sampford Courtenay in 1549 when the corpse of a man regarded as a heretic was given a disrespectful burial. The first casualty of the Prayer Book Rebellion was William Hellions, a gentleman who intervened when objections were raised to the new Book of Common Prayer on the 10th day of June. Hellions was 'hacked to pieces' by the rebels and his coffin was orientated not facing east as was customary but from north to south. That this was intended to indicate contempt is shown when nearly a century later an objection was made in Jacobstowe in 1628 to the rector's insistence on burying the dead north to south. The petitioners noted this was against not only English tradition but particularly that of the diocese of Exeter.[93]

Nevertheless, physical acts were used in church, and elsewhere, to apologise for insults. There were two forms of penance to demonstrate humility. One involved holding a white rod and standing in a white sheet with bare legs, heads and feet. The other was to admit the offence before the victim, who was often in his or her seat, and recite a prescribed apology. During the generation before this period penitents preceded their apology by holding a candle as they walked before the processional cross around the parish church.[94]

Contempt could be shown by merely sitting or wearing a hat in a scornful manner. Thus, as will be seen in the pages below, three Exeter councillors registered their disapproval of the reading of a royal proclamation in the cathedral by putting on their hats. One of these men had a history of objecting to others wearing hats in his presence. Parishioners belittled in this way, by turning their backs or showing their backsides. Parish churches provided the setting for many offensive or slanderous actions. It was in her parish church that one Bradninch woman deployed various gestures to demean a neighbour in 1606. It was claimed that Margaret English 'when she cometh to church to make legs (as men used to do) unto the foresaid Anne Wright contrary to the usage of any good Christian in that place' and that this was done in a mocking and scoffing manner. 'Making legs' was to bow. She also made 'a wry face' and spat. Finally, she was seen 'grinding her teeth and looking so fiercely that this deponent hath often times thought she would forbear to lay violent hands on her'.[95] Spitting was recorded in such other places as Exeter, Bradstone, Okehampton, Axminster and Staverton but undoubtedly it was a more widely practiced act of contempt.[96]

In 1620 complaints were made about Roger Searle, a servant, in Exeter. He had called Jonathan Wood a base rogue, slave, knave, cock leg and pancake. Searle also hummed at Mrs Wood, Christian

Staverton and her daughter. The significance of humming was explained in court: it was said that men 'of that trade do when an unhonest woman passeth by'. Staverton clarified that because her daughter was betrothed the humming 'may turn to her great defame'.

Searle was also accused of using another form of non-verbal abuse: he urinated into rooms which were not his own. Wood asked him why he acted 'so unmannerly' but Searle merely called him more names. It was explained that Searle 'made water into the window that it fell down upon the table when they had been at dinner and supper'. A maidservant castigated him but he replied 'a pox in thee, I would it had been in thy mouth'.[97]

Objects could also be used. In 1566 particular items were left at Alice Barons' door near the Great Conduit in Exeter. This was the great meeting point, the Carfax, where High Street met Fore, South and North Streets. Many residents obtained their water there and most city traffic, whether on foot, by horseback or on wheels, had to pass through. Exonians observed 'certain filthy things' were covered with a white substance, either flour or lime, which were placed in a pan for cooking whitepots, the Devon equivalent to bread and butter pudding. Barons had her servant bring the pan to the mayor and blamed it as the actions of a woman she called Langford's whore. Oddly, Barons was also heard to tell the other woman to 'straw [scatter] raisins upon his codpiece'; raisins were an ingredient of a whitepot.[98] The most common insulting objects, as will be seen, were horns and bones.

Rough justice provided public humiliation by overtly insulting and shaming alleged miscreants without words. William Elliot, an Exeter shoemaker, was involved in a series of verbal as well as gestural ridicule that escalated into attempted rough justice. In 1622 he blamed Edward Searle, a fellow shoemaker, for his being sent to prison. They had a history of enmity and some bad blood was the result of Elliot's appearances before Ignatius Jurdain, the most fervently Puritan justice. In December 1619 Elliot called Searle a baggage knave. It was part of a tirade in the Shoemakers' Hall that Elliot had against the master, whom he gave the same insult, and another member of the company whom he called a puritan knave. Elliot also caused offence by saying that he was a better man than the master and walked in contempt with his hat on in the hall.[99] Six months later, in May 1620, Elliot and Searle had another argument in the market. Elliot insulted Searle by calling him a base rogue and then ridiculed the livery of William Tailor. Tailor's clothing signified he was in the service of Nicholas Duck, the city's Recorder. Elliot said 'he should have as much grace by wearing his own wife's petticoat about his neck as he should by wearing Mr Recorder's livery'. Elliot was sent to prison but possibly not for these words but for telling the mayor that he expected he could not have justice in his courtroom.[100] In July 1618 he had already been in that court for calling a constable a fool and an ass.[101] In September 1619 Jurdain charged him with illegally playing a game and he refused to ask the justice's pardon. Then he stated that Jurdain had 'undone' the Shoemaker's Company and put on his hat in contempt of the mayor.[102] Two years later, in October 1622, Elliot claimed Searle was responsible for his prison sentence and announced that he would employ 'Hart the painter' to draw Searle's portrait and carry it around the city on a may pole. He also said he would give 40 shillings 'to anyone who could give him notice of any [other] Edward Searle that hath [a] *red beard*'.[103] Both men also sought to protect their reputations in the church court: in 1622 Elliot complained that an Exeter woman called him a wittol and a whoreson while three years earlier Searle was named as a drunkard, a base rascal, a lousy rascal and a breeched rogue.[104]

Elliot's intention to humiliate Searle in public with a maypole was similar to other forms such as parading scolds on a pole through the streets accompanied by a crowd and great noisy fanfare (as will be discussed in the following pages). These public demonstrations were intended to mock and were part of a tradition known on the continent as *charivari*, and the best-known occurrences in the West Country were Skimmington Rides.[105] The state punished women found guilty of sexual misconduct by placing them on a cart or being whipped through the streets. Beating a basin enhanced the humiliation. It was this practice which Joan Drewe claimed in 1608 had happened to Grace Corbin of Topsham. She told the other woman she herself 'had never piss pots cast on my head neither basins beaten before me'.[106] Rough justice of various forms was organised within the community and not through the courts. This was the case at Northlew in 1540 when an unmarried woman was allegedly sexually promiscuous and pregnant. A neighbour threatened to make her wear a garland made of a withy, the stem of a willow, which signified betrayal in love. The willow garland

8. *Women humiliating a man, in about 1530, with water or another liquid. A detail from a drawing by Pieter Coecke van Aelst.*

featured in a contemporary ballad which Shakespeare referred to in *Othello*.[107] There was also the use of a hurdle, which was referred to in Exeter in 1619, on which traitors were commonly dragged through the streets.[108]

South Molton and its vicinity were noted for rough justice. In about 1600 John Hooker considered it a 'very ancient market town and is furnished with all kinds of wares and victuals and there dwelleth in it sundry good clothiers. There is in it yearly kept two fairs'. He also commended its 'great peace and quietness'.[109] However, a generation later, in 1630, Thomas Westcote described rough justice and warned visitors not to disparage local women from

32

9. *At a brothel women attack a man, in a contemporary engraving.*

Newland in Landkey, on the road between Barnstaple and South Molton. He wrote:

'They are somewhat dangerous to be passed by strangers; not for thieves or such like, but to those whose tongues are ushers to their wits and walks before them. Such I mean as bring the cause with them for if out of their blindness, or boldness (for it is no other, though they term it valour) they shall but cry out these words (I am almost afraid to whisper them) *Camp-le-tout* [the whole camp], *Newland*, held of the good women very scandalous of their honesty. They are instantly all up like a nest of wasps with the first alarm. The streets are corded, the party (or more, if more there be in the company) beaten down from his horse (if he ride) with stones, or other like dog-bolts, always in readiness, so taken and used at the

33

10. *Dartington Hall, home to Lady Roberta Champernowne in the 1580s, where her servants watched her through a hole in a door. She was the daughter of Gabriel de l'Orge, Comte de Montgomery, the Huguenot leader, and had admitted another man had 'carnal knowledge of her body more times than once'.*

pleasure of the good town's women, washed, shaved and perfumed (and other like dainty trimming, not for modesty to be spoken) that he that travels that way a fortnight after may smell what hath been done there, and he that hath made the trial will confess, by experience, that it is folly for a wise man to anger a multitude causelessly'.[110]

In 1602 Richard Carew wrote a similar description of the Cornish village of Crafthole, which had a reputation for having 12 dwellings and 13 cuckolds. It was said that when strangers reminded the women of their reputation the response was a drenching with an unpleasant form of perfume.[111] Twelve years after Westcote's description Devon's only resident aristocrat came to South Molton and was pelted with stones, and possibly rams' horns as well as most likely less appealing objects, at the start of the Civil War. In this instance their hostility was political.[112] It may have been a similar experience that another visitor had when he visited Bradninch in 1635. A traveller from Norwich wrote the town was 'so poor and ancient as she hath quite lost all breeding and good manners, for I could not pass without a volley of female gun shot which made me hasten away from here as fast as I could'.[113]

The language of slander

Listeners would have judged for themselves whether they were insulted but proving words were slanderous depended on ascertaining the meaning of each term, the circumstances in which words were spoken and the intention of the speaker in delivering them. Thus, in 1634 a witness claimed Joan Banner was deliberately slandered or disgraced at Tiverton as was Alice Hause at Exeter when Joan Parkins spoke 'with a set purpose to defame and slander'.[114] Some slander was referred to as speeches or words which were unfitting while others were described as 'particular words', 'words of anger', or as opprobrious, outrageous, slanderous, unreverent or wild words as well as 'idle words of malice and anger', 'chiding and contemptuous words', 'words of controversy'[115] or they were simply uncivil, abusive, ill, vile, odious, distasteful, scandalous, disgraceful or indecent words.[116] In addition 'speeches' could be unchristian, loud, shrill, foul, bitter, uncharitable, uncomely or ones of displeasure.[117]

The manner in which they were delivered mattered. Thus it was explained epithets were spoken in a 'raging manner', 'moved in choler and anger', 'in quarrelling, chiding or brawling manner' or spoken 'scoffingly and reproachfully'.[118] Others were 'reviling and unreverent speeches in a chiding, scolding and brawling manner' or 'multiplied by him in an angry sort'.[119] When there was a verbal exchange it was sometimes described as a dissension, a quarrel, a 'great falling out and debate in words', 'a multiplication of words', that they 'fell at some difference and fell to hot words', or as an argument or brawl.[120] In Axminster one parishioner watched two women's 'stomachs growing one against another'.[121]

In contrast, John Smith of Bishop's Nympton was unhappy that his wife had fallen out with another woman whom she had accused of having two bastards. He repeated the tale but later explained that although he had not spoken 'in any secret sort or with sorrow' he did regret having repeated his wife's slander.[122] A man of Sampford Peverell in 1558 was unsure of the language his adversary had used: William Shepherd explained he was thick-listed, that is hard of hearing, and unable to hear the abuse.[123] One witness from Cawsand, the Cornish village which overlooks Plymouth Sound, excused the language ('cut pocket old whore') because it arose from upset caused by flooding in the village. It was claimed that the words were passionately spoken because of water damage and that the other woman had begun the argument by calling her neighbour a witch.[124]

Four centuries later the sharpness of some humiliation remains apparent. In 1618 an Exeter woman was called a whore, an idle whore, a scurvy whore and a common whore and the slanderer spoke 'as fast as she the said Justine could utter the said slanderous words'. No doubt John Corbin also felt humiliated when a Topsham neighbour told him 'he was good for nothing but to keep the dogs from the door'.[125] An exchange of words between two women in the autumn of 1593 in a Littlehempston garden was also cutting.

'A cart for thee, a cart for thee', said Julian Curtis.
Jane Dugdale then replied 'A cart is for a whore'.

And Curtis responded 'Yea, and so it is for them, thou foul-mouthed, crook-leg whore'. She also called Dugdale a drunkard.[126]

It was often said that language was 'contrary to the duty of a good Christian', which was at the heart of the immorality of defamation,[127] but some excused their words as being only humorous. George Woodleigh of Upton Pyne explained that when he had described himself and a woman as being married he had done so 'but in sport'.[128] Likewise, in 1635 a Lapford man excused his calling the parson a knave and a woman as his 'quean' (a prostitute, rather than a queen) as words spoken in 'merriment'.[129] In 1566 the church court heard that Sir John Berry, and his two brothers, referred to women, maidens and children by the term 'Joan Down'. It was, according to one witness, 'but a merry word' which was used 'not for any hurt or dishonesty'.[130] A Zeal Monachorum man, who had a history of suspicious involvement with women, claimed that he had offered money for sex 'in jest'.[131] Likewise, a group of men travelling from Totnes to Tavistock in 1583 fell out while they were 'jesting and merrily laughing' about a cousin's intended bride. One suggested a mutual friend had impregnated her but, it was later claimed, they were only talking 'as upon the way men use often times to do' and without any intent to slander.[132] Finally, an Exeter man maintained he had had not intentionally slandered Robert Stone in Castle Lane when he asked if Stone, as a cuckoldly baker, was walking about selling his cakes and bread. It was, he said, spoken in jest.[133]

Occasionally witnesses defined the local meanings of slanderous words but some language was puzzling. This happened at Whitestone, the small village a few miles west of Exeter, where during the early 1600s William Howell had claimed 'in a kind of scoffing manner' that a local man 'did break a colt of Humphrey Bawdon, husband of the said Joan, but this deponent doth not understand nor can judge' what he meant. A secondary meaning for a 'colt' was that of a boy who was newly initiated into roguery.[134] Neither definition seems to fit the wording.

There are occasional references to foreign languages. Lady Roberta Champernowne confused her eavesdropping servants in Dartington Hall when she spoke her native French with an alleged lover in 1582.[135] At Topsham in 1541 Senhor Consallos, a Portuguese visitor, allegedly called two local men 'whoreson drunkards' in English and then 'in the Portyngale tongue or Castilyone tongue he called them *cornudo*'. Jeffrey Frost told the court that he understood the Portuguese language and explained that the equivalent English term was cuckold.[136] There is limited evidence in the statements for the use of Cornish in Cornwall. In 1572 a witness specified that in Lelant near Hayle a woman called another a whore and a whore bitch in English rather than in Cornish. The eyewitness, a tinner, began by noting in Cornish '*Dew Whallan gwa mettng in Eglos de Lalant*' and then provided an English translation of '*that is upon all hallow day last past about the midst of the service in the parish church of Lelant*'. He testified that 'Morris David's wife and Cicely James came into the church of Lelant together and in chiding which words together Cicely James called Agnes Davy whore and whore bitch in English and not in *Cornowoke*.'[137] A few miles to the west, in St Ives, a woman was told in 1608 'thou art a whore, an arrant whore, a scurvy whore, and a mangy whore and thou gettest thy living by thy tail'. The abuse was said in a mixture of English and Cornish.[138]

There is outdated or archaic language. Some is noted in the following chapters and others include a conversation at Filleigh church where a woman, who objected to sitting alongside another woman, asked 'Shall a scorpit sit in the seat with me? I scorn to have such a scorpit to sit with me.' She meant the intruder was a mocking person.[139] In 1607 John Short and Joan Wilcocks

11. *Toads were particularly associated with witches as is shown in this detail from a painting attributed to Pseudo Bocchi in about 1700.*

of Littleham near Bideford were prosecuted for having what was called a 'luxurious life' for more than a dozen years. Closer inspection reveals that their lifestyle was also termed filthy and the term luxurious had been used in its thirteenth-century sense as being unchaste or lascivious.[140] The term 'naughty' had the same meaning.[141]

The word 'toad' had several different meanings. In 1617 a Moretonhampstead cleric was likened to 'croaking toads and fries which lie all day inside mud and in the puddle and in the night leap abroad'.[142] Less clear is why a Cornishman was called a toad in 1567 other than it just being an opprobrious word.[143] Nearly two generations later three Exeter women were also called toads. The first was additionally told she was a whore, rogue, witch and devil, the second was likewise also called a whore, rogue and witch and the third, who was also called a whore, was termed a 'white toad'.[144] There were probably several meanings of the word but the latter uses referred to witchcraft: in Devon as elsewhere in England toads were particularly associated with witches.[145]

Some terms have unclear meanings such as when a Chudleigh woman was called a 'gerbil-tailed' whore in 1558[146] and also nine years later when a Broadclyst woman, suspected of having illicit sex, was described as 'a white hare with two legs'.[147] The term 'mad cat' was used in Exeter. A cat signified a prostitute but a mad cat may have had another meaning.[148] At Exeter in 1616 a woman used the phrase 'to whip the cat' regarding the suspicious visits of a man to a woman's home. Nearly 300 years later this expression was still current in the South Hams and it then described a tailor who worked in private homes because he did not have his own premises. However, it had another meaning. It was also a deceitful and perplexing wager practiced upon rustic men involving a cat pulling a dupe through a pond.[149] Nevertheless, neither explanation neatly fits the circumstances of 1616. One term which appears to have lost its meaning was used in Exeter in 1618: one man was asked to explain the difference between a constable and a Robin Redbreast.[150] One of the most perplexing terms was 'agrimomsie', which was used in Sampford Courtenay in 1583: a woman was asked to 'play agrimomsie' by which she was being for sex for a man's friendship.

Other words and phrases are still used in Devon but have largely become archaic elsewhere. It may be that when scribes wrote 'they', they meant 'the' or they may have intended the traditional local use of the word. Furse is preferred in the testimonies to gorse, drang was used in one instance instead of alley and shippen was preferred to cattle-shed. The word 'foggy', meaning bloated, was spelled with a 'v', which is also a traditional Devon pronunciation.[151] The term 'East Country' was used in one testimony to indicate Dorset. Also, when two men quarrelled at Kingston in the South Hams in 1636 one called the other a 'mazed' rogue.[152] This is also still used in Devon and was defined in Sandford in 1621 in relation to Margery Bawdon as 'one that through her amazedness, sickness, lunacy or insanity of mind is not nor was not able to understand what was or should be told her nor anything that she should be told her, nor anything that she should hear spoken'.[153] In 1569 a slightly different meaning

12. *A mazed man?, as drawn by Leonardo da Vinci in about 1495.*

13. *An array of codpieces in the late 1500s, as depicted by Peter van der Heyden after Pieter Brueghel.*

was given to a man involved in a hurling match at Lifton, near the Cornish border, between the parishioners of Clawton and Milton Abbot. Two men argued about choosing a subsequent game and one said 'he should have the maze' by which it was explained he was drunk.[154]

Several archaic phrases involved kites. In 1635 an Exeter cleric was said to be so ineffective in the pulpit that 'he shall as soon catch a kite with a rattle as save a soul by his preaching'.[155] Kites were then only either birds of prey or a term for a rapacious person but amongst the meanings then in use for a rattle was the seed pod of a plant, a toy, and a boisterous noise which could mean a babbling flow of words. Kites were also used in another expression at Crediton in 1566: it was said of a woman who conducted illicit business in public rather than in private that 'the kite and crow

14. *Carving of a male figure, of about 1600, in the Church of St Peter & St Paul, Churchstanton. His codpiece is particularly prominent.*

should cry out upon them.'[156] Nearly sixty years later a similar phrase was used in Exeter. Witnesses heard a married woman being called a whore and they said 'the crows, kites and birds of the air would bewray [betray] them'.[157] In a number of places another unusual phrase was used: men spoke of 'skinning a mare'. This, as will be seen, alluded to a woman having illicit sex.

Four other phrases are equally curious but possibly not uncommon. In the early 1600s an Exeter woman was said to have been 'touched to the quick' by her master. Magdalene Rutter was told that she had two children fathered by her master before she married and that 'when he had touched thee to the quick he sent thee down for a pack. And thou shalt be sent up again for a fardel'. One meaning for quick then was pregnancy.[158] Another phrase was 'the English of it' which has been in print since at least 1547: a generation later a Barnstaple woman was called a whore and then told to 'pick then at the English of it'.[159] In another instance, Agnes Westcott of Chawleigh, was also told she was a whore and then told 'thy pot boils the better' for the parson.[160] Finally, in 1568 the cleric of Coldridge was denied access through a courtyard and told his wife was an arrant whore who 'weareth a codpiece upon her arse'.[161] This may be what was meant fifty years later when an Exeter woman had what was described as a 'guarded tail', that is, it was ornamented.[162]

There is one instance of a former folk belief, possibly only then current in Devon, which has been forgotten. In 1561 Wilmot Croppe of Kingsteignton was said to have had a longing for apples which was interpreted as an indication of pregnancy.[163]

Seven archaic words meant seduction or sexual intercourse. 'Mell' appears to have been more commonly said in the early 1500s than afterwards. It was in use in England from at least the mid 1400s and was recorded in Trusham in 1540 ('should mell with the said Julian in his *beat* boards'), Fremington in 1541 ('he did carnally mell with Joan Visheley upon a bench within her own house'), Exeter in 1541 ('he melled not with her'), Lanreath in 1542 ('Did you hear Margaret my wife say that I should mell carnally with Thomasine Cornish?'), Crediton in 1541 ('I am not the first that melled with her', 'did see out of a hole the said Rafe & Elizabeth carnally melling together upon a hurdle in the hog's house'), Venn Ottery in 1558 ('when she first melled with him'), Newton Poppleford in 1560 ('he laid the said Agnes down in the floor and did carnally mell with her') and Dawlish in 1566 ('he should not mell with her').[164]

The term 'sard' was first recorded in the Lindisfarne Gospels in about the year 950 and was said in Lostwithiel in 1572 ('he doth sard her more than her own husband'), Poughill in 1575 ('Milton did sard her in that bed'), Kenton in 1577 ('common sarder'), Bovey Tracey in 1596 ('I did hear Pinsent to sard thee') and Chudleigh in 1598 ('thou art like unto thy sister at Kingsteignton that did sard for beans and peas').[165] No instances of either mell or sard have been found in Devon documents for the 1600s.

'Swive', another medieval word, has been found in only instance and that was in 1560.[166] 'Jape', in use from at least the 1300s, however was commonly said. It certainly is more readily found than the word 'fuck' which was recorded less than a dozen times.[167] Its meaning was made clear when an Ashburton man denied having sex with a woman in 1566. He said 'you have seen me lie with her in the bed, you have not seen me jape her'.[168] 'Occupy', another medieval term, was more often used than either. A related term was 'bag', which from the early 1400s had meant impregnation such as when John Pyne of East Down was said in 1624 he would marry Thomasine Downe because he had bagged her.[169] This was also the meaning of 'gravel', which was used in Probus in 1608. A witness explained it meant 'that she was with child'.[170]

Some terms had several meanings. A Tiverton woman complained in 1637 that she had been called a drunken sow and a drunken 'sot'. In the contemporary ballad *Halfe a dozen of good Wives* one of the wives is described:

> 'The third was somewhat cleanly,
> but yet a drunken Sot;
> She'd pawn all things for ale and beer,
> whatever she had got;
> She scarce would leave a smock
> or shoe unto her foot,
> But at the alehouse all these went,
> and somewhat else to boot.'

The term 'sot' most likely indicated that the Tiverton woman was a habitual drinker[171] (it has been recorded in use from 1592) but other uses recorded in Devon are less certain. For instance, when an Alfington woman was called a 'sot' bitch in 1626 her accuser may have been alluding to excessive drinking but from about the year 1000 it also defined a foolish or stupid person. This ambiguity also extends to the insults given to Christian Rumbelow of Bampton: she was called a whore, a base whore, a beggarly whore and a sot whore.[172] A man in Dean Prior used the same insult as was used in Alfington. He said of Agnes Knowling 'thou art a whore and a common whore and thou art as common a whore as a sot bitch and you have been as common as a dog & a bitch'.[173] This was similar to those given to a Honiton woman in 1604. She was told 'thou art a hot whore, a bulled whore & a sot whore & thou hast as many hang about thee as a sot bitch hath dogs'.[174] An Exeter woman in 1599 was given a similar insult: she was 'a sot whore worse than a bitch'. This was part of a longer stream of abuse which helps put the term into a wider context. She was also called 'a whore, an open-arsed whore, a common whore, a whore for every man, and four honest men did see one with boots and spurs occupy thee upon a bed'.[175]

'Stinking' had several meanings: it could mean an offensive smell but it was also used from the 1200s onwards to indicate intense disgust and contempt. It could have been intended with either meaning when women from Barnstaple, Exeter and Cullompton were called stinking whores or when Walter Sainthill was termed a 'scurvy, stinking, proud fellow' in Exeter Cathedral.[176] A Totnes woman was called a 'sinkard' in 1583 but she might have meant a 'stinkard', someone who stank. A woman of Rewe was described in 1631 as being a 'whore and a savage whore'. The latter term might have indicated she was wild or that she was cruel and brutal.[177]

Equally uncertain is the use of the word 'show': in 1638 Charity Finny was called a bastard, a whore and a show. The word could indicate an appearance with the intention to deceive.[178] In 1635 a string of abuse was thrown at a woman in St Peter's Church in Tiverton. She was called a brazen faced slut, a cripple, a fat arse, a fat breech and a hagabout jade. This is not the only use of the word 'breech' (a medieval word meaning the buttocks) that has been found but the term 'hagabout' has not been identified although it is clearly not complimentary.[179] Various men were called simpletons or fools when they were named as a ninny and others, as will be seen, were called a ninnyhammer, ninnypoop or ninnycock. None of these terms, except ninny, are in use today.

There were various terms recorded for genitalia with more for men than women. Only rarely was 'prick' noted. More common were 'yard', 'privates', 'privy parts', 'privy members' and 'members'. There was one use in 1557 of 'knipsey', this may have meant 'nippy'.[180] There was also one instance of the term 'maypole' which was in use nationally from at least 1607. It was said in Great Torrington in 1612 along with other denouncing words including ape, jack, beggarly knave and proud rascal.[181] There was one recorded use of the word 'shaft' and this was in a case of alleged bestiality. A cobbler's son was said to have 'had his shaft out' while drawing a pig closer to him. Curiously, the word has not been found recorded in print in England until 1719.[182] Each of these words meant a penis. Testicles were in one instance called stones: in 1584 two men argued in Tavistock and one told the other that if they fought he would 'cut off both his stones'.[183] The term 'bollocks' was more common. At Tiverton, John Pitt was said in 1624 to have had so much sex that 'the hair of his bollocks' had been 'beaten away' and five years later another man's disease was treated with 'an oil to anoint thy bollocks'.[184] One of the most graphic descriptions of sex was given by a Stokenham man who said of Margaret Spratt that 'he hath been so far in her as he may go for his bollocks'.[185]

Female terms were more limited. In only three court cases has the word 'cunt' been found.[186] One instance was in 1636 when Joan Sincock of Colyton objected to a reduction in her neighbour's taxes which was allegedly the result of sexual relations with the tax assessor. Sincock told him 'Joan Dodge is thine whore and if that my cunt had been as good as Joan Dodge's I had not paid so much to the rate'.[187] Nearly twenty years before a Cornishman in St Keverne called a woman a whore and pocky whore before saying 'Mr Nicholas Buggins did wash thy cunt with drink'. Finally, a Combe Martin woman told another in 1629 that she was a mare 'and thou hast a cunt like a mare'. Only one use of the term 'vagina' has been found: in Exeter in 1622 a woman was called a 'vaginal whore'. There were also several euphemisms used, both in 1614. The term 'wren's nest' was expressed in Ottery St Mary,[188] a Sandford woman was said to have had medical treatment on her 'uncomely' and 'nether' parts, and the term 'secret parts' was used in Brampford Speke.[189] Another possibility is the word 'bottle': in Cornwall during the early 1600s an observer claimed that she had witnessed a couple having sex and noted seeing 'the stopple in her bottle'.[190]

There are occasional plays on words and witticisms. In 1557 William Luscombe was asked about a conversation he had with Mary Roche. He denied having looked at his codpiece and then alluding to having had 'a dainty morsel of fish named a roche'. In Kenton as elsewhere local people were familiar with the fish, the common roach. This was as commonly known as a toll dish, the measure of grain that a miller received for grinding corn. Thus, an Exeter woman was slandered by being called a miller's toll dish in 1627.[191]

Some slanderers implied bad behaviour by stating that none had been committed. For instance, in 1626 one Exeter woman said to another 'thou art no whore and my bed knoweth that thou art no whore, meaning thereby that the said Elizabeth Courtney was a whore and she had played the whore upon her bed'.[192] Likewise, that same year a Totnes man complained that Agnes Wyott had said to him 'Sir, thou art no cuckold, meaning thereby that the said Richard Sampson was a cuckold'.[193] In 1615 William Delve of Sandford was more creative with his wording. A witness testified Delve said to Hugh Mill 'thou art no cuckold holding out two of his fingers to the said Mill in the manner of horns, then the said Hugh Mill demanded of the said Delve what he meant thereby and why he did so, and Delve scoffingly replied again thou art no cuckold'.[194]

Ridicule was also put to music. In 1540 a song was composed in Yealmpton to mock the parson for an alleged affair. Walter Kine sang it throughout the village and then taught it to the younger generation who made it a common song in the area. A 'scandalous' song was also used at the Bear Inn in Exeter at the start of the Civil War in 1642. It was composed by a gentleman to ridicule Parliamentarians but it was the singer, John Gollopp, who got into trouble.[195]

One insulting word, which was used in Devon but apparently

not complained about in court, was 'noddy'. In the early 1600s
Tristram Risdon noted that East Budleigh's church had a memorial
stone to Radolphus Node. Risdon recalled that there was a tradition
that Node had attempted to fly from the tower using 'artificial
wings' but instead he crashed to the ground and was killed. For
this, wrote Risdon, he deserved the name 'Noddy', which meant a
fool or simpleton.[196]

ONE

Drunkards, Beggars and Witches

Some insults were applied to both men and women. This included the term 'scum', first recorded in use in England in 1590. In Devon it was used as part of a phrase in three instances of the early 1600s: in 1617 women from Totnes and Exeter St Thomas were called 'the scum of the country' whereas at St Neot in Cornwall another woman had the more elevated term of 'the scum of the world'. In addition, in 1639 a Bampton preacher used it to describe men then fighting the Scots. They, in his opinion, were 'profane people and rebels to God and the king and that one righteous man would do more good than a thousand thousands of them'. This preacher's use differs with calling women scum: they were being accused of sexual immorality.[197] The two remaining uses of the word were similar but it was used as an adjective: Exeter and Cullompton women were called 'scum whores'.[198]

The term 'creature' signified a reprehensible or despicable person and was used to disparage a court witness ('a simple creature of no credit or estimation and wandereth about the country with her mother a begging'). It does not appear to have been used in Devon's slander cases but an Exeter constable was called 'a base creature, it was written in one parish register in 1581 ('Anne, a lame creature') and in Cornwall it appears as the first name of a fisherman in 1626.[199]

'Baggage' was used to describe both men and women but unlike its use for women, there were no sexual overtones for a male baggage: it denoted a worthless or vile man and was first recorded in use nationally in 1594. Shortly afterwards, in Colebrooke, Exeter and Staverton, local men were called either baggage knaves or baggage fellows.[200] The former term was used in Cornwall at Calstock and men were also called baggages in two other Cornish villages.[201]

Vain, insolent or saucy young men or boys were called princocks in England from at least 1540 and in this sense it was used in Totnes in 1576 when two men were called princocks and cockcombs.[202] A string of abuse said against an Exeter man in 1565 included the word princock but its meaning is less apparent as it was when later used in Kenton church a generation later.[203] However, the term was also used to describe women in Exeter and Lapford where it is likely the intention was to deride them as being insolent and vain. In Cornwall a variant term was used: a Madron man was called a 'proud, pocky prinklet' in 1624.[204]

The term 'carrion', in use nationally from at least 1547, was recorded in Exeter in 1621. It was used by a servant to describe his mistress and he called her a rascal carrion and a foggy carrion. By this he meant she was vile or corrupt.[205] The term was also used against men.

Three main categories of insults applied to both men and women and these were concerned with immoderate use of alcohol, the lack of personal wealth and collusion with the devil.

Drunkards

Being called a drunkard was one of the most common insults and ordinarily involved excessive use of either ale or wine. The denials, along with the rest of the details, would be familiar today. For example, John Easton of Clayhidon explained that he had been

15. *A drunkard, with drink spilling from his mouth, of the late 1400s as painted on a screen in the Church of St Thomas Becket, Bridford.*

merry on several occasions but proclaimed that an honest man would not say he was a common drunkard. Likewise, a potential witness in Totnes admitted merely 'loving a cup of good liquor sometimes'. Many other Devonians also protested but the details of their drinking history could be very explicit and compelling. Clerics were the segment of society who appear to have attracted the most abuse for being constantly overcome with drink.

According to Richard Younge, who wrote *The Drunkard's Character*, a volume dedicated to the bishop of Exeter in 1638, the sins of a drunkard were pride, enmity, ignorance, atheism, idleness, adultery and murder. Younge thought that a drunkard's appearance typically included a 'Brazil' nose, a swollen and inflamed face, and goggle eyes that were swimming, running, glaring, bleared and red. Another attribute was a mouth nasty with offensive fumes and

16. *Drunkards depicted as beasts, who are fighting, smoking and vomiting, in a contemporary engraving.*

continually foaming and drivelling. His or her body was feverish, the brain was sickly and giddy, the stomach was boiling, the teeth were rotten, the breath was stinking and the legs were gouty and staggering. As if this was not enough, gestures were odious and all behaviour was loathsome, nasty and beastly. Perhaps it was to be expected that, in his opinion, a drunkard also had belching, hiccups, vomitting and ridiculous postures.[206] Not surprisingly, given this description, there were many Devonians who objected to being named as a drunkard.

A small number of men or women were only called drunkards. This included Elizabeth Hills of Exeter who was called a drunkard in 1629 and James Beaple of Barnstaple who was labelled a drunkard and a base drunkard in 1638.[207] Most other insults escalated: this included being called a drunken rogue (Leonard Pugsley of Loxbeare), a drunken whore (Catherine Smale of Salcombe), a drunken slut (Helen Rutleigh of Broadclyst), a drunken

17. *A chamber pot, otherwise described as 'a stool pot' or 'shitten pot' in Exeter in 1634. This monkey was carved to embellish a bench end, now in Forrabury's church at Boscastle.*

bitch (Thomasine Hawkridge of Exeter), a drunken old bawd (Sidwell Rowe of Plymouth), a drunken sow (Elizabeth Upham of Exeter), a drunken baggage (Katherine Abbot of Withycombe Raleigh), a common drunkard (George Shurte of Bideford) and a base drunken whore and a spewing drunkard (Charity Colliscott of Barnstaple).[208] Katherine Daniel of St Agnes' in Cornwall must have felt besieged in 1638 when a neighbour told her she was a drunkard, a drunken sow, a scurvy whore and a drunken whore while another called her a drunkard, a drunken sow, a drunken beast, a whore and a drunken whore.[209]

The received perception of a drunkard was given in *A Messe of Good Fellows*, a contemporary ballad. It included the lines:

> 'we scorn to spend money on queans,
>   though sometimes we hunt the fox [get drunk];
> For he that so wasteth his means,
>   at last will be paid with a pox.
> No surgeon, nor any physician,
>   for money their aid shall lend us;
> When drinking hath changed our condition,
>   a hair of the old dog will mend us.'[210]

Some speakers added personal details which gave added bite such as Richard Germans who reminded Edward Searle that he had been inebriated in his house in Exeter while John Jerman of the same place told Thomasine Hawkridge that not only was she a drunken bitch but added she had been intoxicated the whole of the previous day.[211] John Ruggs heard John Fley say that he had come home inebriated from Topsham and John Trender, vicar of Barnstaple, insulted his own wife by calling her 'the most notorious drunkard that is in the whole country'. An Exeter neighbour told William Cosens that he was a drunkard and said 'go thou home drunkard and it is fitter for thee to be at home with thine own wife than here'.[212]

Most slanderers suggested that their target was frequently intoxicated. In 1588 a Slapton man was said to be a common and notorious drunkard and one witness claimed he was so 'over gone' that he was unable to walk steadily.[213] Likewise, in 1636 an Exeter man was named as a common drunkard who was drunk as often as he came to a witness' house while John Chapel was said to be drunk two or three times each week.[214] In comparison, Thomas Drake of Plympton Maurice was unfavourably compared with 'Cutty' who was drunk only two days a week whereas Drake was said to be drunk every day. John Hayne was slandered for being overcome six days of seven and an Exeter woman was said to be drunk every day of the week.[215] Elizabeth Oxenham who, in addition to claiming that Joan Weekes was her husband's whore, said Weekes was so drunk that she fell off her horse in Okehampton market. A similar story was told in Tetcott at a hurling match in which ale was blamed for the fighting. But one man alluded to the other's prior heavy drinking which resulted in his falling off his horse and 'turning up his tail'. The same was said of Richard Venn, vicar of Otterton, in 1631: it was claimed that he fell off his horse and slept where he dropped. Venn, it was said, 'stank' of drink.[216] Fifteen years later he was ejected from the church and imprisoned at Exeter. While in gaol he wrote:

'We were immured in Newgate [sic] by Ro-Duke,
Knave-Clapp, Ro-Boules, Witch-Callard, who did look
as if she had kissed the devil that same morn,
and had received from him those lips of scorn.
such as we took for kindred flock and friends
But found close bloody and malicious fiends.'[217]

A Harberton woman felt insulted when another told her that she had drunk so much before coming home from Totnes that she had lain drunk along the side of the hedge. Another woman, who was a witness in court, was described as a notorious drunk who had lain in the gutter of Totnes High Street.[218]

A considerable number of clerics were called drunks. An alehouse keeper in Denbury refused to renounce his slandering the rector in 1585. William Dolbeare had said in church that Reverend Mendous had been so intoxicated one midnight that he needed to be escorted home. The vicar of Totnes objected in 1619 to the rumour that he had been drinking until six in the morning at a parishioner's house and he also had to be accompanied home. In 1640 the rector of Teigngrace was outraged when a parishioner said he was always drunk when he came home from Newton Abbot.[219]

In 1635 the rector of Clovelly preached at West Woolfardisworthy one morning but allegedly became so drunk at a parishioner's house in the afternoon that he was unable to return home.[220] Far worse was said of the drinking habits of the cleric at Werrington. It was alleged that he had become drunk and disorderly at a banquet for a parishioner's churching and then was thrown out of the house. Reverend Hancock subsequently fell unconscious in an ox stall where he remained the night. He was 'as it were a tosspot' by which it meant he was a drunkard. A contemporary ballad sang of 'Tosspot Tom' of whom:

> 'This fellow will not stay at home
>   Above an hour's space;
> He'll at the alehouse stay,
>   from breakfast time to dinner'.[221]

A wretched case of drunken slander took place in Brampford Speke in 1625. John Triggs was cited for calling the vicar a knave 'again and again before a whole congregation' as well as for being a 'most slanderous and bitter railer against his neighbours and betters'. The abuse of the vicar followed his telling Triggs he was a drunkard.[222]

Many insults reflected familiar effects of intoxication. In 1637 a West Alvington man was allegedly so overcome that he 'did much reel in his going and faltered in his speech' which was similar to a Cornishman who was told he could not speak plainly but had stuttered and stammered with drink. Both an Ottery St Mary woman in 1629 and an Exeter man in 1622 objected to being told that they had been so drunk that they could neither 'go nor stand'.[223] A generation before, in 1582, another Exeter man was said to be so inebriated that he reeled, staggered and could 'not stand nor go'. It was worse for another Exonian who was not able to walk and had to be carried out of a tavern in 1615. Elizabeth Searle of Dartington complained when it was said in 1629 that she was so drunk that she had to be led by the hand and only the wall held her up.[224] Priscilla James' slander was worse: in 1623 she was allegedly so drunk that her 'boy hath carried her to bed drunk upon his back'. Incidents of excessive drinking were also recorded in court presentments in which local people were charged with it as a crime: for example, in the mid 1620s Joan Gonne of Crediton was said to have been 'so drunk that she could not stand nor go, she fell and burst herself'.[225]

It was also in Exeter that a man was said in 1634 to have been so drunk that he 'bear or tear stool pots or shitten pots'. A Cornish woman had far worse said of her regarding a toilet: in 1622 a neighbour told her 'thou art a drunkard, an arrant drunkard and thou was led to the jakes drunk and Roger Yeo brought brown paper to wipe thine arse'. At least her slander involved making it to a privy. A Cornish woman felt insulted when two neighbours called her a drunken bitch and said 'thou were so drunk that thou tookest up thy coats and did piss under the table where thou stood'.[226] Another Cornish woman was also said to be a drunkard who 'didst piss where thou standest'. A woman of Silverton, who was at Lammas Fair in Exeter, was said in 1634 to have been so drunk that 'thou didst spew or piss about the room'. These comments may or may not have been true but a parishioner of St Sidwell's parish was successfully prosecuted in 1630 for coming drunk into the church and urinating on the floor. That same year a Stoodleigh man vomited in church.[227]

In 1640 a married Exeter woman objected to a tale that after drinking excessively she had lain in straw with a man, who was not her husband, and that when they were discovered it was nearly impossible to pull her away from him. Her story was not nearly as lurid at that told of Philip Michelmore of Buckfastleigh. In 1617 he felt himself scandalized about a tale being told of his drinking three years before at a house in the village. A witness explained that Michelmore 'had drunk much and being overtaken with drink he fell asleep and being asleep one Elizabeth Lange then present did take out the said Michelmore's privy members out of his breeches and put them in again and the said Michelmore did not awake or understand thereof.' Fellow drinkers later confirmed what had happened while he lay in a stupor but he did not believe them. Several men allegedly watched, presumably in amusement, as 'his privy members were taken out and laid upon his hose'.[228]

Beggars

Insults alleging poverty were also common and its prevalence could relate to avoiding subsequent prosecution. Elizabethan England's concern was that vagrancy could destablise society. National poor law legislation tried to address this by outlawing begging and attempted to reduce the number of 'masterless men' then roaming the country.[229]

Only men were explicitly called beggars including one of Marhamchurch in Cornwall who was told he 'lied like a beggar' in 1627. The minister at Witheridge was called 'a lowly priest and a beggar' whereas Chagford's curate was also called a beggar amongst a string of other abuse.[230] Most beggar insults involved, in the case of men, being termed 'beggarly' knaves or rogues, or in the case of women, being called beggarly whores, wenches, scabs or drabs. This was also the case with the terms vagrant and wanderers by which it was meant they had no fixed abode or source of income. Four men were also insulted by being associated with bankruptcy. An Exeter man handed out a range of insults one night to local people including calling one 'a beggarly and almost bankrupt constable' while another was called a bankrupt knave.[231] Mr Roope of South Milton was said in 1581 to keep 'none in his house but whores and harlots and bankrupts and that never an honest man came to his house'. Sixty years later Elizabeth Searle called Edward Collins of Exeter a bankrupt rogue and he called her a 'ram beggar whore'. This term was used in one other case and that was also in Exeter. It may have referred to lechery.[232]

Runagate was used slightly more. It had been used in England to define a vagabond or deserter from the 1530s and was said of the aforementioned John Baker in Exeter in 1619, at St Issey in Cornwall in 1558, at Chagford in 1620[233] and then again in 1626 to describe Agnes Heddon who was a witness in a slander case. Heddon was then pronounced to be 'a poor beggarly woman, one that goeth from door to door, or at least one that goeth often to the house of the said Anne Rice for relief and there hath it, a common tale teller and a runagate and such a one as for a piece of bread or for some small piece of money will say or swear anything upon her oath'.[234] It had also been used in 1559 to describe two men who were whipped in Exeter to punish them for their 'runagate and vagrant lives'. A Totnes man was called a runagate and a vagabond in 1579. He was alleged to 'filch' other men's goods and, more importantly, to have run away from his master.[235] In other instances men and women were called a runagate person (Exeter), runagate whore (Salcombe, Cullompton and Exeter),[236] runagate jade (Exeter) or a runagate rogue (Barnstaple and Exeter).[237] An Ipplepen man was called a 'runaway rogue' in 1624 which most likely meant he was a wandering person or perhaps had left his master. Others were called runabouts, a variant of runagate also used by the mid 1500s.[238] Poverty was alleged in other ways: some women, as will be discussed, were said to be so poor that they prostituted themselves for low sums of money.

It was more common to scorn witnesses for poverty; it was regularly claimed that men and women were so destitute that their testimonies could be purchased. Hence, a Bradninch man in 1614 was said to be a poor man of no credit or estimation who was a wandering beggar that went from door to door seeking assistance. Zacharias Pigeon, of an unidentified parish, was in 1626 'a poor, base, wandering, vagrant fellow and a drunkard and one that hath nothing to stake to for his living but wandereth up and down the country from place to place not having any certified settled place of a dwelling to abide in but now here, now there, wandereth hither and thither to shift by any base means for his meat and drink and necessary sustenance to maintain his life and is such a one as will easily be corrupted and drawn for a little gain, reward or profit to say or swear anything so he may get or procure anything to have himself thereby'.[239]

Several Devon vicars were called jacks. It was used in England by 1548 to designate a lowbred or ill-mannered fellow but the slander cases indicate that in Devon it was associated with poverty. A

Cornish example supplements the other usages against clerics and demonstrates the link with hardship: in 1627 William Langford of Marhamchurch was overheard telling George Bowden that he lied like a beggar and also that he was a jack and a baggage.[240]

Witches

Twenty-eight people, all of whom were women except for five men, protested that they had been slandered as witches. They lived across Devon in Bampton, Barnstaple, Beer, Broadclyst, Chulmleigh, Crediton, East Worlington, Exeter, Georgeham, Halberton, Huxham, Ide, Lapford, Loxhore, Modbury, Morchard Bishop, Nymet Tracey, St Marychurch, Sheepwash, Sidbury, Topsham, Totnes and Whimple. The Protestant Reformation sought to remove magic from the church: the supernatural power of saints was denied and it was questioned whether priests had the ability to turn bread and wine into the body and blood of Christ. And yet alongside this was a rise in the belief of witchcraft; magical power resided only in the hands of the devil's servants. Ceremony was also largely discarded by the Reformers but it continued to be an essential part of witchcraft belief. The parallel message of zealous Protestants was to proclaim that the Catholic priests dealt in superstition and were also witches and sorcerers.[241] In about 1590 Hooker recounted an extraordinary tale of Bishop Oldham having been treated for an illness by a Crediton woman in about 1518. This woman had been prosecuted by Oldham for witchcraft and sorcery but she grudgingly consented to treat him with a charm. He, lying in his bed, repeated her words 'Hugh Oldham arise in God's name' and she then told him 'and lie there down again the devil's name'. Hooker commented that he never recovered nor did he leave his deathbed and questioned how a bishop could seek such help.[242]

Two women, Joan Moreman of Broadclyst in 1566 and Elizabeth Crosse of Chulmleigh in 1588, were simply described as witches but the majority had a longer torrent of abuse. This happened to Joan Allan of Exeter in 1615 ('an old jade, an old scurvy whore

18. *Detail showing a pickpocket, as painted by Hendrick Van Steenwijke the elder in about 1590.*

and a witch') and to Leonard Pugsley of Loxhore in 1627 ('a drunken rogue, a bastard, a drunkard, a cuckold, a whoremonger, a whoremaster, a bastard maker and a witch'). Others had slight embellishments added to their slander such as Alice Reynolds of Nymet Tracey in 1624 ('a whore, an old rotten whore for thirty years ago, a pocky whore, an old rotten witch and a scurvy pated whore'), Joan Grantland of East Worlington in 1558 ('that old witch'), Alice Scampe of Georgeham in 1597 ('a witch and arrant witch') and Grace Can of Huxham in 1615 ('an old drunken jade and an ill-favoured witch'). In 1596 a husband and wife living in Topsham were given the accolade of being 'as rank witches as any be in England'.[243]

Witchcraft was a serious charge but even so the wife of a Sheepwash man in 1583 may have hesitated to believe her husband's excuse when she discovered him having sex with another woman: he claimed she had bewitched him. The naming of a man or woman as a witch had the potential for severe consequences: witchcraft was a crime punishable by imprisonment or death from 1542. Devon has the distinction of being the county in which the last execution took place, in 1685, for witchcraft in England. Some slander cases show individuals were not merely named as witches but details were given of practices. Causing harm was legally specified as an unlawful witchcraft practice which was why it was taken seriously when Anne Hunt in Liskeard was accused of having bewitched two men 'to all that trouble'. A woman even claimed her father's fishing nets at Beer had been bewitched in 1619. There had been an argument the day before over the mooring of boats and the cause, she said, for his nets being torn was because they were 'witched'.[244]

It was more common to claim that animals had been bewitched. This included a cow in Halberton in 1629, a horse in Loddiswell in 1582, pigs in Ide in 1556 and Exeter in 1621,[245] and cattle in Moretonhampstead in 1559 and in St Marychurch in 1565.[246] Margaret Fox of Dartmouth was accused of killing her neighbours' cattle through witchcraft. She argued that animals only died through natural causes but conceded that her neighbours thought it could be done by a witch.[247] Slander between two women at St Marychurch revealed suspicions that an inability to make cheese was due to witchcraft. In amongst that discussion it was alleged that charms were chanted and that a cheese had been pricked with sticks to ward off evil.[248] In 1565 a woman claimed charms were also used to cure animals at Whimple.[249]

One particular case suggests an ulterior motive in suggesting witchcraft. The slandering by Richard Giffard of Melior Berdall of Exeter St Thomas in 1561 followed a legal dispute between them. He told an acquaintance that he knew of a better way to settle their suit and promptly pronounced her to be a witch.[250]

In addition to these individuals being slandered as witches there were another six who were associated with devilry. Barnstaple's Reverend Trender was one of the most expressive in his abuse. Not only did he call his own wife a Judas, filth, a rogue and a

witch but he also named her as Satan.[251] Philip Dillon, a servant
of the Italian doctor Bartholomew Jaquinto, testified against his
employer in the early 1600s in Exeter. He called him an Italian
devil but also provided more lurid details including that the doctor
was able to 'commune and raise the devil and drive him into a man
and expel him again'. He swore that his conscience told him that
the doctor was a devil and had said so when Jaquinto attempted
to sodomise him.[252] At about the same time another Exeter man
was said to keep his neighbours awake at night when he conjured
devils. A parish clerk in Yarnscombe was told by his own vicar that
the 'devil did ride' him and the vicar of Totnes was said to be able
to raise devils. In Ottery St Mary it was said that a man had gone
to the devil.[253]

Exeter's mayoral court also heard mocking language involving
witchcraft and the devil. Joan Combe was called a witch, toad and
devil amongst other abuse and another local man said that 'all
such puritan rogues that run to sermons be as bad as the devil'. A
woman told a constable that she wished the pox would confound
him and that the devils of hell would consume him. A husband
told his wife that he prayed the devil would appear to her and 'tear
her in pieces'. Two individuals spoke one sentiment at different
times. Barnaby Gouch, a diocesan official, told the mayor's court
in 1629 'that many which did go to sermons did afterwards go
to whores or whorehouses and that the devil might as well come
out of hell and be saved as well as some of them'.[254] More than a
decade earlier whilst a ballad singer was being imprisoned he told
the constable 'some carried the word of God in their mouths and
the devil in their hearts'. 'Old Beezlebub' was a name uttered by
several women against their neighbours in 1621 along with 'other
foul and odious names not fitting to be spoken'.[255]

These cases heard in the civil court concerned improper
language and scurrilous insinuations but alongside them were
investigations into witchcraft such as in 1601 when a Dartmouth
magistrate interviewed witnesses who testified that a family had
bewitched them causing poverty, insanity, maiming, death and
destruction.[256] But even the church court cases illustrate the harm

that could be done even before coming to court. In one case, which concerned two Crediton women in 1584, Philippa Weavel said to Wilmot Basse 'thou art an old whore witch and I could find it in my heart to fry thee in thine own grease'. She then threw burning coals onto a stack of hay before them.[257]

TWO

𝒦naves, 𝒇ools and 𝒮colds: 𝒩on-𝒮exual 𝒯erms 𝒇or 𝒨en and 𝒲omen

In addition to drunkenness, poverty and devilry, there were other areas of life in which to find fault with friends, family and neighbours. Much of this name-calling concerned illicit sex but there others and these were gender specific. One exception to this was being called a thief. Two Exeter women, for example, fell out over the alleged theft of a chicken in 1638; one said to the 'brazen-faced thief' that 'it was a thievish trick to take up her hen in her own court'. Thievery was especially suggested in regard to taking purses and picking pockets. For example, in 1621 an Exeter man was called a rogue thief 'who has picked my pocket', another was called a pickpocket rogue and a woman was termed a pickpocket whore.[258] Joan Clarke of Tiverton complained that Elizabeth Weeks said in 1638 that 'thou art a whore, a pocky whore, a pickpurse whore and a thievish whore' while Margaret Madgent of Exeter objected to Joan Dawe telling her in 1624 'thou art a whore, a tinker's whore, a cutpurse whore and a thievish whore'. An Exeter man protested after being told he 'was worse than any cutpurse or pickpurse that robbed in the highway'.[259] Other names were restricted to either men or women.

Male Terms

A considerable number of abusive words applied only to men. Some appear to have been widely used but seven others were recorded only once in Devon. In a heated argument at Kingston near Kingsbridge in 1636 one man called another a mazed rogue, a base rogue, a beggarly rogue and a 'pattick'. The intended meaning of the latter term might have been that he was a 'paddock', a term used in England from the 1400s to describe a contemptible, mean or spiteful person. Another uncommon word was 'peasant': a vicar called a Marldon man both a knave and peasant. The two men were arguing about a horse and eventually they brawled in a local green.[260] An Exeter constable was called a 'beefeater' in 1619. By this it was meant that he was a well-fed menial. Nine years later another Exeter man was called a 'pickthank slave'. John Trehane's intention with this word was to suggest that James Tayler was a flatterer and tale-teller.[261]

Three terms used in Exeter have unknown meanings. In 1624 William Morrell said of Robert Hawkins that he was a cuckold and a cuckoldly knave but more interestingly he added that Hawkins was 'a cuckoldly roastmeat'. Roasting was another term for arresting as well as for jeering, ridiculing or banter. Roger Searle used two other unusual terms. In 1620 he called Jonathan Wood a base rogue, slave and knave and, interestingly, a 'cock leg' and a 'pancake'.[262] The meanings of the remaining male ridicule are more straightforward; they suggested dishonesty, low intelligence or unusual physical characteristics.

Dishonesty

In 1626 Thomas Periam, of Sidmouth, was said to have a 'dishonest and incontinent life' and he was further slandered by a claim he had been whipped 'for laying with a wench that now is a man's wife of our town'. Six particular terms were used to mock men for leading dishonest lives such as this. These were knave, rogue, rascal, slave, varlet and sucker. The word 'cozening', which was said of William Griffin at Plymouth in 1574 (he was called 'an arrant cozening rogue'), was often used. It also meant deceitful or cheating.[263]

Knaves

'Knave' was the most frequently used term. For instance, when Giles Ball chose to castigate his neighbours in Bampton he said in about 1600 that every woman who accused him of fathering an illegitimate child was a whore and that any man who said the same was a knave. In many instances a man responded to being called a knave by replying that his female accuser was a whore.[264] It appears to have been a generic or preferred term of abuse. Even the inside page of an Elizabethan church court book has relevant lines of doggerel[265]. A scribe wrote:

> *'Beggarly knaves*
> *shall never be rich*
> *if that their wives*
> *wear the britches'*

Knave had been a pejorative term since the 1200s; it defined a dishonest unprincipled man or a cunning unscrupulous rogue. A complaint by Kenton's church clerk in 1597 confirms its local meaning: one witness overheard him being called 'a knave or a troublesome fellow or a lewd fellow'. In 1573 it was explained in Widecombe-in-the Moor that the word indicated 'a man of evil life' while Peter Palk of Littlehempston equated knaves with being 'unhonest men'.[266] Its meaning can also be gleaned from its use in 1621: Nicholas Spicer of Heavitree chanced upon Thomasine Philips in Exeter and asked her 'Where is thy knave, thy husband?' to which she answered 'I hope he is no knave'. Spicer replied 'Yes, Thomas Phillipps is a knave, for he leesed [unfastened] up thy smock and brought thee with child before marriage.'[267] Likewise, Margaret Vingle's explanation for why she thought Roger Cheek of Exeter was a knave provides another insight: she allegedly said 'thou art a knave and an arrant knave for thou hast attempted my chastity and thou wouldst have had the carnal knowledge of my body'.[268]

Its use as an all-purpose term for a disreputable man is shown in the ways in which two women were ridiculed: Joan Allen of Tavistock was said to lie in bushes 'with every knave' while Joan Harward of Aveton Giffard had a similar insult thrown at her: she allegedly laid in hedges with every knave.[269] It can also be seen in William Tregoe's admittance to being a knave whilst drinking in a house on Exe Bridge in 1599. He had slandered Joan Hayne's reputation which prompted another man to defend her. Robert Western said that Hayne was a more honest woman than Tregoe was a man. Tregoe replied 'then she is an arrant whore for all the world knows that I am an arrant knave'.[270]

However, the word was not disregarded. In one unknown parish it was used to describe two men who promptly objected. On 16 May 1558 John Wood testified that at the beginning of Lent 'this respondent and one Pilson, a cutler, went along by the said Mogridge his [own] door unto whom the said Joan [Mogridge] said *there goeth two vile knaves* (meaning this respondent and the said Pilson) then said this respondent to Pilson *I am sure she calleth not me knave* then Pilson said that *she said as much to this respondent as she said unto him* the said Pilson. And then this respondent said that *the said Joan spoke more like a whore to call this respondent knave who said no evil unto her*. And then Mogridge asked *who it was that called his wife whore?* Then this respondent said *thou scabbed squire, I do not call thy wife whore but she calling me vile knave going by the king's highway she is more like a whore than an honest woman*. Likewise, in 1619 an Exeter man warned a woman that 'if any whore in England called him lousy knave, he would pull her nose from her face'.[271]

The term's use was sharpened by adding adjectives such as in Tavistock in 1617 when Richard Rowe was called a cuckoldly knave or in Exeter in 1624 when one man called the other 'knave, old knave and beggarly knave with divers other uncivil words'.[272] Likewise, in 1571 two men argued in the churchyard of Zeal

Monachorum and one called the other 'naughty knave, harlot knave and bawdy knave'.[273] The term knave was often used with other disparaging words, such as rogue or whoremonger, but in many instances it was the only term used albeit with a tirade of stinging adjectives. These provide insights into the alleged characters of those being ridiculed. This includes the vicar of St Erth in Cornwall who in 1634 was called a knave, a base knave, a greedy knave and a dangerous knave.[274] Robert Gun of Exeter St Thomas was likewise called 'a base knave, a base livery-coat knave and the basest knave that ever was kept'. Likewise, an Exeter man was termed a knave, base knave and 'pockerly' knave in 1621.[275] The rector of Dodbrooke, Otho Morcombe, had more reasons to feel aggrieved. In 1622 he was called 'a knave, an arrant knave, a very knave, a dissembling knave and a shit breech knave'.[276] Two years later an argument in Exeter resulted in one man calling the other 'a knave, baggage knave, paltry knave and a rascal-like veriest knave in the parish'. In 1631 the cleric at Sheepwash was called a knave and a cheating false knave, in 1618 a Halberton man was both a wooden-faced and brazen-faced knave and in St Veep in 1627 a Cornishman was termed not only a knave but a bald and rascally one.[277] In Topsham one man was described as being 'as rascally a knave as any within the town' and another exceptional knave was a Drewsteignton man noted in 1616 as 'an arrant whore-maker knave as any in Devonshire'. An Ilsington man was credited with much more prowess: he was slandered in 1636 as being the greatest bawdy old knave in the country.[278]

In 1559 a Shirwell man admitted calling another a knave but denied saying he lied or was false. He regarded him as 'no less than a knave' but added 'as for other men let them take him as they list [liked]'.[279]

Rogues

This term, which has signified a disreputable man since the late 1400s,[280] was also highly used but less specific than others: it was cited in more than 70 slander cases in the church court and there were other instances of it being complained of before local magistrates. It was said in every part of Devon and much more commonly applied to men than to women. It was often used on its own but there are many examples of it being preceded by adjectives such as arrant thievish, bankrupt, base, beggarly, burnt-tail, common drunken, cuckoldly, full of lice, lousy-breeched, mazed, pocky, reprobate, runagate, runabout, runaway, tallow-faced, thonging or thong cutting, very, whoremaster, whoremongering and whoring. The terms drunken or drunkard rogue were among the most commonly used variants.

Rascals, slaves, varlets and suckers

Rascal was said far less frequently than either rogue or knave. While today it is used more lightheartedly to suggest an appealing scamp, from at least the early 1400s it defined 'an unprincipled or dishonest person, a rogue, a scoundrel'. Its sense in 1623 is indicated when Thomas Dobbins was called a rascal for being found at midnight with a 'quean', a prostitute, in Barnstaple's churchyard.[281] Although not commonly used on its own, it was nevertheless recorded in such widely dispersed places as Uffculme, Staverton, Great Torrington, Exeter, Christow, Plympton St Maurice, Slapton, Willand, Bishop's Nympton, Kingsbridge, Barnstaple, Southleigh, Sheepwash, North Petherwin and Berry Pomeroy.[282] Knave and rogue were often used alongside rascal: in 1619 Edward Searle was said to have become drunk in another man's house and was called a base rascal, lousy rascal and a lousy breeched rogue while in 1637 a Willand man was said to be a knave, a base knave, a rascal and a rascally knave. Along with a longer string of abusive terms, another Exeter man was called 'rascal-like' in 1624.[283]

An alternative term to rascal was slave which had this secondary and now archaic meaning in the sixteenth century. It was cited in nine court cases of which six occurred in Exeter and the earliest recorded use was in 1571 when two men called each other a string of names including whoreson slave and bastardly slave.'[284] The next recorded instance took place in the cathedral in 1583. An official asked several gentlemen to leave the building and when one refused he was called a knave and slave.[285] Of the remaining

19. 'How now, mooncalf?', The Tempest *by William Shakespeare, Act II Scene ii, c1610.*

four Exeter cases two were sexual insults: Margaret and Richard Tucker complained that Robert Weare said in 1627 'thou art a cuckoldly slave and thy wife meaning the said Margaret Tucker is a whore and a base whore' while eight years later Gregory Woolcott complained that John Loone said 'thou art a whoremonger, whoremaster and whoremongering slave and thou were found abed with Joan Follet'.[286] The remaining two uses involved alcohol. One man in 1617 was called 'a drinking beast, a drinking slave and a drunkard' while two years earlier a woman, while standing in Mr Prowse's shop near the guildhall, said to Henry Lay 'thou art a drunken rogue, a drunken slave and a common drunkard'.[287]

Its meaning is perhaps best understood from a dispute over tithes in North Huish church. In 1569 a brawl broke out between parishioners in the chancel. Two used the term slave. One man called out 'where is that vile slave?' while a second man objected to another sitting while talking to his social betters. Witnesses did not agree on the precise wording: one thought Richard Cleveland had said 'What a slave art thou to sit upon thy tail when that thou dost talk with thy better' while another remembered it being 'Arise slave, thou dost talk with thy better, if thou wilt give my master, Mr Collins, no more reverence get thee out of this seat and go and sit down among thy fellows'.[288]

There were also two early-seventeenth century instances, both sexual, which show its use outside Devon. From Padstow John Bishop complained that Henry Pawlyn said 'thou art a cuckold and a cuckoldly slave' while Richard Butland of Mevagissey objected to a man of Gorran telling him in 1624 'thou art a black liver slave and thou didst fuck thy mistress before thou wast married to her'.[289]

Three instances were recorded of the term 'varlet', a dishonest man or one of a low disposition. It was said of Robert Rich of Down St Mary who was a court witness in 1565. He was scorned as being 'of small honesty or of credit and a common varlet and tale bearer and no credit to be given unto him'. The vicar of Tavistock, as will be seen, called his parishioners varlets in the 1650s and a man of Sheepwash was also called a varlet knave in 1568.[290] Hooker thought it was the place of a varlet to look after horses and not one for an honest and wise man.[291] Another term, in national use throughout this period, was recorded in Cornwall but has not been found in Devon. In 1572 a Cornishman near Boscastle was described as a drunken 'sucker', from the early 1500s this defined a man who lived at the expense of others.[292]

Low Intelligence

Twenty terms were used to demean men for having insufficient intelligence or being impudent. These were fool and ass, innocent, cockscomb, woodcock, calf, bull, mooncalf, lubber, lobb, puppy, jackanapes, ninnyhammer, ninnycock, ninnypoop, bull head, blockhead, hardhead, slug and patch.

Fools and asses

The term 'fool' featured in a number of court cases. In one instance it was used to describe a woman who probably had extreme cognitive disability. Thomasine Palmer of St David's parish outside Exeter in 1619 was called 'a very fool, idiot and a natural' who 'had not so much wit as a child of ten or eleven years old'.[293] The other references to fools were made in a scoffing manner. In 1623 Daniel Rowcliff of Burrington complained that Hugh Perceley called him an old fool but he also objected to being termed an 'innocent', by which Perceley meant he was deficient in intelligence. 'Innocent' had been written in 1554 in Barnstaple's parish register to describe a woman. Perceley also called Rowcliff a 'trout', an unidentified term, and added that his sons 'were drunkards and rogues with many other disgraceful speeches'. A Totnes woman, who in 1576 was ridiculed as leading an immoral life, replied to her adversaries that they spoke like fools.[294] On 27 December 1616 Joan Snow, while in church at Puddington, accused her neighbour Humphrey Melhuish of being a fool and the cause may have been because she regarded his wife as a social inferior. Snow said that Melhuish's wife 'was brought up at the pigs' trough. Let her go home to the swine's bucket and then she will know where she is.'[295]

Two men in different parishes independently used the same unusual phrase in 1583. A Sampford Courtenay parishioner admitted having had illicit sex and explained it as 'a foolish part of me'. In contrast, a Sheepwash man sought his wife's forgiveness but explained his behaviour was not his fault. John Hayne told his wife Anne, on finding him naked in bed with another woman, 'I must confess I have done a foolish part, I think I am bewitched to her but forgive me for this. I will never do the like'.[296]

The term ass was often used concurrently with that of fool and turned it into a phrase. For instance, in 1601 John Follet was called a fool and an ass while in Honiton church.[297] The same insulting phrase was applied to the husband of Elizabeth Wolcock in the early 1620s. She was told 'thy servant John Philipps kept thee and was as familiar with thee as thine own husband and thy husband was a fool and an ass that he did not perceive it'. In 1597 one man called another, whilst in Werrington's churchyard, not only a fool and ass but also a cozening knave, beggarly knave, 'powling' knave and proud knave.[298]

In 1579 a Rackenford servant was called both a fool and a 'dizard'. Nearly fifty years later this same unidentified term, along with fool, was used in Burrington. In 1580, less than a generation after it was first in print, it was said that a Paignton man was a 'patch', another term for a fool or an ill-natured person.[299]

Cockscombs and woodcocks

In 1618 a man walking through Southernhay in Exeter was called a fool and a cockscomb. From at least the 1600s the latter term meant a conceited fool if not a fop. When Alice Stephens and Caleb Saunders exchanged insults in a Bradninch street in 1637, she was called a whore and he was termed a drunken knave and a cockscomb.[300] The term woodcock, which denoted a dupe or a fool, has been found in one instance. As will be discussed later, it was used to mock the vicar of Churchstow. The best-known Devon use for this word took place in 1521 on Maze Monday otherwise known as Cockwood Fool or Woodcock Fool. That year it was rumoured that a French fleet intended to plunder the Exe Estuary and the effect it had in Exeter was panic, referred to by John Hooker as a 'hurly burly'. The mayor locked the city gates in order to stop a stampede of people. A Cockwood inhabitant started the rumour but Hooker wryly renamed him (or her) as the Woodcock Fool.[301]

Calves and bulls

There was one recorded instance of the term 'calf'. It signified a dolt or a stupid man. Only some ten years after it was first recorded in print, the term was used in Devon. In 1577 a dispute broke out in Halberton regarding the election of a way warden, the local official who oversaw the maintenance of public roads. An older man, Richard Berry, tried to impose his candidate but a younger parishioner, John Sanders, pointed out that his actions were illegal. Berry resented Sanders' comments and told him 'thou hast an oar in every man's boat'. He also said 'Hold thy peace, thou art a calf' to which the younger man replied 'If I am a calf, thou art a bull'. Tempers increased as Berry told Sanders he himself was not a bull given he was unmarried and therefore could not have (cuckold's) horns. Sanders replied by instructing him to take his thumb, 'put him in thy arse', bite it off, make a crook of his nose and use it to draw out his thumb.[302]

Another term to imply a simpleton was 'mooncalf'. It was deployed in Crediton in 1616 but a second meaning, used by Shakespeare in the *Tempest*, was that of a deformed animal or monster. This may also apply in this particular instance. A neighbour told Priscilla Cleeve 'you are a notable whore and they say you are with child but it may be none of your husband's for ought I know' and then added 'I think it is a mooncalf or it may be a *noon* calf '. Three years later a conversation at Topsham about illegitimate children included the word calf but in a different sense: one resident said to another 'whosoever bulled the cow . . . shall have the calf.'[303]

Lubbers, Lobs & Loggerheads

There are three recorded instances of the medieval term 'lubber' which from the 1300s denoted idle and big, clumsy, stupid men. Hartland men, as noted below, were on one occasion called abbey lubbers. In 1635 a falling out at Winkleigh church between James Hernaman and Samuel Luxton was overheard by witnesses who reported Hernaman had called Luxton 'a lubber and a foul mouthed lubber' and asked him 'what is the reason thou dost speak so hoarse?' He also advised Luxton 'to have a bramble to scour thy throat' before asking a further question 'what is the reason thy breeches are not clean?' The two men argued over taxes: Hernaman was a churchwarden and Luxton disputed the amount he allegedly owed.[304] The term appears to have been more widespread than is indicated by its prevalence in the records or it became so later. In 1884 Ugborough men were known as lubbers because it rhymed with Ubber, the name by which the parish was known. It was part of a rhyme:[305]

> 'Ubber lubbers,
>   Harford gads,
> Cornwood robbers,
>   and Ivybridge lads'.

Lob, in use through the 1500s, had a similar meaning to lubber in that from the early 1500s it defined a country bumpkin, a clown or a lout. A Crediton man was called a 'foul-mouthed lob' in 1581.[306] A generation later, in 1619, an Exeter man was called both a great fat lubber and a loggerhead, another term, recorded in use only from 1595, for a stupid man.[307] It was also used in Exeter in 1621 to describe an assize judge.[308]

Puppies and jackanapes

Two Cornish men were called 'puppies' but only one Devon occurrence was recorded. In 1629 Ralph Payne of St Gluvias near Falmouth was called 'a puppy, a ninnyhammer and a cuckold' while a man of Withiel was also said to be both a cuckold and a puppy. It was used from at least the mid 1500s to denote a foolish, conceited or impertinent young man.[309] The curate of Hartland, William Churton, who was in office from 1628 until 1646, called his parishioners abbey lubbers, rascals, reprobates (unredeemed sinners), base epicures (disbelievers in an afterlife or in the divine government of the world) and puppies. In addition to these terms, some of which were not recorded elsewhere in Devon, in an infamous sermon he preached that the children of a Protestant and a Catholic would produce mongrels. The latter term was also used in Bishop's Nympton in 1601 when a local man, who was said to have syphilis, was also said to have been 'a mongrel bastard'. In these instances mongrels signified individuals of mixed descent.[310]

Jackanapes was used to describe impudent men such as one in Totnes in 1639. A number of Exeter constables were called jackanapes with one woman adding 'I did think how proud thou wouldst be when thou were put into office'. The term had been in use through the 1500s.[311]

Ninnyhammers, ninnypoops and bull heads

'Ninny' was recorded in three instances. It had then its current meaning: it has denoted a simpleton or a fool since the late 1500s. It could also mean a small child such as when used by Tavistock's Richard Peek in his play Dick of Devonshire in about 1626. One of

20. *St Mary Major Church, painted by Edward Dayes, in about 1800. In this parish in 1565 it was alleged that Richard Gervis was called a bull head knave amongst other insults.*

his characters said 'the very name of Drake was a bugbear to fright children. Nurses stilled their little Spanish ninnies when they cried *Hush, the Drake comes*'.[312]

The term 'ninnyhammer' was less common. It signified a man who was a blockhead, fool or braggart and was first used in print in 1592.[313] Three Cornish instances, dating to the 1620s, were cited in the church court: Richard Gaine of Madron was called both a cuckold and a ninnyhammer, Thomas Seymour of Launceston was named as a wittol and ninnyhammer and Radolphus Payne of St Gluvias was called not only a ninnyhammer but a cuckold and a puppy.[314] It may be relevant that no use was recorded in Devon except in one West Devon parish, Tavistock, which also occurred in this decade. In 1624 Alexander Skerret of that town was called a hardhead, wittol and a ninnyhammer.[315] This is intriguing because a generation later, in the late 1650s, Reverend Thomas Larkham, the Anglican vicar of the town, was alleged to have used the term, from the pulpit, when he described local people. He subsequently disputed this when questioned by justices at the Quarter Sessions in

Exeter. Larkham even claimed to be ignorant of its meaning. The justices, he later wrote, informed Larkham, or so he maintained, that a ninnyhammer was 'nine times worse than a cuckold'. His Tavistock parishioners responded 'one thing which he is accused for is that he hath an unwashed mouth and is a common railer in the pulpit; calling the people Ragged Rogues, snarling curs, devil's dish clouts &c, to plead himself guiltless of this he calls them varlet, brute, monster in the press'. Larkham was a controversial figure across Devon and beyond: he became a leading Puritan figure after having served in several Devon parishes. Larkham was licensed to preach throughout the dioceses of Bath and Wales, London and Exeter in 1626 and was the vicar at Northam from 1626 to 1641. He also served as curate of Sandford where he had been involved in a case of alleged misuse of the church house. Married men were said to have behaved there in a 'beastly and filthy manner' with a local woman. Just before the Civil War he emigrated to New England where he had a child born outside of marriage. He returned to Devon, was court-martialled for insubordination while serving as chaplain of Sir Hardress Waller's regiment and then imprisoned at Exeter on another charge. His alleged use of the term ninnyhammer was perhaps even more public in that it culminated in a series of printed attacks and retorts with his parishioners who also claimed he was over-fond of alcohol and playing bowls.[316]

In 1601 Richard Harris of Bodmin complained that it was said to him 'thou art an arrant cuckold knave and a ninnypoop ten times worse than a cuckold and thy wife Jane Harries is a whore and a pocky whore and hath been laid for the pox'. A poop could mean a backside and the words' combination suggests this was a highly derogatory word. It also was used to suggest someone who cheated or deceived. This may have differed from the term ninnyhammer in that ninnypoop could have been an earlier version of nincompoop, which has been defined as a simpleton or foolish person. Its meaning may be better understood in its context: it was also said that Harris' wife hid a man under her bed when her husband came home unexpectedly. The earliest printed reference to the word nincompoop is 1673.[317] It is interesting, when considered alongside the use of the word ninnyhammer, that the example is Cornish. Another possible version was used in Exeter in 1637. A married woman complained that she was called a whore, a base whore and a ninnycock whore.[318] This presumably meant that a fool paid her for sex.

Similar in meaning to ninnyhammer was 'bull head' which was recorded in use in England only from 1624 to describe a stupid fellow or blockhead. However, it was five years earlier, in 1619, that Richard Downe of Bideford complained that John Clement of Monkleigh had said to him 'thou art a cuckold and a bull head'. Another instance took place much earlier in Exeter: in 1565 an exchange of words between Richard Gervis and one Mrs Hose resulted in the former being called not just a bull head but a knave, cuckold, princock, slut bone and whoreson.[319] A 'hardhead' was similar to a bull head in that, from at least the 1570s, both meant a blockhead. It was recorded not only at Tavistock as mentioned above but also in Cornwall in the early 1600s.[320] The early sixteenth-century term 'blockhead' ('an utterly stupid fellow') is documented for Yarnscombe, as noted earlier, and also in Cornwall where a husband was said to be a blockhead or 'slug', which was in use from at least the early 1400s to denote a slow or inactive man, to allow another man to sleep with his wife.[321]

Physical deformities

Three terms, blinkard, crookback and cripple, were used to ridicule physical attributes. In 1605 Drewsteignton's rector was called a series of names including a pilled parson, a medieval word which meant he was either wretched or bald. The rector was also termed 'a fucking priest' as well as a blink-eyed priest.[322] Further to the west, in 1594 at North Petherwin, which was a part of Devon until 1966, men were in a field 'Devonshiring', otherwise known as beat burning, when John Pope was called an old whoremonger knave and an old fornicator as well as an old blinkard.[323] A blinkard was 'a reproachful name for one who blinks or winks' but it was also 'one who lacks intellectual perception'. Either of these definitions may be appropriate but for another Cornish case, that involving a man of St Teath in north Cornwall in 1561, it is clear that poor eyesight was meant. Alice Cowlyn was unhappy with her family's choice of a man for her to marry and said she wanted 'some honest young man that she might fantasy', that is fancy. She rejected William Raw of nearby Warbstow because he 'was a man that had an impediment in his sight and looking somewhat a blink or blearied-eyed'. It was also thought she called him 'spore blind' which would be better known today as purblind in which there is blindness in one eye or partial sight.[324] More than a generation later, in 1597, a Launceston woman was called 'an arrant blinking whore' which may also have indicated poor eyesight. It was probably this meaning that was intended in yet another Cornish case. In the early 1600s Henry Johns of St Issey, near St Teath, was called a blinkard and a blinking slave. Johns was also termed a crookback, that is a hunchback, and told to stick his nose under a lamb's tail. The secondary modern meaning for blinking is much later.[325] Stoodleigh's parson and a woman of Tiverton were both called 'cripples' but the word 'lame' was not used although it was written into Barnstaple's church register in 1581 to describe a burial ('Anne, a lame creature').[326]

Female terms

In Devon young unmarried women have been traditionally referred to as maids and they were noted as such in court depositions. Occasionally one was called a wench and this does not appear to have had a derogatory meaning. It denoted a young woman or a working class girl.[327] For example, Elizabeth Hill of Pilton, for example, was described in 1596 as being 'a maid and unmarried and accounted and taken to be a very honest wench' while Katherine Holman of Modbury in 1619 was noted as 'a poor simple wench and can hardly tell her tale except she be schooled and taught what she should say'.[328] Likewise, two young women on the verge of being betrothed were described as wenches in the 1530s. An Exeter woman was approved of when she was told that she spoke like an honest wench and a prospective groom in Hartland was asked 'will you have this pretty wench for your wife?'[329] 'Goodwife', a term which defined a female head of household and was in use from at least the 1200s, was said once in Exeter's diocesan court but 'Goody' was not noted as a title although it was recorded in a mayoral court in 1621: Goody Harris was an Exeter widow.[330] Other documentation shows the term Goodwife was used elsewhere in Devon at this time.[331]

Interestingly, the word fool was nearly always only described men: only one use of it has been found directed at a Devon woman. In 1573 Faith Bond of Bishop's Tawton was described as being 'a very fool'.[332] It may be that society agreed with John Knox who wrote in 1558 that women by nature were not only weak, frail, impatient and feeble but also foolish.[333] It could therefore be argued that because women were not expected to act in an intelligent manner, they were less likely to be defined as fools.

Animals inspired some insults and one contradicts the lack of women being called foolish. A parishioner called Mary Arundel of Lapford an arrant sow and he spoke of her 'goodly increase of pigs'. He added 'if I were a young bore I would see if I could bore thee'. It was claimed that she had called his wife a goose, by which she meant the woman was silly. That term had been used in England since at least 1547.[334] Nearly all instances of women being called sows were associated with an excess of alcohol in that they were named as drunken sows. The insult had been used since at least 1508 to denote a fat, clumsy or slovenly woman but there are only a few instances in the church court where women complained of it being used on its own. For example, in Stoke Gabriel in 1612 one woman called another a sow and a gentlewoman whore whereas in Thurlestone in 1638 the slur had a more farmyard flavour. The curate testified that he heard John Pearse say of Joan Elly in a West Alvington house 'many uncivil words of her, but this deponent being somewhat hard of hearing did not certainly hear the same what they were saying that he said she was a sow and bored or bulled sow, which of the two he doth not know'. Another witness thought he called her an open-arsed whore before naming her a bored sow.[335] As will be discussed later, the term 'mare' described a woman in a sexual manner similar to the way in which vixen is used today. In 1560 a man in Topsham was called an Irish cow but it is unclear what was meant by this phrase although it was also suggested he had horns and was a cuckold.[336]

The term 'giglet', in use nationally from at least the early 1300s, was cited in two church court cases in Exeter in 1635. In Holy Trinity Church one woman sat in another's seat and caused offence. Places in churches were prescribed and the order reflected the social hierarchy. Susan Richardson refused to allow Mary Bligh to sit in her accustomed seat. She mocked Bligh by calling her a giglet and young thing as well as a proud minx. Richardson also said 'thy husband hath better fed thee than taught thee, go home and learn more manners'. An incident in Cathedral Yard concerned which woman should give way while walking. Alan Penny took

21. *Plymouth's ducking stool. It was reported in* The Western Antiquary *in 1881 that a chair had been recently discovered 'amongst a quantity of lumber' near the quay. This might have been the town's ducking stool but there also was a rival seat held at the Athenaeum.*

offence at the behaviour of Mrs Margaret Spicer. He said to her 'What do you mean you will give us the way? Come you forth, here are better women than you be coming after and you are a giglet.' The original meaning of giglet was a lewd or wanton woman but it also came to mean a 'giddy, laughing, romping girl'. It may be that the second meaning was implied in both instances.[337]

The term 'trash' has only been found applied to women and may have been similar to the male term, 'knave'. It signified a worthless or disreputable person and its uses include 'trash whore', 'scurvy trashing jade', 'base trash', 'common trash', scurvy trash' and 'scurvy whore trash'.[338]

Particularly vivid are some scatological terms given to women. Two objected to being called a jakes, a term in use nationally from the 1530s meaning a privy or merely excrement. In 1570 Joan Knowles of Littlehempston was called both a scold and 'old jakes' while a woman of St Uny in Cornwall was called 'but a shitting jakes' by her neighbour in 1567.[339] Similarly, a Dartmouth woman was called 'a shitten whore' in 1598 and a Chudleigh woman in 1558 was called 'a shitten-heeled whore'.[340] Also, some prostitutes, as will be discussed, were particularly associated with chamber pots.

Whereas most insults for a woman relate to the misuse of her sexual organs, there are many others which concern the inappropriate use of two others, the ear and tongue: women were ridiculed for improper hearing and speaking. A contemporary ballad entitled *A New Medley or A Mess of All-together* highlighted three 'good wives': the slut, the strumpet and the scold.[341] Women, as will be seen, had name-calling which reflected each of these 'qualities'.

Crimes of the ears and tongue

One crime had no correlating slander: women could be prosecuted for overhearing private conversations but they do not have appear to have been slandered for it. In Dartmouth three married women were brought to court between 1491 and 1502 for being 'common listeners' or 'a common eavesdropper' at neighbours'

22. *Carving of a woman with her tongue out, possibly depicting a scold, at St Peter's Church, Dowland.*

doors and windows.[342] Similar wording was used when a man, John Acland, was prosecuted before Barnstaple's mayor in 1583: he was 'a common night-watcher and listener at a man's window'.[343] Curiously, the lack of it as slander in the courts may indicate it was not used as an insult in Devon or at least very rarely. Also, as will be seen, in Exeter such behaviour was not only encouraged but rewarded in the early 1600s.

The tongue was the principal organ that was referred to in verbal exchanges and almost exclusively it was only a woman's tongue that was cited. The author of *The Drunkard's Character* wrote in 1638 that a lewd tongue was a loud tongue, and a loud tongue a lewd one. He also compared impudent speakers with gaping oysters; when opened they 'either stink or there is nothing in them'. In 1600 one woman of Berry Pomeroy was called 'a common whore both of thy body and tongue', another of Heavitree was said in 1626 to be 'a whore and a whore of thy tongue' and in Exeter a local woman was described in 1561 as being 'a very wavering women of her tongue'.[344] In contrast, yet another Exeter woman was called 'a quean of her tongue' in 1617 while Ricarda Cole of Littlehempston was slandered in 1557 as 'an honest woman of her body but a shrew of her tongue' and ten years later Agnes Hewett of Great Torrington was called 'a drab of her tongue'.[345] In comparison, Agnes Berry of Exeter was termed a 'troublesome woman of her tongue' in 1566 and eight years earlier yet another woman was called both an unquiet woman and evil woman of her tongue.[346]

When two women exchanged words in Broadclyst in 1565 one said the other was 'a slanderous woman of tongue and that she were better to be a whore of her tail rather than of her tongue'.[347] The variants of the phrase 'whore of her tongue' was used during various arguments. For instance, in Kenn in 1558 one woman called her neighbour a cuckold knave and he replied she was a whore of her tongue for using those words. Likewise, a few years earlier a similar exchange in Chudleigh produced a comparable phrase. Two parishioners disagreed about pulling down a hedge and one called the other a cuckold knave. The other responded by saying 'she was a whore of her tongue and an unquiet woman of her tongue and a shitten gentle woman' but by time he had finished talking she had dealt him several blows. His neighbour, he claimed, was 'ever taken amongst her neighbours for an evil woman of her tongue'.[348]

Women were more likely to be accused of spreading rumours such as Agnes Heddon, described as a poor woman who begged from door to door in an unnamed Devon parish, who was called a 'common tale teller' in 1626. Her credibility as a witness was questioned.[349] But men were occasionally noted such as Robert Rich of Down St Mary who in 1565 was described as a 'tale bearer'.[350] In 1585 two men were in a workshop in Alphington and one asked the other if there was any news of a common acquaintance, Joan Mitchell. One had forbidden his servants to talk of her but added 'my Cowick close can tell tales if it were able to speak – for the old Tuckfield saw Mitchell's wife and William Corben both in the close together and there the deed was done as they say'.[351] It would be more likely today for such tale tellers to be termed gossips. There were 16 civil prosecutions of women for being 'common gossips' in Dartmouth between 1503 and 1509. Nine actions were against two married women, Petronella Stone and Agnes Wellys, and a third woman was prosecuted twice.[352] In these instances the term gossip defined a woman who maliciously talked about her neighbours. However, it had several other meanings which were not insults including that of a woman's friends who were present at a birth.[353]

One meaning was a close friend. It was in this sense that witnesses denied being either a 'gossip or familiar' of an Exeter woman in 1635. It was possibly this sense of the word that was implied in 1556 when the circumstances of a betrothal and marriage were questioned at West Alvington. Peter Hopill's mother and wife, it was explained, were concerned at his familiarity with a servant girl and had her removed from his house. After their deaths Hopill brought the young woman back into his household, married her and they had triplets. She had been, it was said, 'his gossip'. This might have been the implied meaning in 1561 when one Alphington man said of Katherine Hayne 'she is a whore although she be my gossip'.[354] Likewise, in Littlehempston a woman, who was outraged at her daughter's sexual conduct, called her a whore while beating her with a rod outside of the church. Her lover tried to speak to the mother whom he called 'Good Gossip' and claimed he considered both to be his gossips.[355]

The term also could designate a godparent. Hence at St Stephens near Launceston in Cornwall in 1637 a local man accused another of being a gossip to his own illegitimate child. It was explained in court that a second man had married the child's mother but the father acted as godfather.[356] It may have been either definition that was meant at Barnstaple in 1599 when Lettice Wichalse visited Thomas Edwards' workshop and asked him 'Gossip, the speeches goeth that there is one here by us which is with child'. Edwards called her 'Mistress Wichalse' which might imply she was an older woman and therefore possibly his godmother.[357] A similar exchange took place in Kenton in 1604. It was rumoured that Richard Frost fathered illegitimate children while working in Somerset's herring fishery. Fishermen spent several weeks there in the autumn. John Folkes said to William Scorche 'Gossip, I can tell you news, I do hear say, said he, that Richard Frost hath a bastard or two at Porlock and that Gawen Baker told me' but Scorche had been with Frost for two fishing seasons and replied 'Take heed gossip what you say for I do think it is a lie.'[358]

Scolds

The most common non-sexual abusive term for a woman was scold. It had been in common use nationally from the 1200s. A scold signified 'a woman who disturbs the peace of the neighbourhood by her constant scolding', that is a woman who persistently railed with the effect of disturbing her neighbours.[359] There were a number of individuals named as such in Devon's courts.

Scolding was punishable in civil courts and prosecutions can be found in sixteenth-century, and earlier, records for Barnstaple, Dartmouth, Exeter and Plymouth. Smaller places, such as Colyton, also had cucking stools. In 1881 it was claimed that it was as late as 1808 that the last woman in Plymouth to have been cucked was Nancy Clarke, 'an aged fishwoman, a great drunkard, for an assault on Kitty Ware, in the same line of business, also for cursing, swearing and using obscene language'.[360] By 1808 there had been five hundred years of prosecuting Devon women as scolds: in the mid 1300s Barnstaple's mayors punished married women for being 'common destroyers and disturbers of the peace'.[361] The town's accounts show repairs to the cucking (or ducking) stool, where some women were punished, in 1525, 1555 and 1567. In 1567 it was referred to as the 'skilfying' stool whereas in 1606 a woman named Comer as having been 'cucked'.[362] In 1495 and 1500 Dartmouth was deficient of a cucking stool although in 1494, 1495, 1497 and 1500 seven women were punished for being common scolds.[363] Plymouth's borough accounts show that in 1508 the corporation paid three shillings for making a new 'cage', the seat on which a scold was fixed. It had been there by 1486 as it was in that year that the pit was cleaned by two men. The stool was renewed again in 1560. In 1599 four pence was paid for 'hauling the ducking stool to duck the cook's wife and James Coyt's wife'. Seven years later 2s 6d was expended for 'ducking a woman and for a swifting girdle and cords to make her fast'.[364]

In Exeter there had been some 150 indictments of scolds in the late 1300s and prosecutions continued through the 1500s. In 1562 Anne Fryer, a married woman, was 'washed' at the cucking stool because of 'her scolding and her slanderous words and evil report'. She was then banished. That same year four women were also convicted of being scolds but their punishment was to be dragged behind a boat along the river Exe.[365] In the early 1600s some twenty Exeter women were likewise named as scolds, often as 'common scolds', and punished. Between 1618 and 1621 seventeen women were prosecuted and most were ordered to be 'well washed' by ducking. Anne Trivett, Joan Sampford, Alice Thomas and Joan Cassil each had 9 neighbours testify against them. These women were accused of continually berating their neighbours with abusive language, to have been physically violent and to have stolen clothing. The insults allegedly given to their neighbours included pocky jade, tallow-faced whore, bawd, thief, cuckold, rogue, whoremonger, murderer, bulled bitch, truckle whore, carted whore, turned coats, whoremaster and scabbed whore.[366] In June 1621 four of these women, who appear to have engaged in a physical and verbal brawl, were each punished by being ducked. Their behaviour had clearly caused great public offence, and it must have been viewed with some irony when Joan Sampford mocked her neighbours in Paris Street in saying there was not an honest man or woman living in that street.[367]

The most unusual recorded punishment for a Devon scold also took place in Exeter. According to various witnesses in 1621 Goody Harris had called Thomasine Loder old Beezlebub, old whore and a bawd. Loder then commented in a like fashion of Harris and added that her son had died of the pox and piles. What happened next was a form of rough justice not sanctioned by the law. Loder initiated punishment for her adversary by procuring a rule staff, a long pole. She said that Harris 'ought to ride to water upon a rule staff'. However, it was Loder that her female neighbours placed upon the pole and then they carried her on it as they paraded up and down Paul Street. Nearly 200 people gathered to watch what was described as 'sport'.[368]

It was important to avoid being called a scold to prevent prosecution in the civil court but there were other benefits in not being regarded as a scolding woman. The testimony of one Modbury woman as a witness was dismissed in 1619 when it was claimed that 'she did ride in the cucking stool and was dipped in the water for her lewd tongue and this deponent sayeth that in his conscience the said Prudence careth not what she sayeth or sweareth'.[369] Likewise, some Exeter witnesses were disparaged for being 'poor scolding & brabling people' who 'often times scold with their neighbours in the open street and are people or little or no credit or repute'. It was also said that they had 'many brables', that is arguments.[370] A Davidstow woman was noted as 'a common scold' in 1601 whereas another woman of Throwleigh was called in 1616 'a notable' or 'an over' scold. She was told she had 'caused much money to be spent as thou are like to undo thy husband'.[371] In contrast, another woman was said on the road from Berry Pomeroy to Littlehempston to be regarded 'as very a scold as any is in the parish'.[372] Elizabeth Ebbotson of Exeter was regarded in 1638 not to be a scold in comparison with her neighbour Mary Cholwell who had not only called her a jade, a beggarly slut and a rogue but also said she was not worth a quart pot or a groat. In contrast, Ebbotson was regarded by a court witness as 'a woman of far better life and conversation & far better rank & quality than the said Mary Cholwell, meek and lowly, peaceable amongst her neighbours and such a one as is no way given to scolding nor would speak a disgraceful word of any one unless mightily thereunto provoked'.[373]

At Dartmouth in 1618 the word scold was used in an incidental manner and was secondary to another insult. In 1618 two merchants exchanged heated words at the Hardness end of the Fosse, between the two mills which were situated there. The argument between Thomas Holland and William Bogan took place in front of nearly forty witnesses. One recalled that Holland said to Anne Bogan 'Away thou strumpet, dost thou scold in the street?' while another thought he had uttered the words 'Art thou not ashamed to scold like a strumpet?' What happened next appears to have been Mrs Bogan asking 'Dost thou call me strumpet?' on which Holland dismissed her by replying 'I have nothing to do with thee, I talk with thy husband'. It was at this point that Anne Bogan repeatedly told Holland that his own wife was a whore and strumpet. The term scold seems to have been the minor insult.[374]

Some court cases show that the use of the term preceded or could trigger a string of more serious abuse. For instance, in the spring of 1572 Martin Grosse, a Moretonhampstead tinner, was hacking, that is breaking up, ground along the north hedge of Yalworthy Down when he was interrupted by Elizabeth Laskey who 'began to rail' at Grosse and told him he was diseased. He called her a scold and told Laskey to go home. Scolding was also said to have taken place at a well in Gnaton at Revelstoke a week before Easter in 1604. One man testified that he heard two women scolding while they were washing clothes and then the mistress of one called out 'Wilt thou stand there with a scurvy scold?' The other woman then called her a whore and named the man who kept her.[375] Likewise, an Exeter woman was chatting to her neighbour in 1560 when a man passed by and called her a scolding drab. She asked him to leave but he responded by calling her a priest's whore, among other insults, and she then named him a knave.[376]

The accusation of scolding was also incidental in a case involving two Silverton women in 1618. Bishop Cotton preferred the village to his palace in Exeter and spent at least eight months a year there. He may well have heard that Grace Luscombe had shouted through the courtyard gate of Elizabeth Facey 'Art thou come out, thou old beetle-browed whore, thou old drunken whore?' upon which Facey's daughter Alice appeared. Luscombe then asked her 'Art thou come out, thou young whore, thou shouldst get in about thy work, thou shouldst not come out to scold.' Luscombe later admitted she was angry that Mrs Facey's son threw stones at her door and when asked why she thought she was being prosecuted, she answered 'I cannot tell, except it be because I called Alice Facey whore, I think she be too young to be a whore'.[377] Being called a scold was clearly not as important as another insult given to Jane Everie of Chudleigh in 1597. She was told by two neighbours 'Go thy ways whore, go scold, go thy ways, thou art like unto the woman that did sard for a bushel of beans and peas'.[378] Likewise, a string of abuse involving a considerable number of Georgeham parishioners followed in the churchyard from what was later described as one woman's scolding with the parson and his wife in 1594.[379]

THREE

Insulting Authority: Challenging Civil and Church Figures

Authority figures generated abuse unlike that which was hurled at other men and women. They were ridiculed and demeaned in a variety of ways, one of which was to denigrate their social status while at the same time asserting or elevating the speaker's position. In this John Stokes' defiant words were typical. In 1616 he told his Aylesbeare vicar 'setting thy ministry aside, I am as good a man as thou'. The same phrase was used about Okehampton's mayor in 1638 and against Burrington's vicar in 1613.[380] In 1627 an Exeter man claimed to have been wrongfully sentenced and said he was as good a man as those that punished him. He was then told he should be whipped again for saying so and replied 'I will go hang myself rather than I will come into their hands again'.[381]

Perhaps the most striking example which goes beyond mere affirmation of status, but shows a direct challenge to the social order, was said in Dartmouth in the summer of 1625. One evening several men were fulfilling their duties as night watchmen when they came across three soldiers, John Horwood, Richard Lane and

Thomas Currington. An exchange of words followed in which one soldier proclaimed that the poor were about to rise against the rich. He allegedly said:

> 'poor men were put down by the rich and that ere long the poor and the rich would go by the ears and that if they did, they knew who would have the worst of it and thereupon John Horwood said *I will begin,* Lane said *I will be another* and Currington said *I will not step back.*'[382]

A year later, in 1626, another soldier in Dartmouth refused to toast George Villiers, 1st Duke of Buckingham, then Lord High Admiral, and said he would rather see the duke hanged and his soul damned.'[383] His comments preceded Buckingham's assassination by a soldier two years later in Portsmouth.

Such direct threats to the overall social order are highly unusual whereas men and women across Devon used insulting language to question and challenge local officials. The only countywide outbreaks of civil disorder occurred at the start and end of the period with which this study is concerned: the Prayer Book Rebellion, known locally as the Commotion, took place in 1549 and the Civil War in 1642. Nevertheless, the tensions caused by national politics and changing religious policies helped generate insults against authority figures on a local level. The issues of these two violent disorders were reflected in the invective uttered across Devon.

Secular figures

Insults flung at a ruling monarch were not dealt with like other slurs: words spoken against those in the church, the judiciary and members of the government were legally considered sedition and punished as misdemeanours. But they were treated as treason when it concerned the monarchy.[384] Thus on 10 August 1538 John Bonefant, an Exeter gentleman, was executed as a traitor in Southernhay. He had, unwisely, discussed written prophesies while dining with two friends. The three men deliberated on 'the present state of the world' before examining the foretelling that a mole would 'come cursed of God's mouth and vengeance should befall him'. Moles were recognized symbols of destruction and the three men concluded that this prophecy, and another, concerned Henry VIII. They burnt the writings but later that same night Bonefant's companions conspired against him. He was arrested the following morning, tried and subsequently hung, drawn and quartered. The Elizabethan chronicler John Hooker noted of the surviving two men, who were equally guilty of making these comments, that one 'fell amazed and was distracted of his wits, his tongue rattled in his head and died most miserable'. The other lived in Bonefant's house 'in great infamy' and his children led poor lives. In a separate incident that same year another Exeter man insulted the monarch when he said that he 'set not a turd by the king neither by his council'.[385]

It may be that the bloody consequences of the Prayer Book Rebellion, with the deaths of possibly thousands of rebel Devonians, imbibed a greater sense of caution during the subsequent reign of Queen Mary in the 1550s. The hanging in 1549 of the vicar of Exeter St Thomas, in his vestments, and the execution by Plymouth's Council of the 'Cornish Traitor' must have had a considerable effect on the public. For many days the cleric dangled from his church tower and the Cornishman's head sat on a pole at Plymouth Guildhall. The other rebels were likewise called traitors.[386] Various slanderous statements were later made of Queen Elizabeth including one uttered in 1560 by Thomas Burleigh, known as 'the drunken Burleigh', who said in Totnes that Robert Dudley, 1st Earl of Leicester, had 'swived' the queen.[387] His punishment for suggesting that the queen had sexual intercourse with the earl was not recorded. In the Cornish parish of Landrake

▶ 23. *Okehampton, drawn by William Brockedon, in about 1800. In this town in 1635 Edmond Cann's tongue was said to be too great for his mouth.*

94

one man objected in 1570 to having been called a false knave, traitor and a 'rebellion', probably meaning a rebel, but he said he would be as faithful to the crown as any other.[388]

Mayors and councillors

Relations between some councillors were poisoned by the early sixteenth-century fragmentation of belief between the existing Roman Catholic faith and the new Protestant interpretation of Christianity. The subsequent divisions in the emerging strands of Protestantism also caused fractures. Religion became a discordant factor in local politics and insults reflected these differences. This can be seen as early as the mid 1530s in Plymouth which witnessed a power struggle between an evangelical faction and religious traditionalists in the council. One man insulted another by calling him a 'naughty heretic knave' but the reformers, led by William Hawkins, the prominent merchant, then prevailed. Religion remained a continuing factor in abuse: two decades later,

24. *The Guildhall, Exeter, where the mayors held their court.
As drawn by Thomas Girtin in about 1797.*

in 1557, when the country was once again Catholic, Hawkins'
son was maligned as 'a traitor, thief and a very villain'.[389] In 1545
Henry VIII had implored his subjects, in his last speech, to refrain
from calling each other heretic, Anabaptist, papist, hypocrite or
Pharisee. Fourteen years later, in 1559, his daughter Elizabeth
had similar words spoken in parliament.[390] State policy was to
demand uniformity in religious belief but alongside it the concept
of personal conscience developed through the sixteenth century.

Exeter's councillors also struggled to keep a sense of decorum in
the mid 1500s. For nearly a decade John Levermore was involved
in a dispute with his fellow councillors which originated with
his failure to lease a property in 1581. He first verbally abused a
councillor, then the mayor and finally refused to attend council

meetings. His punishment escalated from fines to imprisonment and then ultimately to being barred from trading. However, Levermore continued merchandising with the consequence that his goods were seized and forfeited. It was only after the intervention of the Lord Chief Baron, Sir William Periam, that relations were restored between Levermore and his colleagues.[391]

Levermore understood the consequences in insulting the mayor, the 24 councillors or other city officials. In 1557, in the midst of the Marian changes, the council had revived an earlier agreement that any councillor who slandered another would pay 40s as a fine for his first offence, forty days imprisonment would be levied on a second charge and then finally a third offence would result in dismissal from the council and disenfranchisement as a freeman. Thus, in 1517 a councillor who had called the mayor a wretch, churl and knave was fined 40s. In 1559 Peter Lake was given the same fine for calling the city's sheriff a dissembler, knave and beast. That same year it was imposed on the sheriff for his verbal attack on Lake. But Lake suffered a further punishment, imprisonment, when he called the sheriff and a constable knaves.[392]

It was shortly before this that John Midwinter named Griffin Ameredith a knave and then termed his own brother Robert a 'knypsy'. This was probably a 'nippy' which in Devon was a nursery term for a penis. All three men were councillors and Midwinter's fine was twelve pounds.[393] John Hooker, who knew the men, later wrote in his official chronicle of Exeter about the brothers' relationship. He noted that John Midwinter was 'a man of high grain, proud and malicious' and that 'he could not bear with a better nor love an inferior' whereas the slandered brother Hooker regarded as being 'both of one complexion but not of like conditions'. Hooker added that Robert Midwinter was 'somewhat hasty and choleric yet without malice and forgetful of injuries and ready to do good to any man'. Perhaps most appropriately Hooker added 'the more that he prospered and was beloved, the more his brother was angry and disdained him'.[394] The reason for Ameredith being called a knave may have been because of jealousy of his prosperity and popularity but as Hooker noted the

25. *Justice being dispensed in a contemporary engraving.*

brother 'had many good parts in him though not without some imperfections for as the common adage is *nothing is good all the way through*'. Hooker noted that a considerable number of other men, and one woman, were prosecuted by the council for 'unseemly words', 'unseemly speeches', 'unhonest, unseemly and evil names', 'slanderous words', 'disordered words and railing speeches', 'unseemly terms and words', 'outrageous words and terms', 'very unseemly, ungodly and taunting reproaches' and 'unseemly, irreverent and unhonest speeches mixed with scorns, threats', all against the city's officials.[395]

Not surprisingly, maintaining decorum and civil order was also expected in other boroughs; it was assumed that the mayor and his fellow councillors would be treated with appropriate respect. Dartmouth's mayor entered into a heated exchange after being shown contempt by a servant of the Lord High Admiral in 1558. The debate centred over the legal rights to the river Dart which from the early 1300s had rested with the Duchy of Cornwall. The

26. *Late Elizabethan carving of what might have been intended to be a drunk, in Exeter Guildhall.*

Corporation of Dartmouth had leased the rights, in the office of bailiff, from 1508 but the admiral, then Edward Clinton, 1st Earl of Lincoln, challenged its authority.[396] In June 1558 the mayor, Thomas Gourney, travelled to Tavistock where he testified before John Russell, 1st Earl of Bedford.

Gourney related that a Flemish mariner had appeared before him complaining that John Reynolds, the admiral's servant, had illegally confiscated his safe conduct papers and imprisoned him at Kingswear. The Fleming had escaped, crossed the river Dart and fled to the sanctuary of Dartmouth's guildhall. At that point Reynolds arrived with three armed men. The mayor reminded Reynolds that the Fleming was a friend of Queen Mary and subject of Philip II of Spain, who had become king of England upon his marriage to Mary. He also recapped an earlier discussion over solving the disputed jurisdiction between the borough and the admiralty. Reynolds retorted that he had authority to act in Dartmouth as if he were on the high seas and accused the mayor of holding £500 which he intended to spend in legal proceedings against the admiral. At this point the exchange turned heated.

The mayor said '*No honest man could have spread such a report*'.

Reynolds replied '*I tell thee, thou mayor, that thou shall't answer.*'

The mayor responded '*Doest thou know where thou art and to whom thou speakest?*'

Reynolds said back to him '*I speak to thee, thou knave mayor*'.

The mayor then ordered his sergeant '*Take Reynolds unto the ward*'.

However, Reynolds drew his dagger and said '*Who dare of you all villains to put hand on me?*'

Violence then followed. The mayor's man took the dagger, Reynolds struck the mayor on the head with his fist and called for his sword. Gourney appealed to those assembled to keep the peace but Reynolds remained unhappy and said '*God's blood be you all that point*' as well as '*Do what you dare villains for your lives*'. Nevertheless, the mayor prevailed and Reynolds was escorted from the guildhall to be imprisoned. En route to the gaol and while in the street the latter made one final act of defiance: he removed the mayor's cap from his head, placed it on his own and said '*Thou shall not wear a cap and I to go barehead*'.[397] Reynolds may have given an alternative account of the proceedings but they do not appear to have survived.

Various Okehampton mayors received verbal abuse from two men who had just consumed excessive amounts of alcohol. In 1635 Edmond Cann, 'who was overcome with drink and his tongue too great for his mouth', called a local man a cuckold and a beggarly knave. When he was fined five shillings it transpired that he had also said that 'a company of knaves' ran Okehampton. It was probably these very same men that he came across having supper fifteen months later: Cann told them 'what a company of cuckolds and whoremongers here. All the town are cuckolds and whoremongers'. Cann was rebuked but then excused himself by claiming that the mayor had given him permission to 'rail' during the Christmas period. This suggests the possibility that the borough had retained a lord of misrule during the holidays. If so, it did not help Cann's case.[398] On two occasions, in October 1638 and again in June 1641, a butcher by the name of Michael Vougler bid the mayor 'kiss my arse'. On the first occasion he admitted to

27. *Mrs Mary Hooper, 1658, in St Petrock's Church in Exeter, who is wearing restrained dress more suitable for a Puritan woman.*

having been so drunk that he had no memory of what he had said. But even his mother confirmed it. Two and a half years later he did not offer the excuse of over-drinking when he once again repeated the phrase.[399] It may have been more insulting when in another case a local man, Richard Reynell, a tailor with a history of over-drinking and not attending church services, openly said in 1638, whilst in the bowling green, that he was as good a man as a former mayor and principal burgess.[400]

Not surprisingly there were slanderous words spoken between councillors in Barnstaple, a fervently dissenting town by the late 1500s. Pentecost Dodderidge, a leading merchant who was elected three times to serve as an MP for the town, reported slander uttered by John Delbridge, another leading merchant who had served as the town's MP on six occasions. Dodderidge admitted that he was in contention with Delbridge but said they had no 'deadly hatred'. He reported that Delbridge called a mayor in 1609 'a cowardly captain' and his comments on a potential church lecturer was that he was 'a boon companion and a tobacconist'. He was informed that the cleric had preached before the king and Delbridge replied 'so have many dunces'. The differences between Delbridge and Dodderidge were apparently more personal than religious.[401]

Ignatius Jurdain

Whereas John Hooker was Exeter's most compelling Elizabethan personality, Ignatius Jurdain was his equivalent for the following four decades which led up to the Civil War. His biographer termed him 'the wonder and phoenix of his age and place' but to others he was 'the principal patron of factious and seditious persons in all the western parts'. The king thought Jurdain deserved hanging.

Jurdain came to Exeter from Lyme Regis, probably in the early 1570s, in order to be apprenticed to a wealthy merchant. His adult interests may have been better served through a career in the church. Jurdain married two Exeter women; the second marriage took place only four months after the death of his first wife. Altogether he had 17 children and Exeter remained his home until his death in 1640. In addition to his mercantile career

Jurdain had two other over-riding interests. The first was holding public office: he was a bailiff, councillor, receiver, sheriff, Member of Parliament, mayor and alderman. But secondly, and probably of greater importance, Jurdain was known for his low church devotion which gave him a reputation for being Exeter's leading puritan. His daily routine began between two and three in the morning with personal prayers and they continued until six. These were then followed by family devotion. Jurdain used his time in the House of Commons to introduce legislation to punish adultery and fornication and when the parliamentary debate began his fellow members ridiculed Jurdain by crying out 'Commit It, Commit It!'

28. *Broadgate in Exeter, as drawn by William Brockedon in 1800, which was the scene of a riot in 1638 in which the bishop's clerk told the city's sheriff he 'did not care a fart' for him.*

In Exeter Jurdain led a morality campaign against drinking, fornication, Sabbath-breaking and swearing. The response was a counterblast of invective.[402] His biographer, the correspondingly fervent rector of St Mary Arches, proudly boasted 'drunkards and frequenters of the ale-house were afraid of him, he was their usual bug-bear, the Mememto in the middle of their excess was *It is time to be gone, Mr Jurdain will come by and by* . . . the stocks and whipping posts could testify what swearers, drunkards, unclean persons and such like notorious offenders were punished principally by his executing of justice . . . he was very diligent both to prevent and remove disorders so that he would go with the constables in person to search for idle and disorderly persons on Sabbath days at night, and at the end of the assizes and sessions and fair weeks.'[403] The pages of Exeter's mayoral court books confirm the diligence with which Jurdain pursued his moral crusade. The first court book coincides with his term of office and the binding has an elaborate copy of his signature.

These documents also recorded reactions it had from some of those Jurdain prosecuted. A number of Exonians expressed contempt. In 1619 William Elliot, a shoemaker, appeared before Jurdain on charges of playing a game of shuffleboard. He was told to 'crave the said Mr Jurdain's good will' but instead replied he 'could tell six before Mr Jurdain was a justice', urged him to 'take his wits about him' and pointed out that his own guild, that of the cordwainers, had been 'undone' by Jurdain. Finally, he rose and put on his hat.[404] Jurdain fully understood this was a display of scorn: he himself, in 1639, would put on his hat while a royal proclamation, with which he disagreed, was read in the cathedral. The Privy Council called Jurdain and two fellow councillors to London, the men apologised and disingenuously pleaded that they had kept their hats on because of the cold.[405] Not long after being brought before Jurdain, Elliot was jailed for a month for contemptuously abusing the mayor, recorder and other justices: he had said that the recorder had rash judgement.[406]

In 1619 another Exeter man also indicated contempt for Jurdain by keeping on his hat. Edward Baseley was interrupted while drinking at home one Sunday by a visit from Jurdain and two constables. Baseley refused to accept that Jurdain had any legitimate reason for being there. Another constable there also disputed Jurdain's motives. He claimed the visit was driven by malice and ill will. Baseley rounded off his contempt in saying he 'did not care a turd for him'. Likewise, the following year, in 1620, Gregory Wolcote was arrested for drunkenness and said that he 'cared not a fart for Ignatius Jurdain'.[407] Another man composed lewd songs about Jurdain. One was cited in court:

'They kept me in prison seven long hours,
until the sun was almost down.
They bound me with cords and whipped me full sore,
and this was their saying Do thou sing no more,
You know it was for singing marking stones and for no other thing,
that they made me weep when I should sleep and sorrow when
    I should sing'.[408]

Jurdain's nighttime searches through the city for misbehaving people resulted in a drunkard fleeing his home in 1624 to avoid arrest. Nevertheless, he was captured on his return and then asked 'what is Mr Jurdain gone? If I had so much counsel before as now I have, I would not have gone away for Mr Jurdain nor any Jurdain in Exeter. If Mr Jurdain come again, whether it be for treason or for felony, I will make his guts garter over his heels'. Shortly afterwards he appeared before Jurdain and was faced with the additional charge of insulting the justice.[409] Even Jurdain's second wife, the daughter of Thomas Baskerville, a renowned apothecary, received verbal abuse. One Exeter man sarcastically called her gentlewoman and apothecary drug.[410] The term apothecary was one of abuse amongst those in the criminal underworld. It implied the speaker was talking nonsense because there was an 'assumed gravity and affection of knowledge generally put on by the gentlemen of that profession who are commonly but superficial in their learning'.[411]

The city's court books show that constables were regularly sent to discover bad behaviour. In 1615 councillors took this process further by establishing that informers would receive half of any fine from a successful prosecution.[412] One curious incident five years later refers to civilian informers. In 1619 a Taunton man, wearing only his shirt, was found in Mrs Elizabeth Brownscombe's bedroom. Some eighteen months later she discovered a friend had surreptitiously climbed through her shop window at midnight one July evening. The woman was drunk, fell into a tub of water and remained there nearly an hour. Eventually she explained she was there to see if the Somerset man was in bed with Mrs Brownscombe. She claimed, most likely with a sense of irony, that Jurdain had sent her.[413]

This abuse, and that given to city officers acting under Jurdain's instructions, was the direct consequence of the moral campaign. A second wave of insults came from Jurdain's political activities which helped widen the schism between the cathedral authorities and the council. Jurdain's role in Exeter's council was influential in leading it to support parliament rather than the king during the Civil War.

When in 1638 Richard Commins, the Broadgate porter employed by the cathedral, was convicted by Jurdain of being drunk, he refused to pay his fine of five shillings and said 'he had no money for Jurdain to boil his pot'. By this he may have been implying that the fee was being appropriated by Jurdain or this may have been an allusion to the moral capital that Jurdain was accruing through his crusade. Interestingly, in 1615 the city's councillors had agreed to raise money for better conditions for prisoners and Exeter's chronicler noted of this decision that they 'have agreed to *boil the pot* for better relief of the poor prisoners'. In any case, Commins eventually admitted that he spoke the words 'unadvisably'. Before that point the dispute had erupted into a melee in Cathedral Yard with a large crowd and the constables, who had been intent on collecting money, were locked inside the gatehouse. The key disagreement lay in the city's claim to jurisdiction within Cathedral Close. For several hours there was pandemonium and 'uncivil' and 'unfitting' speeches directed at the city officials. It ended only through the intervention of the city's sheriff who was told by the bishop's clerk that 'he did not care a fart' for him.[414]

Hostility towards Jurdain continued long after he was mayor in 1621. Ten years afterwards one woman was prosecuted for telling another 'to kiss Mr Jurdain's arse and come home by hers'.[415] Of course Jurdain was not the only Exeter mayor to be insulted: in 1625 a constable attempted to stop the rector of Parracombe from playing a game in an alehouse late at night. John Hayne's response was 'I'll fart in Mr Mayor's mouth'. Shortly afterwards the cleric moved to Somerset.[416] However, on the day in 1621 when Jurdain set off from Exeter for his first session of parliament, one local man said 'Mr Jurdain is gone for London' and his friend replied 'the devil take him by the way'.[417] There were many in Exeter who would have agreed and would vocalise their feelings.

Civil court officials

In the early 1600s Nicholas Gill, parson of Brentor, refused to pay his poor relief tax, was arrested and then insulted the Devon Quarter Sessions' judges with 'very great contemptuous speeches' in calling the bench 'an ale bench'.[418] Another incident took place in 1624 when the jury in Exeter's mayor's court were ridiculed as knaves.[419] Abuse towards justices or juries may have been less common than that directed at the men sent to investigate crime or arrest suspects. Some were highly inventive. There were a fair number of law officials to rail against. Exeter had two salaried constables to serve each quarter of the city and there were also volunteers who were watchman.[420] Other boroughs had similar arrangements. Those individuals who were enacting court business in other ways also received abuse. In Exeter one litigant, who had obtained court papers, 'showed the same to one John Glanville, who perusing the same, one Hugh Atkins took the said precept out of the said Glanville's hand and told this deponent he would wipe his arse therewith and tomorrow he should find it on the dunghill'.[421]

Constables

Ignatius Jurdain was eulogised for having prosecuted men and women who sold fruit and herbs on Sundays. Exeter's court records show he also fined a man for selling a basket of pasties in 1622[422] but four years earlier radish sellers were prosecuted. These traders called Constable Robert Trescott a knave as well as a cockscomb goose, by which they meant he was a fool. Another hawker threatened to throw his can of beer at the constable and called him a hungry knave, rogue, drunkard and catchpole (a word of contempt for a petty officer).[423] Another arrested man called Trescott that year a knave, fool and an ass. He appears to have become disenchanted three years later when Jurdain instructed him to interview an actor who had just performed a play but a

29. *In 1582 the bishop was allegedly called a whoreson ape and ass. This ape, which holds a urine flask, was carved in the 1500s on a bench end in St Helen's Church at Abbotsham, lampoons medical men.*

disagreement followed in which the player drew his sword against the constable. Trescott subsequently informed the court 'he will never go more for Mr Mayor nor for any of the justices and further bid the justices to do what they did please.'[424]

Other constables faced continual abuse when attempting to arrest Exonians: a Londoner told Robert Sherwood he was a fool and instructed him to 'kiss his arse', Nicholas Carwithy and William King were also asked to kiss a miscreant's backside, Nicholas Gregory was called a dissembling rogue and slave as well as a base creature, Constable Nott was told to 'go shit in Southernhay' before Samuel Isacke 'played' with his nose, Robert Lewes was called a Puritan drunken rogue, Richard Kingdom was told he was a 'pallafoot' before he was likened to the devil, John Robins was called 'a busy fellow and that he was very busy in his office and did live by stolen goods', Nicholas Clarke and John Sprague were both called rogues and knaves and finally, Nicholas Brayley and Nicholas Carwithy were called not only rogues but jackanapes (impertinent people). Physical violence, in some instances quite serious, was also inflicted.[425]

As aggressive as some Exeter people were, few were as creative in their disrespect, and yet also baffling, as Nicholas Rowcliffe of Okehampton who quarrelled with the town's constable upon being arrested: he told the law officer 'he would shit first' and then brought his three children for 'the cuckolds of the town' to maintain.[426] Okehampton's constables faced abuse like those in Exeter: Edmond Townsend of Milton Dameral was called in 1601 a knave and a 'scurvy, ragged, scabbed, pocky constable' while John Chapel of Chittlehampton was told in 1631 he was 'a drunkard and a base drunken constable and thou art drunk twice or thrice every week'.[427]

Church figures

In 1630 a drunken parishioner of Stoodleigh called his rector a cripple before he spewed all over the church.[428] A few years earlier another had called his curate in Great Torrington 'a rascally proud priest, a jack, a maypole, a beggarly knave' who had come 'a begging to my door'.[429] Jeering at a physical ailment or lack of wealth appears straightforward enough but many other insults given to churchmen were the consequence of national religious politics as the country swerved from King's Edward VI's Protestantism during 1547 to 1553 to Queen Mary's Catholicism from 1553 to 1558 followed by the return of Protestantism from 1558 onwards of Queen Elizabeth I and her successors. The years 1558 through to the Civil War, the Interregnum and the Commonwealth fragmented the Church of England through the rise of dissent including that of the Puritans. These developments gave birth to new insults.

Comments that were considered offensive in one reign would become acceptable, if not encouraged, in another. At Exeter in 1531 Thomas Bennet called Pope Clement VII the Antichrist and the whore of Babylon among other names. Bennet was executed for his comments but the same words a few years later would not have conflicted with government policy. Likewise, it was unfortunate for Agnes Prest that when she repeated similarly disparaging comments in Exeter during Queen Mary's reign she suffered Bennet's fate.[430] Mary had even outlawed the use of the words 'heretic' and 'papist'.[431] Less than a year later, when Elizabeth came to the throne, there would have been no arrest let alone execution. Insults were not just in the ear of the beholder but in those listening from afar. Similarly, it was safe to condemn friars as knaves while England was Protestant but unwise before the reign of King Edward VI or during the subsequent reign of his sister Mary. Plymouth's James Horsewell uttered that insult in 1533[432] during the earlier years of rapid transition. The starkest example of the difficulties in 'safe' speech centres on the visit of Hugh Latimer to Exeter in 1534. Henry VIII had sent him to preach the gospel. Latimer was evangelizing to a considerable crowd in the Close when a gentleman insulted Latimer by calling him a heretic and knave. The accuser was subsequently out of favour with the king but twenty-one years later it was Latimer, under a different monarch and religious policy, who was burned at the stake for continuing to have the views he had expressed in Exeter.[433]

Devon's leading sixteenth-century writer, John Hooker, poured particular scorn on Catholics but he did so from the safety provided by a Protestant monarchy. For the year 1416 he noted there had been only one notable event in Exeter: 'one John Rolfe, a grey friar, was accused for the carrying away of the wife of one John Perott and his goods, and for his unchaste life with her'. It was during the reign of Elizabeth, who he noted had suppressed 'the false and popish religion' and had set up the true service of God and the preaching of the gospel, that he criticised Bishop Edmund Lacey ('drowned in Popery'), John Welshman ('too much blind prophelising'), William Smith ('a most inveterate Papist and an enemy to all such as were known or suspected to be true professors of the gospel'), Walter Staplehill ('over much blinded in Popery . . . the many good virtues in him were blemished and spotted'), John Woolcot ('too much addicted unto Papistry') and even his godfather John Ryse ('marvelously blinded in the Popish religion').[434] The most outrageous comment he made concerned the nuns at Polsloe Priory. He noted the priory was dissolved in 1535 and added 'what the chaste life of these nuns so ever was before, it fell out that at the time when the house was suppressed, so many of them had tasted so much of the fruit in the middle of the garden that the most part of them and, as some said, 12 of 14 were with child'.[435] During Elizabeth's reign his disparaging descriptions would have been slanderous had they been untrue but during the years of Queen Mary such words would have been seditious.

There was a range of name-calling and many comments were repeated at other times and in other parishes. Some were recorded only once. This includes words spoken in 1635 to William Tilor, vicar of Witheridge, that his parishioner 'did hope to have his ears in his pocket ere long'.[436] The judicial punishment for removing ears was unusual but clearly well-known enough as a practice to have reached this small mid Devon parish.

Bishops and church court officials

Perhaps it is not surprising that bishops were the focus of abuse. Fifteen men between 1500 and 1650 served in that position. One, Miles Coverdale, the illustrious translator of the Bible into English, was preaching in the cathedral when news arrived of the accession of Queen Mary. He suffered the ignominy of being deserted by his congregation, who knew which way the religious wind was about to blow, and left him standing in his pulpit. Whilst bishop he had endured, so wrote John Hooker, 'open railings' and 'privy back-biting'.[437] In the mid 1530s Philip Gammon of Axminster insulted Bishop Veysey when he said that 'the blessing of a bishop was as good as the blessing of his old horse'. When he was reprimanded and reminded that bishops were anointed with holy oil, Gammon replied 'there was as much virtue in the oil of a beast's foot as was in the oil that the bishop was anointed withal'.[438] In 1581 a Werrington parishioner was convinced by his cleric to petition the bishop for a divorce but when Reverend Hancock asked for 20s for his services William Finnimore only offered him 6s 8d. Hancock told him 'that would not serve to grease my lord bishop's hands'.[439]

On a November evening in 1582 a dozen people were dining together in a house just outside the North Gate in Exeter when Anthony Halstaff walked in. His breeches were befouled as if he had just fallen and he was so overcome with drink that he could neither stand nor walk. Halstaff commented that he was as good a man as Bishop John Woolton and while he made a number of odd comments, some of which were incomprehensible, his most offensive words were probably calling the bishop a whoreson ape and ass.[440]

Twenty-five years later, sometime around Christmas 1606, Bishop William Cotton was called a Sabbath breaker and it was suggested, with irony, that he condoned high fees from his officials while he preached about conscience. Christopher Potter, town clerk of Bradninch, added he would as soon hear a cow bellow as hear Cotton preach. Part of the dispute lay in trying to arrest Robert

Milton on a warrant from the Court of High Commission.[441] It was just before this time that another court official, William Moore, had attempted to serve additional papers on Milton who was then in Uffculme. Moore presented the papers over a quart of wine in a tavern. Despite the wine, or because of it, Milton threw bread and cheese at Moore and called him 'apparitor knave, drunken knave, rascal knave, beggarly knave, bribing knave and that he was a notable fool and a liar and that this deponent for 15s would have let him go if he would have given it, but he would see this deponent hanged first'. The situation escalated with the arrival of Milton's son and a crowd of local people. Moore requested that the local constable keep Milton in his custody and returned three hours later with another warrant. On this second occasion Milton attacked Moore by giving him 'two or three strong thumps on the breast with his fist' and placed the constable in the stocks. Strong words followed but Moore left Uffculme without success as he did later at Bradninch.[442]

As noted earlier, church courts in general and the national Court of High Commission in particular became increasingly unpopular in the late 1500s. Their officials, such as apparitors and pursuivants, similar to constables in civil courts, were similarly caught in verbal abuse. For example, when Roger Withycombe tried to serve court papers in Combe Raleigh in 1639 he was called a base knave and threatened with whipping. In 1630 another apparitor at Payhembury had 'a bowl of urine and other filth' thrown at him.[443]

An unidentified man stated he would rather his case was heard before honorable men than those of the archdeacon's court at Great Torrington which he said was a court of knaves.[444] The Exeter court had similar criticism. In late November 1604 William Dewnes found the diocesan chancellor walking in the cathedral and asked for a copy of the charges against him. Chancellor Morrice refused and told him he could have only one act. Dewnes called for witnesses to note that he was being illegally deprived and Morrice declared that Dewnes would now face the High Commission. He responded 'I would very willingly, for there I shall be sure of justice and at your hands I can neither have law nor justice'. He also said that the officials were 'small birds' and one in particular was a 'paired fellow'. When Dewnes appeared before the chancellor it was claimed that he offered a bribe of forty shillings to have the matter dropped and during the subsequent hearing Dewnes was said to 'be very full of words and of rude behaviour'.[445]

Possibly the most challenging ridicule given to an Exeter church court official was uttered in August 1617 by Richard Doddridge of St Sidwell's parish. He resented being examined by a junior man. Doddridge told the scribe 'I care not a dog's turd for none of you all: I am more in the king's books than the greatest of you, a pox on you all for me; you may pack up your libel and wipe your arse with it'. Doddridge was then brought before Barnaby Gooche, the chancellor, and once again questioned status. Doddridge asked 'of what rank be you of? I am as much in the king's books as you. There was a chancellor here not long since that was blown up for taking of bribes.' Gooche was a senior man: he was chancellor of the Worcester diocese, a judge of Devon's Vice Admiralty Court and would become a Member of Parliament for Truro and Cambridge University as well as hold a string of national offices.[446] Doddridge repeated that he was 'as good a man as thou', put on his hat as a mark of contempt and said to the chancellor 'You will make shit, *Sir Reverence*, worse than wax'. 'Sir Reverence' was an expression of apology that was used before a statement that could be seen as vulgar or offensive. It was similar to saying 'begging your pardon' but it also meant human excrement. In addition, it was also an ancient custom and in the eighteenth century it was explained that it:

'obliges any person easing himself near the highway or foot path, on the word[s Sir] reverence being given him by a passenger, to take off his hat with his teeth, and without moving from his station to throw it over his head, by which it frequently falls into the excrement; this was considered as a punishment for the breach of delicacy. A person refusing to obey this law, might be pushed backwards'.[447]

Two other Exeter cases provide more background for the phrase. In 1618 a man said to another he 'did not care Sir Reverence a turd', or fart, 'for him'. In another instance a woman was told to 'reverence', that is venerate, a man's backside. Similar was said of a Staverton cleric: in 1607 a parishioner used what appears to have been a common saying when he told him 'your Reverence, a turd in his teeth'.[448]

Doddridge was told he would be excommunicated, responded that he was returning home, cocked his leg at the chancellor and said 'I will be upon the jack of you'. Doddridge also told him that he loved his church but if excommunicated then he would shun it for seven years. The chancellor responded 'I think I shall do good service' and Doddridge replied 'they will say that you do the devil good service'. The chancellor then dismissed Doddridge from his presence and instructed him to face the court in the morning. Their war of words was not over. It was harvest time and Doddridge threatened to charge the chancellor for his reapers' costs and told him that if the two men had been elsewhere he would have 'set him by the heels'.[449]

Rectors, vicars and clerks

In 1599, the year after his arrival, Bishop William Cotton drew up a list of the 'common disorders' in the diocese. He claimed atheists and Catholics were common, that there had been a marriage of a goose and gander, and that animals had been baptized including a dead horse and a cat wearing an apron. He relayed a joke in the diocese: was it better to hang all the preachers or the dogs? The answer was the preachers because the bishop could ordain more ministers but the supply of dogs and bitches was limited. Among Cotton's other complaints were that clerics were railed on by lewd persons and that a minister had recently been forced to 'kiss the bare hinder parts of a man'.[450] These may appear to be exaggerations but later, in 1630, a lamb was placed in a Devon river, baptized with the sign of the cross and given the name Welcome. In the early 1600s four men were imprisoned for baptizing a mare and another was prosecuted for christening a dog he named John.[451] As outrageous as these slights or insults were, those recorded in the courts were more personal and wounding.

Some clerics were described as forsworn, by which it was meant that they had perjured themselves. This insult was almost exclusively reserved for churchmen and this included men at Staverton, Knowstone, Barnstaple, Halberton, Diptford, Witheridge and in Cornwall at Lezant.[452] Being false was an insult levied at a wider range of society but it had a particular sting for vicars as it called into question their ministry. Sheepwash's curate was named as a 'cheating false knave' in 1631, a Barnstaple cleric was told in 1604 that he lied as if he were a bishop and the preacher John Nicholson was mocked by a parishioner who told him 'thou preaches false doctrine'.[453] Tiverton went further: a group of Brownists in 1622 were unhappy with the preaching and one said the town's preachers were 'false prophets and that they go up into the pulpit to tell a tale'. Perhaps the most unpleasant insults regarding a churchman's honesty were those levied at Robert Sparke, the parish clerk of North Tawton. In 1626 a parishioner overheard him being told 'thou didst skulk to my house in my absence and did slock away my goods. And thou art an alehouse haunter and doest commonly rail in the alehouse. And thou art a liar. Who is a liar but Sparke? You may go to Bow and there lick men's pots thereby terming him a lickpot'.[454]

In 1613 a Burrington parishioner challenged his vicar's right to question him and, perhaps more seriously, told the vicar he was not his superior. Reverend William Harvey had advised Richard Pennacott 'not to go to law without cause or causelessly with your neighbours' and Pennacott responded, in what was said to be a 'scolding violent manner', that 'if you say that I go to law causelessly, you lie or whosoever says so doth lie and tell me not thereof, for I am as good a man as you are'.[455] Two years later the vicar of Aylesbeare heard the same phrase from a parishioner but with the caveat 'setting thy ministry aside'. He also told Reverend Stokes he was a knave, was covetous, did not care what wrong he did, that there was no truth in him and that he was the falsest man he knew.[456] Both men disputed vicars had elevated positions and their insults were typical of many others thrown by fellow Devonians at their clerics.

Parsons could also be insulted by gestures which broke social protocols[457] such as inappropriately wearing a hat. It was improper to wear one during a church service but elsewhere it was unfitting when a man of a higher status did not wear his. The correct use of a hat, whether wearing one or removing it to hold in one's hand, was fully understood. It remains to this day one of the most prominent civic symbols of Exeter. In 1497 Henry VII gave his own cap on condition that it was carried before the mayor in civic processions. His hat remains a conspicuous symbol of his personal identity with Exeter.

Clerics also understood that it was possible to show contempt by sitting or standing in an unsuitable manner. Thus, in 1622 the vicar of Brampford Speke watched the 'indecent and unseemly' behaviour of John Prescott who sat directly in front of him in church. Reverend Tristram Haycroft observed Prescott 'sometime turning his back towards me, sometimes with his hat on his head, and sometimes smiling, deriding and laughing in my face openly in mere derision as on St Stephen's Day last at the time of the exposition of the gospel in the afternoon and when he had done rose up and went out of the church in absolute contempt'.[458] On 14 August 1569 the rector of North Huish took offence at a parishioner, Philip Harvey, who sat before him in a pew whilst holding his hat but wearing his night cap. The two men were in a tithe dispute and the cleric had angered Harvey by referring to his mother. The argument escalated into a brawl. A servant of the parson told Harvey 'What a slave art thou to sit upon thy tail when thou dost talk with thy better', took him by the arm and said 'Come out, if thou use thyself so unreverently, thou shalt not sit here.' Before long a dagger was drawn and Harvey told the cleric he would 'send thee packing' if he repeated any comments about his mother.[459] Likewise, Truro's rector in 1636 watched one parishioner, who had previously called him a knave, keep his back to the cleric during the service. John Rowe then 'reached out his tail' in what was regarded as an unseemly and irreverent posture. Augustine Parker also showed his contempt at North Tawton in 1630 when he 'turned his tail towards the minister'.[460] Presentments in the church court include men being cited for inappropriate hat wearing such as Andrew Langome of Crediton in the early 1620s.[461] These were all disparaging gestures.

In 1566 Dean Prior's vicar felt insulted by different behaviour: he disliked John Fox placing a child on his lap. Reverend Drake was 'troubled and unquieted' by the two talking through the service and insisted the toddler be removed but Fox refused and laughed, an act the vicar thought showed scorn or derision. Seventy years later children were banished from services at Exeter Cathedral.[462] No doubt Reverend Drake would have approved. It was not just the cleric but the entirety of Padstow in Cornwall that was allegedly insulted by the actions of David Edwards, the parish clerk. On Whitsun he was said to have taken the pulpit cloth and used it to 'make a play or May game'. Edwards had a list of offending behaviour including being an uncivil, lewd and 'rising fellow' as well as a haunter and common frequenter of alehouses.[463]

One clerk endured some of the most biting and varied abuse recorded for a Devon parson. It included a physical insult. In the late 1630s Amiel Slade served as vicar at Yarnscombe near Great Torrington on a yearly wage in place of Thomas Cheek, the sitting incumbent. Cheek fell out with Slade and accused him of attempting murder through poisoning the chalice, said that the devil 'rode' Slade and wished that the vengeance of hell would take him. He also violently assaulted Slade in church. In addition, Cheek's son told Slade to use a court warrant to 'wipe his arse with' and another family member, Dorothy Cheek, called Slade a blockhead and compared him with Balaam, the Old Testament prophet who manipulated the Israelites into cursing themselves. Her gesture to Slade was to receive communion on her buttocks 'in an unseemly manner'. John Baylie's insults were more accomplished. He repeated part of Slade's sermon in shouting 'Arise and go to Nineveh, that great city'. Baylie's implication was that Slade's pride was as great as that of Assyria and that God would also bring him to destruction. In addition, Slade was insulted by a comparison made with the story of a horse which fell off a bridge carrying his rider to the devil and hell: Baylie said it would be a fitting steed to take Slade to Nineveh. The allusion to the devil was an insult particularly given to clerics and the citing of the Nineveh story was also used in another part of East Devon at the time.[464]

Amongst these insults Baylie also told Slade that he was but a hireling 'as a servant that had wages to wipe horse heels'. Other vicars had similar slurs regarding their fitness to be ministers. One parishioner said openly in Halberton after morning prayers that the vicar was 'worthy to keep a stable for horses rather than to be of the ministry'. Cornworthy's curate had a string of abuse in 1639 including being called a knave, an arrant knave, a base fellow and a jackanapes. Robert Perrot also said to him 'come hither, thou base priest, and cobble my shoes'.[465] At Malborough near Salcombe the vicar had a torrent of insults. William Gannycliff was told in 1556 that he was not only a whoremonger but a knave, a flea carrier, a maggot carrier and a 'fuckery'. As if this was not harsh enough, Gannycliff was also called a fish driver, a fish 'witer' and a fish jowter by which he meant that the vicar sold fish. The vicar of Pancrasweek suffered less abuse from a parishioner in 1606: he was called a knave and a bad fellow but perhaps more importantly his slanderer, whose illegitimate grandchild was not baptised in the church, threatened to stop him working in the diocese.[466]

An inability to perform their duties was also hurled at clerics. In 1635 Elizabeth Blackall said of the rector of Exeter St Mary Major that 'he shall as soon catch a kite with a rattle as save a soul by his preaching'. Holne's vicar had the longstanding enmity of one parishioner who announced in an alehouse that he thought Reverend Jones had also been employed as Exeter's hangman.[467] At St Gerrans in Cornwall a parishioner commented in 1600 that his parson was a damned dog as were all ministers that could not preach. Some insults implied poverty such as when Chagford's curate was told he was a beggar as well as a full of lice rogue and that one day he would 'pick lice under a hedge again'.[468]

A more common insult, but possibly less inflammatory, was that of knave. This term was given to Brampford Speke's cleric in 1625 whereas in 1594 an argument in Diptford descended into a preacher not only being called a knave and a rascal knave but also a scurvy pilled parson. Knave was more often a part of a general string of insults. That of Newton St Petrock in 1588 was named as a rascal knave, at Okehampton in 1629 the parson was called a scurvy, lop-legged knave, Willand's was termed not just a base knave but also a rascal in 1637, and in Knowstone in 1640 he was called a false knave, base vicar and base priest amongst other abuse.[469]

Equal in offence and similar in meaning to knave was the term rag. This referred to a contemptible person and was used in about 1593 against the vicar of Hittisleigh. He was verbally assaulted during a wedding feast in Cheriton Bishop by William Eastabrook who called him scalled (scabby), a pilled (wretched) priest and a bally rag (a contemptible person who was verbally abusive). Amongst these insults the vicar was also said to be 'like unto a fart': Eastabrook said he did not know from whence the vicar came nor did he know where he went.[470] He was not alone in his reference to gas. In 1637 a parishioner of the North Devon parish of West Down dismissed his vicar's tithe claims: 'I owe thee nothing and I care not a fart for thee.' In 1615 a Payhembury parishioner, after having put on his hat before the vicar, said 'I care not a fart for the pilled priest'. In the same parish twenty-four years later a parishioner refused to pay his church rate and was threatened with being prosecuted by the bishop. He told the churchwardens that they were knaves and of their threat 'he cared not a fart for it'.[471]

Being called pilled was not uncommon. Like his counterpart at Hittisleigh, the curate at Werrington was also named pilled.[472] During the harvest of 1600 or 1601 the cleric at Drewsteignton was also called a pilled parson as well as a blink-eyed priest and, unusually, a 'fucking priest'. A blinkard could imply deception or trickery and that term was also used against the vicar of St Issey in Cornwall in 1618. He was also insulted by being called a blinking slave and a crook-back.[473]

Some insults concerned hypocrisy: clerics were slandered for having committed moral crimes for which courts prosecuted parishioners. Thus the vicar of Ilsington was described in 1569 as 'the greatest swearer in the world'.[474] As mentioned earlier, a common charge was drunkenness. The cleric at Teigngrace was said in 1640 to be a base drunkard priest and to be 'drunk so often as thou has come from Newton'. Likewise in 1618 the cleric at St Sidwell's Church was said to be a drunkard and to have been prosecuted in court for his excessive drinking.[475] The 'arch puritan' Ignatius Jurdain claimed that in the West Country 'there are no greater drunkards and disordered persons than the ministers'.[476] Presumably he would not have been surprised by the antics of the clerk of Ashbury who one witness said 'was so distempered with drink as that he both vomited and fell asleep at the table board where he sat and this deponent conceiveth he was very drunk'. Another man testified he saw the clerk 'reel and stagger and fall under the stairs in the court and was afterwards asleep in the porch.' Jurdain would have been outraged, but probably not taken aback, by an earlier vicar of St Issey who used his Cornish vicarage for the sale of wine 'as a common tavern'.[477]

The loss of reputation through alleged sexual misconduct involved a considerable number of clerics. For instance, in 1613 the vicar of Dunsford was said to have offered £3 to a woman to have sex with him and two years later a Paignton woman was alleged to have had an illegitimate child with her vicar who was then called a tallow-faced rogue.[478] The controversial preacher of Plympton St Mary, Alexander Grosse, complained that he was slandered when it was said he 'did travel over the moor and did lie with a wench in a ditch and one coming suddenly upon thee you rose up in haste and left thy cloak behind you which cloak the party so coming made a suit of clothes.'[479] In 1541 a roomful of Exeter people turned the conversation to 'jesting upon priests' with an emphasis on their sexual antics with married women. Similar stories were told in Brampford Speke and at Yealmpton where it was turned into a song.[480]

Sexual probity was complicated by changes in national religious policy. Clerics were officially permitted to marry in 1549 but this freedom lasted only a few years until the reign of Queen Mary

30. *Carving of a cheeky lad who is exposing his buttocks to another behind him at St Mary's Church, Offwell.*

when it was again abolished. Married men were removed from office unless they sent their wives away. Queen Elizabeth restored clerical marriage a few years later. Before this, early in 1553, Elizabeth White married William Lamb, parson of St Keyne in Cornwall, but was forced to separate from him. He later became ill and she went to him, stayed overnight in the parsonage and shared a bedroom with a servant. That night a justice arrested the separated couple and placed them overnight in stocks on the charge of having an unlawful marriage.[481] Accusations regarding the sexual activity of clerics could hinge upon the date in which they were made.

Suggestions of clerical misconduct were more current in 1568 following the High Commission trial of Richard Gammon, a canon of Exeter Cathedral. The tale of Dr Gammon and his illegitimate child became well known in Exeter, where it was said to be 'the common fame', as well as in Staverton, Brixham, Rockbeare and Cullompton, the four parishes in which he held office as either vicar or rector, and probably much further afield. Gammon had met Isotte Rich at Staverton in 1566 and shortly afterwards employed her in his household. She later testified that they agreed to marry and that they had sex on many occasions until she found herself carrying his child. He then refused to marry her because, he explained, he would lose his position if Catholicism returned. He then made private arrangements: Gammon promised her maintenance costs, sent Rich to Somerset to have the baby and tried to persuade her to move to London. Rich had undertaken to name another man as the father but identified Gammon in the parish register of births. Publicly Gammon disputed he was the child's father and accused the cathedral's dean and treasurer of pursuing him 'tooth and nail'. He feigned outrage at the insults to his reputation. However, an impressive number of witnesses revealed the duplicity of Gammon and his servants. During the trial it was alleged that he had previously fathered other illegitimate children but it may be equally significant that eight years previous to his trial Gammon had preached doctrine which supported Catholicism and he had been forced to retract it. Gammon died a few years after the trial but not before his misbehaviour had become common gossip.[482]

Other parsons were accused of merely trying to have illicit sex. The cleric of Zeal Monachorum was alleged to have failed in his advances to the wife of Walter Merrifield. Her husband claimed that Rector St Hill, who was called, probably sarcastically, a 'lantern of light', 'would have had the pleasure of my wife's body but she was too honest a woman & would not yield to him'.[483] There was also discussion amongst men drinking at Bicton House in 1566 about the vicar of Dawlish. One man 'did reprove Edward Ward of divers slanderous words that the said Ward had spoken'. Ward had warned that the vicar would 'jape your wives and maidens all them that be in your parish'. One man responded 'he should jape none of his and the said Ward swore by God's blood that he would'. Several Dawlish residents later recounted an episode in which the vicar had attempted to have sex with Elizabeth During. Her husband William, a weaver who was then in bed, testified that they had a visit at home from Hugo Drover, the vicar, one night and that he had asked for a pot of ale. At that point 'the vicar begun to take this deponent's wife and wrestled with her minding to have his pleasure of her is so much that she was fain to come unto this deponent's chamber and the vicar came as far as the chamber door after her. And at last he departed when he might not have his purpose'. Elizabeth During said that he had taken her 'in his arms and showed his privates' but she appealed to his conscience: she told him 'if he were a man that he should not mell with her'. Afterwards she told a neighbour what had happened. The vicar castigated her for revealing his behaviour and told her to never speak of it 'that all might be trod under foot'.[484] The vicar at St Austell was also alleged to have tried to rape a local woman; he was called a whoremaster priest and it was claimed he had locked the church doors in order to have her. The witness said 'Hark, do not you hear her cry? I hear her cry'.[485]

Yealmpton's vicar, Richard Lallington, also appeared at a parishioner's home late at night. He called up to a window and asked John Philips to let him in as he was cold. Philips refused and may have known that Lallington had already pleaded with Philips' daughter who had likewise denied him entry and was called a drab by the vicar. Finally Philips' wife opened the door to the vicar but, according to an observer, 'what he did there or how long he stayed' he could not say.[486]

One woman heard that Chudleigh's vicar had a mistress and another of Bradworthy said that the cleric had paid a crown, a ewe and a lamb to a woman for her 'labour' when she was 'occupied' by him in a garden. It was a Cornish parson's reputation that suffered when in a Lostwithiel street Julian Anthony was called his whore and that he had had to be 'plucked from her tail'.[487] There were also suspicions about John Bagbeare, rector of Ashreigney. In 1562 the cleric's intentions were questioned when he was found loitering one Sunday afternoon in some woodland in proximity to a local woman. His reputation also suffered.[488]

Slanderous arguments sometimes escalated into violence. In 1562 parishioners of Spreyton attempted to recover money from Oliver Bennet, a former churchwarden, and enlisted the help of their vicar, John Shelston. Bennet called him a pilled priest, whoreson priest, whoremonger and bawdy priest and then struck him in the chest with his fist. In July 1557 the vicar of Morebath asked for tithe money from one of his parishioners but there was a 'multiplying of words' and the two men 'went by the ears together and were both down and then the vicar would have had this respondent's sword out of his hand and wrestling thereabout the vicar clasped the naked sword in his hand and this respondent had the hilt in one hand and the stabbard of the sword half drawn in the other hand and plucked the sword through the vicar's fingers

◀ 31. *Totnes Mill, as drawn by William Brockedon in the early 1800s. It was here that Joan Knight described the alleged antics of the town's vicar.*

which were then cut therewith'. In contrast it was the curate of Colebrooke who was violent: he called a parishioner a vile knave for which he was hit on the head with a hazel stick. The fight escalated with the parishioner being thrown over a hedge.[489]

Some insults implied financial impropriety on behalf of the clerics. There were continual tensions in many parishes between tithe payers and clerics. This is shown in strained relations in Kenton in 1557 when one parishioner paid his Easter tithe and then said that the vicar 'went about to suck his blood'.[490] The afore-mentioned parson of Drewsteignton was called 'a fucking priest' because of a dispute over the payment of tithes of rye that year. In 1618 the vicar made a financial pronouncement about the parish which he excused as being for its 'good' upon which one parishioner shouted 'A vengeance upon such good . . . By God, Mr Isaac, if you take such courses no poor man can live by you.'[491] In 1634 the vicar of St Erth in Cornwall was slandered as a knave who was base, greedy and dangerous, and it was also said that he had 'cozened' a parishioner, by which he meant defrauded, of 33 shillings. The two men disputed the tithes. A complicated slander case involving the vicar of St Issey in Cornwall included the latter being told to put his nose under a lamb's tail. It too appears to have arisen from a dispute over tithes.[492]

Two Kingsbridge vicars

Edward Hill, who served as Kingsbridge's vicar in the late 1500s, was identified as the minister who was rumoured to have stayed overnight in a Newton Abbot hostelry where he had paid for a woman's services. The gossip in Kingsbridge related that a boy had been dressed in woman's clothing, sent to the minister's room and the two spent the night together. In the morning the cleric was said to have given the boy an additional eleven pence. Hill admitted only to being physically similar to the rumoured minister in that both had 'yellowish' beards and the same complexion. Nevertheless, one parishioner shouted to him in the street that he had been overcharged given the standard rate for a prostitute was only 18d instead of the 36d which he allegedly paid.[493]

His successor also faced substantial slander. In 1617 a sideman complained that Reverend Costard and Marmaduke Dove, a parishioner, chided in church despite being requested to stop. In the midst of the argument the sideman cautioned Dove 'that he should not meddle with Mr Costard for Mr Costard will be too hard for him whereunto the said Marmaduke then and there presently replied saying his head (meaning the said Mr Costard's head) might be harder than mine but my horns may be as long as his'. It was the sideman's opinion that the congregation was not offended by Dove but he also thought it inappropriate to speak of a minister in that manner.[494] Reverend Costard was himself guilty of slander. He was accused of calling Dove, in the open street in Kingsbridge, a fool, ass, woodcock, rogue, knave, sinner and shutman (a spendthrift). He then 'bid the said Dove kiss his arse and held up his coat behind to the said Dove.' Costard's time in the town was marked by extraordinary litigation from Dove who pursued him in the mayors' courts of Totnes and Exeter, in the stannary court, in the consistory court at Exeter and in London at the court of arches.[495]

Henry Hill of Totnes

Totnes was one of the leading towns of the South Hams and well-situated for exporting cloth and tin down the river Dart to Dartmouth. Henry Hill served as vicar from 1610 until his death in 1621. Two years before his death he was ridiculed by Joan Knight, a parishioner. Among the words Knight said to him were 'Thou art no minister. Kiss my arse. Do as my smock doth. Thou didst dance naked and thou was drunk in Christopher Farwell's house by six of the clock in the morning and thou art a raiser of devils and dost at thy will suppress them again'.[496] Some seven months later five witnesses confirmed Knight spoke similar words in three different parts of the town. It was claimed that whilst having a meal at Mary Babb's house Knight told her fellow guests that Hill had 'lay drunk in the street of Totnes and was not able to go home until he had somebody to help him to go home'. He had danced naked by which she explained 'the said Mr Hill did putt down his breeches and take up his shirt and taked his buttocks and turned round'. On another occasion Knight met Joan Goodall at the water conduit. While Knight filled her pail with water Goodall was scandalized to hear that the vicar had danced naked. On yet another occasion three witnesses listened to Knight tell the same tale at the town mill near the bridge. Edward Venton, the miller, heard different details. Knight allegedly told him 'Mr Hill is a drunkard and he was found drunk in the street of Totnes and some came along and found him so and did lead him home to his house and he was not able to come to church the next day to read service at prayer time because he had hurted his face with a fall'. Also there were Reverend and Mrs Hill. They had what was described as a 'great falling out and debate' in which Knight told Hill to kiss her arse. He responded that she was a whore to use such words.[497] Ten years later it was Knight herself who was accused of being drunk. Agnes Yate said she was 'a drunkard, a drunken sow and a drunken jade' while Margaret Norwood told her she was drunk at Anthony Langworthy's house as well as in Dartmouth where she was carried home drunk.[498]

John Trender of Barnstaple

John Trender served as Barnstaple's vicar for nearly thirty years, from 1593 until 1622, despite extraordinary episodes with unusual name-calling. In about 1600 he was called a lying varlet and false, forsworn knave before being physically assaulted.[499] The reason for this attack is unclear but there were other incidents which may have contributed. In 1909 he was remembered as being 'of a jovial temperament, his amusements were the pipe and tabor, and it was also whispered the bottle'.[500] This questionable assessment was based on an observation by the town clerk that on the evening of 14 November 1600 the mayor and aldermen:

> 'going about their search in the evening as usual found the vicar Mr Trender in John William's house, being a tippler, with other company and having amongst them a pipe with a tabor a little after nine. And because Mr Trender would not come down to Mr Mayor from the

chamber upon commandment and for other his . . . was committed to ward where he abode till . . . morning following.'

Trender then wrote to Bishop Cotton that he had been arrested without cause. Edward Bourchier, 4th Earl of Bath, who lived nearby at Tawstock, received a letter from the bishop and commanded the mayor to see him. Trender was released and on the 'Sunday following he preached 2 hours, being a cold day he wearied all his audience'. The dispute continued with the mayor determined that there had been just cause for the arrest and Trender was compelled to appear before the High Commission in London. The town clerk wrote 'there is no likelihood of good government while such dissensions last'.[501]

Trender had been in trouble with Barnstaple's councillors since at least 1596, three years after his arrival. The town clerk noted that Trender had:

'inveighed in his sermon against the aldermen for not coming to church whom he said were like two fat oxen that they would not hear when Christ called unto them but drew backwards and drew others from Christ. The aldermen were present but unseen. For this and his indecent behaviour on being questioned for this abuse he was committed to ward for want of sureties. The Earl of Bath next day discharged him'.

In 1604 he was called a paltry jack (an ill-bred man) as well as a scurvy companion.[502]

It may have been Trender's wife who did more to damage his reputation. In 1596 he married a widow, Mrs Joan Lindgo, and the ceremony took place less than three months after the burial of his previous wife. Her thoughts on the propriety of such a hasty marriage are unknown but she may not have been surprised that her husband would remarry six weeks after her own death in 1615.[503] By then it was common knowledge that Trender and his second wife had a stormy marriage.

Relations with her mother-in-law were obviously strained by

32. *A woman dressed to impress, in a contemporary engraving.*

1607 when she called Mrs Christian Trender a rogue, Satan, an old filth and a witch. Mrs Joan Trender also told her husband that she could never live quietly with him until he turned out 'the old Judas and vagrant'. That same year she sought a legal separation with maintenance costs. She explained in court that Trender ranted and raged; on one occasion he accused her of keeping assassins under their bed and told neighbours she was a drunkard and whore. Moreover, he had beaten her with an iron rod until she was black and blue and he struck her with candlesticks.[504] Her testimony was corroborated by a couple who had travelled with them to Bath where they shared a bedroom. The vicar and his wife slept in a high bed while Thomas and Joan Lugg shared a truckle bed. The latter heard Trender say to his wife 'thou beast, I will make thee be quiet, come I never be at rest for thee, thereon she heard him take a sword from the bed's head and strike the same . . . the bed post'. It is perhaps ironic that he later supplied a testimonial for a woman who was the victim of domestic abuse. Trender died on 17 November 1628 and his memorial stone proclaimed 'many are the troubles of the righteous but the Lord delivereth them out of all'.[505]

Clerics' wives and their children

Clerics' families came in for particular abuse. It was for excessive pride that Alice Tucker chided the rector's wife in Lawhitton in 1617. She called Mrs Elizabeth Cole and her family a 'company of ragnals or bally rags' and declared 'they be so proud now, that the highest seats be too bad for them, they were bare enough and had scarce a rag to their tail when they came to our parish first, we are polled to maintain their pride'. Mrs Cole's 'great ruffs' were, according to Tucker, paid for by the parishioners' rates and she likened them to beggars on horseback.[506] Ruffs, an ostentatious symbol of Elizabethan status and wealth, were also mentioned in the slander against a South Molton woman in 1596 who was told that a local man 'maintaineth thee in thy long ruffs'. Without her patron, Margery Paynes was told, she would have to return to her mother to wash dishes.[507]

Sexual ridicule dominated the abuse given to cleric's families. In Newton Tracey Nicholas Thomas scolded the rector in 1627 before saying his wife had 'a filthy report so filthy as thou sayeth thou wert ashamed to speak of it'.[508] The virtue of Rackenford's vicar's wife was also questioned in 1581. A parishioner accused another not only of having had 'the foulest whore in the parish' but stated that he had the parson's wife in his chamber and had hugged and kissed her behind the locked door.[509] When the horns of sheep and bullocks were placed over the church pulpit in St Clether in Cornwall it was the vicar's wife that was being slandered. Mrs John Old and a parishioner, Mrs Trevelyan, were in dispute over the illegitimacy of their children. The latter had called the vicar's children bastards as well as hinderlings by which she meant that they were base or degenerate. Mrs Old insisted that it was her

33. *Painting of a woman who might be intended to represent lust, painted on a screen in the Church of St Thomas-a-Becket at Bridford.*

rival who had a child before marriage. It was also in Cornwall that Padstow's vicar was named as a cuckold and his wife was called a whore.[510]

The aforementioned changes which had made it possible and then illegal for clerics to marry resulted in some parishioners not recognizing the validity of these marriages. Some speakers may have retained their Catholic beliefs despite these legal changes. Hence in Cornwall in 1601 a woman said that 'the ministers' wives were but priests' whores and arrant whores and that Agnes Powell the wife of John Powel, clerk vicar of Davidstow, is a priest's whore and an arrant whore'. She also declared that their children were priests' bastards. The vicar she scorned as an old knave and mocked him when he catechized. Similar words were spoken at a wedding feast in Sidbury in the autumn of 1606. One guest asked what Leonard Palmer's name was and upon being told declared that all 'priests' children are bastards'.[511]

Christian insults

In one marked respect the insults recorded in Exeter's two courts differed. In the mayoral court there were seven complaints that men or women were called puritan whores, puritan rogues or puritan knaves. No such complaint was made in the diocesan court. In 1618 and 1619 two men called two women 'puritan whores'. One of the latter was also told 'go look in her dissembling bible'. A constable was also told he was a dissembling knave scab and a dissembling scab as well as a puritan knave and a drinking knave. Another constable was called a dissembling rogue. In total four constables were told they were puritans or dissemblers. This may indicate that they were seen as agents of the justices' puritanism or possibly they had been recruited because of shared views. Two name-callers were children of those that they insulted. Joan Truman testified against her son who had allegedly said to her 'all such puritan rogues that run to sermons be as bad as the devil' upon which she asked who the puritan rogues were. He replied 'they be such as you be and you be one of them' and then he called her a dissembler.[512] A number of Elizabethan terms applied to those Protestants drawn to a lifestyle of bible reading, sermon going and psalm singing and the most popular was 'puritan'. It was often used to ridicule men and women but grew to become an accepted term among some. The term 'dissembler' indicated someone who deceived by concealing his or her real purposes.[513]

An East Devon gentleman defined puritans in verse in the early 1600s. It was entitled 'A puritan'.[514]

> If any ask me what is a right precision
> I answer a right precision is, God pardon me If I think amiss
> A state disturber, a proud distractor
> God's chiefest foe, the devil's chiefest factor
> An hypocrite, denied he that can
> This is a proud pernicious Puritan.

Name me but one of them that is not proud
And never more, let my words be allowed
Name me but one of them that is not miserable
Cruel hard hearted, and uncharitable
And I'll be bound to love a Puritan
And count him for a right perfect honest man
which now I think to be as rank a knave
as the earth can breed, or the world can have.

The Pharisee as we in scripture read
professeth God in word, the devil indeed
They make a show of zeal, & great devotion
As though they scorned wealth, honour or promotion
With this prescription the Puritan doth agree
Ergo the Puritan is a Pharisee
But though many of them bad members be
And use deceit and all hypocrisy
Yet I know some that lead a godly life
They love their neighbours & their neighbour's wife
Let not a Puritan think I'll deceive him
A knave I found him & a knave I'll leave him.

The language of these lines, if not the meaning, would have been insulting to some. In the early 1590s the term 'knave' had been used to describe a puritan by a former cleric of Newton Ferrers. Richard Johnson later became vicar of Mevagissey and was accused in the church court of leading a licentious life. He explained that on one occasion he was in a private house in the Cornish port when a puritan condemned the playing of cards and dice. Johnson explained that he began by asking him:

'What say you then to him that hath devised how God should be served upon the cards? and thereupon this respondent showed forth a pack of cards lying then upon the table, and said in manner and form as followeth and laid down an ace, said by the number of 1 may be signified God, by the number of 2 may be signified God the father and God the son, and by the number of 3 may be signified the 3 persons in Trinity, by the number of 4 the 4 Evangelists, by the number of 5 the 5 Wounds of our Saviour Christ, by the number of 6, 6 of the 12 Patriarchs, by the number of 7 the 7 petitions contained in the Lord's Prayer, by the number of 8 were signified the 8 Beatitudes, and by the 9 the 9 words which Christ spake at his Passion, by the number of 10 were signified the 10 Commandments. All which were showed by this respondent by demonstration of the cards, and this respondent turning up the knave of clubs unto the supposed puritan then present said here is such a knave as you that should serve God'.[515]

Johnson's account is the earliest version of a text which was printed in 1776 in Newcastle but it was also noted in a Hampshire manuscript at about the same time. It was popularized as a recitation song, 'The Deck of Cards', by Tex Ritter in 1948 and afterwards by other artists.[516]

FOUR

Sex and Misconduct: Bawds, Incest and Disease

In about 1590 John Hooker loyally characterized Devon's gentry as being disinterested in the games, plays, wantonness, nightwatching, riotness, banqueting, incontinences, 'disorders and filthiness' that were found in what he described as 'the courts of Bacchus and the palaces of Venus'.[517] His confidence was misplaced: insults show, not surprisingly, that Devonians across the social classes were caught up in such pursuits. Moreover, public ridicule provides the only means to understand their sexual misconduct, or at least allegations of it, and reveals extraordinary background details into its various forms.

Prohibited behaviour and the consequences of those sexual acts concerned a great proportion of insults. In response, many men and women protested that their reputations were sullied and they expressed outrage at the aspersions cast upon them. But it was their alleged behaviour that caused family members, neighbours, friends and strangers to castigate them. Men and women told other men and women that they were not fit to be in their presence. 'Get thee in whore' was said by one woman to another in Chawleigh while others were told 'Get thee home to thy whores' (Stokenham),

'Get thee in, thy parboiled whore' (Kenton), 'Get thee away, thy bastardly slave' (Exeter), 'Get thee forth of the churchyard, thou old whore bawd' (Welcombe), 'Get thee home, whore scold' (Chudleigh), 'Get thee home, scurvy whore and have no to do with me' (Launceston in Cornwall), 'Go, go home, what makest thou here? thou harlot? Home, harlot home' (Stoke Climsland in Cornwall), 'Go home and learn some manners' (Exeter), 'Go home like a whore as thou art' (Bideford), 'Away you whore, away you whore, away you whore' (Exeter) and 'Get thou home, drab' (Great Torrington).[518] The court testimonies not only reveal sexual insults but also unveil carnal activity, some of it perhaps surprising, that provides the background to understand name-calling.

Witness statements indicate that it was easier than today to snoop: men and women claimed their knowledge of illicit behaviour had been observed first hand. The comparatively large households of yeomen, merchants and gentlemen exacerbated this. Those in Devon averaged between 9 and 10 persons.[519] Houses had a shortage of accommodation and servants' beds were often placed in semi-public rooms. In 1567 George Berry, for example, slept in a gallery in his master's house in Dowland. From his bed he overlooked the main hall and heard the private conversations of fellow servants sitting by the fire.[520]

Others had to be more inventive spies. At Tawstock the miller was unlucky when in 1613 a neighbour looked through the keyhole of his door and saw him 'occupying his dame being the wife of Simon Whitefield'. Testimonies indicate that it was commonplace for doors and walls to have holes which allowed spectators to watch sex. It was through one such chink in a door at Dartington Hall that Lady Champernowne's servants spied on her with a man who was not her husband.[521] Various servants and relations also peered through a hole in a brewhouse door in Littleham near Bideford and saw John Short with a woman. In Topsham in 1573 a man went to his employer's house at sunset and at the hall door 'did trust his hand against the wicket of the said door and the same was so fast that it would not go open therewith as it was wont to do, and this deponent then looking through the chink of the said wicket did see the said Winifred Carter and Thomas Major within the hall of the said house, the said Winifred having her clothes above her knees and the said Thomas Major having his hose down about his legs and when they heard the said thrust against the wicket separated themselves one from the other, and thereupon this deponent went his way leaving them in the said hall without any further ado.' It was this same phrase, 'his hose down about his legs', that was repeated about a servant at Kilmington caught late at night attempting to have sex that same year.[522]

An interruption seen through a hole was also alleged in Crediton eight years later. William Tremlett testified that his wife had told him that Robert Gullock 'did often in this deponent's absence repair to his house [and therefore he] came from his work to see whether he could find him then at his house. And at his coming home he this deponent, hearing him within his house to talk with his wife, stepped aside from the door and got him behind the house where through a chink he plainly saw the same Gullock to lock fast the door. None then being in the house but the same Gullock and this deponent's wife and a child lying in the cradle, by reason whereof this deponent, suspecting the matter, got him to the door and through the chinks of the same saw them both lying on the bed together and called unto his wife who immediately opened the door to this deponent and the said Gullock forthwith skipped from the bed and sat him down by the fire hard adjoining to the bed. His shoes being off from his feet and being by the fire'.[523]

It was through another chink that illicit sex was discovered in Sheepwash that same year of 1581. Honor Denford stated that Anne Haine was searching for her husband John and found the 'parlour door being closed to and looked through the chinks in the door and came back again and willed this deponent and Agnes Man to go with her. And so the said Anne opened the door and they went in all together and there saw the said John Haine and Mary Scamme in the bed together between the sheets naked committing the act of adultery together.' She told him 'John, it had been better for you to do some other deed than this.' He

34. *'The Church Walk' in Totnes as drawn by William Brockedon in the early 1800s. It was in a house in this town that Katherine Peron allegedly caught Bernard Smith* in flagrante *with his maid.*

responded, 'Faith, I must confess I have done a foolish part. I think I am bewitched to her, but forgive me for this I will never do the like'.[524]

It was through yet another hole that Cheriton Bishop's curate was found with two women. William Hawkin testified he was in Thomas Parker's house in a bedroom beneath one in which John Grant, the curate, was staying. Hawkin observed Grant leave through the back door that night and return with Elizabeth Hanmer, 'a very strumpet'. Hawkin 'suspecting the matter by reason he heard a great rustling over him in the same Grant's chamber, arose and went up to the said Grant's chamber door and there he heard them talk very softly' and saw Grant 'through a hole of a wall upon the bed in the chamber aforesaid with the said Elizabeth in his arms'. Another witness unlocked the door 'and went in and there found the said Grant tumbling between the said

Elizabeth and one Anne Stiggans, which Anne they could not through the hole perceive'.[525]

It was through holes in the spurring or enterclose (a partition) that Newton Poppleford neighbours of Agnes Merrick watched her having sex with her brother-in-law. They observed 'the fashion of them' from a neighbouring house as they had sex against a seat, in a window and then finally on the hall floor. In Crediton in 1541 a servant watched a couple through a hole in the wall of a pig house. He walked in 'and was even upon them afore they spied this deponent or the other maid and there this deponent did see the said Raffe lying upon the said Elizabeth having all her clothes about her heels and his hose so far down as his knees, and that this deponent did see by reason that he had nothing upon him but his shirt and a doublet and a short red jerkin which were all about his buttocks'.[526]

One woman claimed she had grew tired watching sex in Cullompton: in 1576 Anne Cole discovered Margaret Lendon on her knees peering through a chink of a wall in John Rawe's house. Lendon held up her hand and asked her to stay silent, watched 'a pretty while' and said 'now look you in there, for I have looked so long that I am weary of looking'. They saw Humphrey Paris and Thomasine Trott together but it was questionable whether sex had taken place. However, later they were seen under an oak tree 'the said Thomasine lying down upon her back and her clothes half way up her thigh, and Humphrey Paris lying upon her'. However, in Uplowman one witness denied that there was a hole to see any untoward conduct. Robert Hobhouse deposed in 1571 that he 'did never know any such chink or hole in the said wall'.[527]

While some had to spy through holes others observed illicit sex taking place much more openly. At Warbstow in Cornwall William Furse stood on his hedge and watched Elizabeth Bragg and Hugh Mill 'in carnal copulation together in a certain garden of the said Bragg'.[528] Other witnesses claimed to have seen sex in such places as under a bay bush (Dartmouth), under a boat (Teignmouth), in a mill (Tawstock, Down St Mary, Tavistock), against a pair of bars (Lympstone), in a chair (Shebbear), in a meadow (Down St

Mary), in a hayloft (Langtree), in a field of broom (Kenton), on a bundle of straw (Exeter),[529] in the clavel of a chimney (Littleham near Bideford), in a lane (Sampford Courtenay), in a chimney corner (Chudleigh, Littlehempston), under a furse bush in the snow (Alverdiscott), in a field of furse (Chudleigh), in a furse brake (Kingsteignton), against a furse rick (Great Torrington), in a field of wheat (Farway), between two hazel bushes (Frithelstock), in aller bushes (Crediton) and even in a nettle bush (Broadhembury).[530] However, gardens were, perhaps not surprisingly, often pointed to as a place for sexual rendezvous but so too were hedges including at East Budleigh where a couple was seen in the trawe, the hollow, of the hedge.[531]

The circumstances are unclear but it was claimed in 1599 that after an Exeter man called Joan Hurrell a whore he told her 'four honest men did see one with boots and spurs occupy thee upon a bed'. Likewise, it is not known how Gilbert Caseman of Poughill knew the exact location where Julian Giste had illicit sex: he

35. *A couple making hay while the sun was shining, in a contemporary engraving.*

'pointing with his hand said that Milton had to do with her upon a bed that was in the same parlour'.[532]

Illicit sex would, one could assume, be more prudently conducted clandestinely but some witnesses claimed to be so close as to see the points (laces) of a man's breeches. Whilst haymaking a Colyton man discovered his sister with a neighbour and 'he came so near them that he could have pulled off John Restorick's shoes'.[533] An onlooker in Honiton told a local man in 1634 'thou didst occupy Elizabeth Michell and I saw her coats up and thy breeches down lying upon her'. Mary Lyde of Pinhoe complained that it was said in 1630 'that she was found in an orchard with a man and the man had his breeches down and her coats up lying upon her and the man ran away with his shirt hanging over his breeches'. In a kitchen in a private house in Callington in Cornwall a woman encountered another woman who had her clothes above her navel and 'the stopple in her bottle'.[534] She was presumably fairly close to see such detail.

The accounts illustrate the means by which sexual misconduct was discovered at close quarters. Some encounters took place indoors. At Alverdiscott William Pugsley's suspicions of a couple were confirmed when he heard the 'crack' of the bed while at Fremington another couple were discovered by their bed 'knocking'.[535] In Totnes Katherine Peron climbed the stairs to encounter Bernard Smith 'in his chamber with his maid (meaning his maid servant) and he had one of her legs in one arm and another leg in the other arm (meaning thereby as he thinketh that the said Bernard Smith was found by her committing of fornication with his servant)'.[536] In St Germans in Cornwall Emma Moore 'went to a room near to that where this deponent was and afterwards she hearing some noise went to the chamber door where they were and there hearing the bed creak & Bonyfant fetching short breath saw him & the said Emma lying on the bed, he upon & she under & saw her clothes up above her waist & his breeches untrussed before & there committed incontinence with her'. It was also indoors that in Chagford an observer 'saw John Hill take Joan Lant against a form near a table board in one Brent's house . . . and saw the said

Joan Lant's clothes above her navel and the said Hill between her legs, his hose down'.[537]

Neighbours said that they had happened upon couples in various outbuildings such as when Elizabeth Somer of East Budleigh went to a brewhouse and pulled back a curtain to find 'there lying Mark Varley on the floor and his breeches down'.[538] It was in a Broadclyst barn that another couple was seen. Three witnesses, who were weeding in 1616, heard the slander slightly differently. Eleanor Grady thought Agnes Voysey said to Margery West 'thou Margery didst lie with John Holmead in Mr Moore's shippen and there were 3 or 4 boys looked in through the door and saw it, and Margaret Drewe called to thee and bid thee come out for shame, and when thou came out the boys were ready to ride on thy back'. Mary Adam, a widow, remembered it being said 'John Holmead did lie with thee in Mr Moore's shippen and the boys did look in through the door and make a game of it, and Margaret Drewe did bid thee rise for shame for the boys did make a game of it to see how you two did tumble'. Finally, Ellen Perry recalled 'thou were in a house with Mr Moore's man and the boys did look in through the door and laugh at it and when thou came out the boys were ready to ride thee'.[539]

Many sightings took place outdoors. John Yendall was on his wagon in a Sampford Courtenay lane in 1582 when he 'saw by chance Robert Durant alias Paris and Joan Hockaday lying together athwart the way, the said Paris being lying upon her, his hose down about his leg and the said Joan's clothes up and as soon as they had espied this deponent the said Paris rose up hastily from the said Joan holding up his hose with his hand and his shirt hanging out over behind and ran away speedily and this deponent now knowing him at the first called after him and told him he would speak with him and so he having tied up his fore points came back to this deponent again and requested him that he would not make any idea of it for said he it is a foolish part of me'.[540] William Rowe may have been in a drang (an alleyway) in Silverton when in 1636 he saw Jane Combe with Thomas Walter who 'did fuck her against a garden gate and was not so contented but went into a drang between two houses and there had to do with her again'.[541] In Egloshayle near Padstow a group of Cornishmen were with their horses at a well and one of them 'somewhat higher than the other called him and there showed him a woman and Henry Peers standing in the highway and the woman's smock up as high as her breasts and saw a hole in her smock that the red did show through the white and did see the man stand up higher against the woman'. Outside Exeter four women watched a couple in an orchard and concluded their 'motion, action and stirring' proved they were having sex.[542]

In contrast, in the North Devon village of Pilton two men were too distant to declare with any certainty what Robert Northcott was doing on top of Christian Heal in a field but three boys had a better view. They watched Northcott pull up her clothes, put his legs between her legs and then observed him being 'very busy awhile'. The boys bid him 'God Speed You', she fled, Northcott readjusted his codpiece and tied his points.[543]

It could be argued that the closest another person could have been to a sexual act was recorded at Exeter in 1625. Two couples gave contradictory evidence about their behaviour late at night in an attic room in which a newly married couple was sleeping. The four denied there had been any untoward conduct but one wife admitted that she had sat on the stairs outside the bedroom and watched the young newly-wed man, Lewis Rowe, come down with only his breeches on. She acknowledged that she had put her child to bed in their bedroom but the other wife also admitted that all four had visited the couple. The newlywed man remembered different details. He testified that the other two couples 'drawing away the clothes from the bed where they lay uncovering them, and said that they would feel where they were wet or dry, and taken the man by the members and did the like unto her which was a great grief unto them both, which things being done it was more like brute beasts than like Christians'.[544]

As intimate as these details were, several other cases reveal another form of familiarity. Bed sharing was common amongst servants and this custom provided opportunities to observe sexual activities. For example, in the early 1580s John Lane of Payhembury became accustomed to nightly visits of a fellow servant, Agnes Farrant, and of her using 'certain wanton ways' with his bed partner, James Salter.[545] Likewise, in 1566 at Chudleigh while two male servants were sharing a bed, a female servant joined them: John Bushel later pointed out that he lay along the side facing the wall.[546] James Webb, a servant living in Silverton, was more explicit about his bed partner's activities. He said in 1566 'Elizabeth Parker came to bed where John Palmer lay and this deponent being in the same bed, and she the said Elizabeth Parker said that she would be gone and he said that he would first kiss her and therefore tarry and let us kiss before you go, and she said no, yet he plucked her into the bed whereas he lay and this respondent sayeth that they lay together for that time by the space of a quarter of an hour and he this respondent sayeth that they had carnal knowledge together for this respondent sayeth that he was broad waking and did hear that one was upon another but he durst not to go out of his bed for to speak for fear what would happen unto him . . . And this respondent sayeth that they had carnal knowledge together as is before said by the shaking of the bed.' Palmer also allegedly visited Elizabeth Parker in her bedroom where she shared a bed with Joan Roger. The latter said 'John Palmer came into this deponent's chamber whereas this deponent and Elizabeth Parker did lie and this deponent being abed and lying waking did hear Elizabeth Parker coming to bed and being unready and in her smock John Palmer came unto her and played with her when the said Elizabeth Parker was a bed and would have had his pleasure of her but the said Elizabeth would not and said that this respondent was waking and the said John Palmer said that this respondent was asleep and for that the said Elizabeth had a hole in her smock he would do it that this respondent should not hear'.[547]

Despite this apparent sexual license, there were social conventions on sharing beds and miscreants could be punished in civil courts. This included Ann English who was carted through Exeter for having shared a bed with a couple in 1562. At about this time and also in Exeter, a man was whipped in eleven places for having brought with him two 'wives'. He and his first wife had five strips at each place while the second, and younger, woman had three.[548] In 1620 Francis Geale confessed that Julian Smale came into the bed that he shared with Edward Michell 'where they had both the use of her body' but Smale and Michell denied it and protested that only Geale could be the father of the illegitimate baby. Two years later Nathaniel Barker tried to make it sound commonplace that a tinker slept in the same bed with him and his wife but he also admitted that their 16-year-old maidservant regularly lay with them.[549]

A couple in the Cornish village of Stratton also appear to have broken convention. In 1610 Dorothy Corey complained that a neighbour had reported 'there came a man to the house of Ciprian Corey and told him he would not lie in his the said Ciprian Corey's house unless he might lie with him and his wife all night and thereupon he did lie with the said Ciprian Corey and his wife all night or between them and then the said Ciprian went to

36. *A Sheila-na-gig, on a boss in the Church of St Andrew, South Tawton. These images of immodest women can be found across Europe. The carving would have been in the ceiling when Mary Hole was called a maggot-arsed whore in 1640.*

Whalesborough two miles from his house and at his return found the foresaid party [still] in bed with his wife'.[550] The behaviour of Helen Docton of Dolton also raised questions. She denied having had sex with Mathew Hodge when she shared his bed with him and his wife in 1555 but admitted that 'one night when her father had strangers and lacked lodgings for his household and his strangers, this respondent lay in the said Hodge's bed with Hodge and his wife. And the wife lay all the night between this respondent and her husband and prayeth God she may be damned body and soul if ever she had carnal copulation with him or any of them both'. However, she admitted to having had an illegitimate child with another man and moreover, Mathew Hodge confessed he also had sex with her on several occasions.[551]

Several phrases were used only to describe sexual activity. There were variants of one used of a Salcombe woman: it was said she 'didst ride upon Owen Bebel's back'.[552] Similarly, a Paignton woman was told in 1588 that she was a whore 'that thou dost ride upon every man's back', a Cullompton woman in 1634 allegedly let the boys 'ride' her and some Broadclyst boys were said in 1616 to have been ready 'to ride on the said Margery's back' after watching her have sex in a barn.[553] A similar term was used in Crediton when a husband told his wife that two men 'had the carriage of thee'.[554]

The term 'men's heels' was recorded in four North Devon parishes. In 1614 at Alverdiscott a woman said to another 'I scorn to be such a runabout as thou art to run up and down after men's heels' whereas in Barnstaple a neighbour called Honor Gribble the whore of William Kelland and 'did bid her run after his heels again'.[555] At Great Torrington a neighbour said to another he would rather be hanged 'than to be such a one as thou art, for thou art an arrant knave and I might have drawn thee out by the heels from Grace Zegar out of Campe's pigs loose.' A loose is better known now as a pigsty. Thomas Short of Littleham near Bideford was embarrassed by his father's longstanding behaviour with one woman. He was overheard to say that he saw them having sex and that he 'might have plucked his father out by the heels saying he was more ashamed at the sight thereof than they were committing the act'.[556]

Lusty had several medieval meanings, including being cheerful and being pleasant in appearance, but it may have in the sense having sexual desire, otherwise of being lustful, that was intended to describe a 'lusty young wife' of an old man living in North Devon. It was said that this woman gave birth while she was milking her ewes and afterwards admitted the baby's father was not her husband.[557] She may have agreed with the woman who, in a ballad of 1614, explained why she preferred young men to old.

> 'An aged man is testy,
>   and set to hoard and hide;
> With lame legs and resty,
>   bewailing back and side.
> A young man he is beautiful,
>   courageous, trick and trim;
> And looketh with a merry cheer,
>   when aged men look grim.'[558]

'Lusty' was also used to describe a Totnes woman ('an arrant whore, a whoresoring whore a gouty-legged whore and a lusty cut') in 1582 whereas in Cheriton Bishop a man boasted by saying he was lusty ('I am lusty. I will occupy her'). When it later became apparent that he had fathered a child he said 'it is but a lusty part of a man, what is done cannot be undone'.[559]

Recalling misconduct

Alleged sexual miscreants were reminded of their behaviour such as at Exeter where one woman was asked 'Thou art a whore and dost remember the trumpeter?' or in Topsham when another was bid 'Remember the man with the long beard?' The latter may have been a man referred to as 'Blue John'.[560] One witness after another asked similar questions such as 'Thou damned whore, dost remember when thou playest the whore at Chudleigh in a barn?'

(Exeter), 'Remember where thou was when thou wentest with a lantern and a candle when thy sides were tallowed? (Crediton), 'Sherren, Sherren, remember the top of the sanctuary where thou layest in the ditch with Bond's wife and Mr Chudleigh leapt over thy backs?' (Dunchideock), 'Remember when Robert Peter came out of John Tottell's stable with his breeches in his hand?' (Ide), 'Do you remember when you brought a man with you down into the country and came to my brother William Payne's house and there kept him under lock two nights?' (Topsham), 'Oh Joan, Joan, remember the butcher that dressed four quarters with one prick?' (Dartmouth), 'Remember that she wiped his brow in a handkerchief after he had done?' (Newton St Cyres), 'Dost thou remember when that thou did jape for three half pennies?' and 'Remember when thou were japed in the woods going after wool?' (Chudleigh), 'Remember when thou were so common that any man might have had thee for 3 pennies a night?' (Dartmouth), 'Remember thou arrant whore drab when the candle was turned at thy tail and remember when the slippers were left behind?' (Cheriton Bishop), and 'Bid her remember the time when Vicar Wills was plucked from her tail' (Lanliverry in Cornwall).[561]

Men cajoled, induced and enticed women to have sex. One man's promise is similar to those repeated in every generation since 1566: John Palmer promised Elizabeth Parker in Silverton that 'I will not bring thee with child'. She still refused him.[562] Financial payments were alleged in a number of cases ranging from the aforementioned halfpennies to a piece of gold. One woman was actually called a Three Halfpenny Whore.[563] One Exeter woman was said to charge nine pence for sex, another woman was offered a shilling in Chudleigh while one more there was said to have had only a bushel of beans and peas.[564] It may not have been unusual to exchange sex for food: in Tintagel two women were offered a peck of barley for sex. Churchstow's vicar was ridiculed in the street for allegedly paying two shillings for sex when the going rate was only 18d while Dunsford's vicar was said to have offered a woman three pounds to be his mistress for a year.[565] A man in Brampford Speke was alleged to have told a woman 'that her

37. *Carving of a man and woman engaged in what could be idle talk, on a roof boss in the Church of St Peter, Ugborough. Those women who called others 'burnt tailed whores' would have walked under this roof boss.*

husband did not love her and that you would be a friend unto her and use means to get her her husband's love whereupon the said Joan went from her clothes that were there drying and went into her husband's house and you the said Tailor followed after her into the house and there being privately with her (her husband and family being from home) did again kiss her and embrace her and told her that her husband did not love her, and that her husband (staying at Colyton) it was likely that he had a wench there that he loved better than her and that he intended to surrender his living in Brampford Speke to his son to deceive her of her widow's estate and that the only means to prevent it was to be with child and holding her in his arms and embracing her and kissing her, allured her to have had the carnal knowledge of her body and felt her secret parts and took up her clothes and put forth your prick and used all the persuasive means you could to have had the carnal knowledge of her body, telling her that if she were with child that would be the only means to gain her husband's love & to take off his love from his son that he had by his former wife'. It was claimed he succeeded.[566]

A perplexing example of soliciting took place in Sampford Courtenay in 1583. Agnes Sommer testified 'she sayeth that the said Paris is a lewd man and attempted to have his wicked and beastly pleasure of this deponent, for the said Paris about this time twelve months then in a certain close adjoining to his house in Sampford Courtenay came to this deponent passing over a certain bridge and said unto her as followeth, *that is*, wilt thou play Agrimomsie with me for a groat? Agrimomsie, said this deponent, what is that? Doest thou not know? Said he, shall I have my pleasure of thee if thou wilt, thou shalt have of a friend of me as long as thou livest and this deponent denying him earnestly the said Paris held a groat in his hand and desired her instantly to grant his request and this deponent said she would not consent to him in that place but at length after great denial promised to consent to him if he

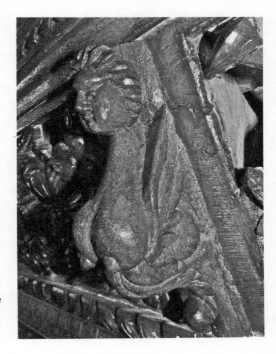

38. *Carving of an amply-proportioned siren on the rood screen of Church of St Mary the Virgin, Washfield. The screen was erected in 1624 by which time puritanism had been on the rise in Devon for more than a generation.*

151

39. *Medieval wall painting of a couple, possibly intending to symbolize lust, at St Winifred's Church, Branscombe.*

would go the other side of the hedge and immediately the said Durant went over the hedge and thereupon this deponent came away and escaped from him.'[567] The definition of 'agrimonsie' is uncertain.

There were also women who were alleged to have paid for sex. In South Tawton one gave two pence for her cows to be milked so she had sufficient time to engage in illicit sex. In Tawstock another was said to hide her lover in an outhouse until her husband left for church and she gave him gifts of clothing including shoes and a doublet. In Northlew in 1578 a woman was alleged to have paid 12d for sex[568] while Joan Cudmore of Rackenford admitted that she had given her servant Robert Coliford four shillings for sex as well as better food, including mutton pies, than that given to her other servants. She also baked him 'ten acre' loaves of white bread. Mrs Cudmore divulged that they had had sex in the middle chamber over the hall, in the barn and stable, and on the kitchen floor.[569]

Bastards

While illicit sex was commonly alleged, illegitimate children offered conclusive proof. Some women allegedly tried to avoid this by travelling to distant places such as Taunton, London and Wales.[570] A woman of Bishop's Nympton was known for having two bastards while a Crediton woman was alleged to have had four.[571] It was said of an Axminster woman that she was able to ride a horse and keep one bastard in her pannier and another in her husband's. In Down St Mary it was claimed that a woman had three cradles filled with one man's bastards.[572] It was a Crediton man that was told he 'had a bastard and it was like him, and the very picture of him, and that it had his own nose'.[573] In Nymet Rowland a woman was told 'thou hast done so much to have a hundred bastards' while a Cornish woman heard her neighbour say that she had had sex with a glover and was subsequently 'full of young glovers'.[574] In Honiton one woman allegedly 'had a bastard by her master Mr Hassard of Lyme Regis and that he gave her a crock and a pan and forty shillings in money to shut up the matter'.[575] Others were told that they themselves were bastards or even that both they and a parent were illegitimate. There were a few instances of the word 'brat' being used but it was not always a word used in contempt.[576]

Bawds and panders

At Exeter in 1620 William Marker's wife was called a 'pander', a fifteenth-century term for a person who procured women for others to have sex with.[577] In contrast, three years earlier at Kingsbridge John Lapp was called a bawd, an earlier term, which also signified a go-between but he was also named a wittol which defined a man who consented to his wife's adultery.[578] Many others were also called wittols, including a Crediton man in 1618, which was then explained it signified 'a man that should be a bawd to his own wife'.[579] Bawds, like panders, procured women and this was alleged in such places as Morchard Bishop and in Denbury in 1585 where a parishioner was said to have sold his wife for sex.[580] The definition was made clear in Plympton St Mary in 1627 when it was explained of William Pitt and his wife that 'thou and thy husband did counsel my maid to be Mr Sharrock's whore, meaning thereby that the said Pitt and his wife were bawds and did brook and solicit women to be whores and provide whores for other men and conceal the crimes and in that sense the witnesses then present did understand the said words'. In 1583 a Barnstaple woman was said to have been 'as often times a bawd as there were sands in the sea'[581] while in 1622 an Exeter man may have been admitting to procuring women when he said to one woman that he kept 'and had to his command 40 better whores than she was'.[582]

Procuring could involve family members. In the early 1600s, in Plymouth, a woman complained that it was alleged she was a bawd to her children.[583] An Exeter woman was accused of being 'a bawd to thy own son' which presumably meant she found women for him.[584] Two witnesses heard similar words spoken of a Tavistock woman in 1623. One thought it was said 'thou are an old bawd, a loose bawd and a scurvy bawd and thou art bawd to thy own children and thou wert occupied in the cellar against a hogshead and some looked at the window and saw it' whereas another remembered it as 'thou art an old whore, an arrant whore and a foggy whore and thou wert a whore by the Queen's days and who so would go into her house and give her two pots of beer might occupy her'.[585] In 1541 it was said that a woman procured her daughter-in-law for sexual services in Brampford Speke, a Cornish woman was alleged to have been a bawd to her daughter and another in Newton Abbot was told she had procured her two daughters and that she herself was an old whore.[586] In Exeter it was said in 1618 a woman was 'an old bawd, a scurvy bawd, a whore and an old rotten whore and the old whore, meaning the said Alice Drake takes the young whore's part meaning her daughter Ann Baron's part'.[587] Another Exeter woman objected in 1622 to her daughter's behaviour with a man and told her she will not allow herself to be known as a bawd. The daughter appears to have married this man shortly afterwards but was then alleged to be having sex with a second man. Her mother called her a whore and she responded 'if you had not been a bawd [then] I had not been a whore'.[588]

What would be called a brothel in current usage had several other terms in the 1500s and 1600s. In Exeter in 1613 John Bingham allegedly kept a 'bawdy inn' which 'no man of credit will come into thy house and thou dost keep John Tailor's wife in every corner of the house'.[589] Thomasine Vinecombe complained it was said she had a bawdy house in Crediton and among her staff

40. *A man with the symptoms of syphilis, including damage to his nose, engraved by Marco Aurelio Severino, 1632.*

was Thomas Basse's wife, a 'light' housewife. The church house at Sandford was said to have had 'base and evil order' kept there in 1624 which resulted in it being called a 'stews' and bawdy house.[590] Women were also called whores in supposedly bawdy houses in Broadwoodkelly and Exeter.[591] A London woman was said in 1615 to have had a bawdy house in London and had plans to open another in Bovey Tracey.[592]

Unusual ridicule was said by Walter Periman, an Exeter man who was known for idleness and physically assaulting his wife. He mocked Nicholas Mills as a cuckold and called Mills' wife Eleanor a whore who sold herself to men for nine pence. More intriguing was that he said to their daughter Anne that she was a young whore whose mother would bring him 'from Cuckold's Bridge to Bawdy Bush'.[593]

Incest

Allegations were made of sex with family members including a claim in Colyton in 1558 that an Axminster man had been intimate with a woman and her daughter.[594] Similar allegations were made in Kingsbridge in 1597.[595] There were claims at Sherford in 1627 and Halberton in 1617 that siblings had had children.[596] In 1594 at Yealmpton a wife discovered her husband was having sex with her daughter: a neighbour overheard Mary Reed call her husband an arrant beast and her daughter a whore. Another family member said 'she had seen them doing that thing which was not fit for them and said that she came in upon them into the hall'.[597] In 1621 Exeter's mayor heard George Clotworthy testify that since his marriage his wife shared a bed with her father and mother. The father slept between his daughter and wife.[598] Incest was recognized as a crime through consanguinity, that is blood relationships. However, it was also illegal through affinity, that is marriage, and thus some conduct described as incest in this period would not be classified as such today: a Newton Poppleford woman was castigated for having sex with her husband's brother.[599]

Disease

Talk of sexual depravity was accentuated by adding disease to the insults and venereal diseases, both syphilis and gonorrhoea, dominated the ridicule. Eventually it was thought that syphilis had been brought back in the early 1490s from the Americas by Christopher Columbus' sailors but initially in England syphilis was known as the French Pox (in other places as the Castillian, French,

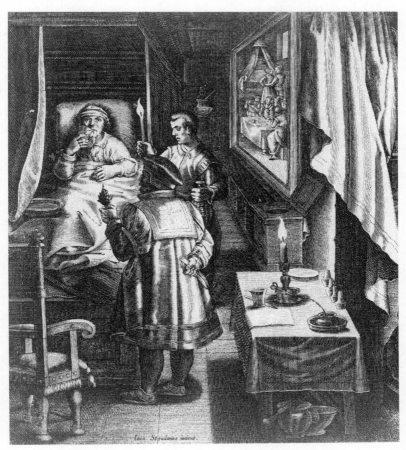

41. *Detail from engraving of patient with syphilis, 1660, by P. Galle after J. van der Straet.*

German, Polish, Portuguese or Spanish Sickness) as well as 'the clap' although the latter term has not yet been found for Devon in this period. The symptoms include skins sores, which were called pocks, and these formed part of most ridicule. Gonorrhoea was not as well known possibly because it was less prevalent but is now thought to have been in England longer than syphilis. Both diseases, as will be seen, were treated with mercury.[600] There was a strong social stigma to having both diseases and it was this sense of disgrace that defined the insults.

Various terms were used including 'bulged' such as when Martin Grosse of Moretonhampstead was called a bulged knave in 1572. One witness explained that it 'doth signify him which is burnt with a whore' while another thought that 'that the words bulged knave are slanderous words and so accounted . . . for that it doth signify a man of any evil life and chiefly him that is burnt with a whore'. A third parishioner added it was 'according to the opinion and inter-pretation of this deponent and as he hath heard it often and sundry times so to be accounted and taken in those parts whereas this deponent doth now dwell and that among honest persons his good name and fame is hindered greatly which is so spoken of and so common people do take the same'.[601] More women than men were called bulged and a Dawlish man thought that the term 'bulged whore' meant she was a woman of an incontinent life. In 1566 a Belstone woman asked why her son was called bulged and the speaker said it was because she was a whore and that in a broom close 'three men did look into it that thy shoes did fall from thy feet'.[602]

A number of men and women were called 'burned' which had no relation to fire. For example a Burrington woman was said to have been burnt but she was also called a polecat, another term for a sexually licentious woman.[603] This was a commonly used term which signified having a venereal disease: for example, it was said in 1606 that a South Molton man 'hath occupied his maiden and hath burned her'.[604] Chawleigh and Ugborough women were called burned or burnt tail whores while a Stoke Gabriel woman had a slightly different epithet: she was a burnt-arse jade.[605] Another of Berry Pomeroy was similarly called a burnt-arse whore and a burned bastard whore and a man of Bishop's Nympton was called a burned-tail rogue. Other phrases were more imaginative: a Stowford woman was told that her guts were 'almost ready burnt' while a Barnstaple woman heard she was a burned-tail whore who was not wholesome.[606]

Other slander not only alleged that a man or woman was burnt but also 'pocky',[607] which could mean pock-marked skin but more likely that she was infected with syphilis. In one case a witness from Broadclyst explained in 1630 that the phrase 'pocky arse and the pox' meant that the accused 'had committed adultery, fornication or incontinency and thereby was infected with a filthy disease'.[608]

Some men and women were accused of infecting others. In 1635 a Barnstaple woman was told 'thou art cursed out of the church for burning John Witheridge his prick and guts. Thereupon being reproved for speaking such words and advised by some one that heard him to take heed what he said, the said Lane replied again and said that she was the last woman that the said Witheridge did commit the act with or fuck or occupy or commit an act and that she was as hot as all the ovens in the town meaning thereby that she was a whore and a poxy whore and that she had committed adultery with the said Witheridge and burnt him or infected him with the pox or to that effect'. More than fifty years earlier, in 1635, a similar comment was made of an Alphington woman. It was rumoured Richard White 'had taken a disease of Elizabeth Barnes and that by occasion thereof the said Richard White's wife had taken the like disease of him the said Richard whereof he thinketh she meant burning'.[609]

Other ridicule was about medical care. An Exeter woman was said in 1571 to have had treatment for being burned after having been 'naughty', that is licentious, and nearly a generation earlier, in 1540, it was claimed in Kenton that 'Body's wife had the pox and Pitt healed her'.[610] In 1576 Alice Maunder's customers stopped buying her bread and the reason lay with gossip that she had the French pox. It was said the Bow baker 'was laid for the pox, and had one pock upon her arm, and another upon her shoulder, and that she had been so skewered that she had no hair upon her head without it were a lock here and a lock there'. Another parishioner was told that her hair was stripped away 'like a goose foot'. A man of Bradninch had heard 'she hath the pox sure enough and that which is nine times worse than the pox the green *greingoomber* for, said she, leeches come over the backside to her'. A neighbour confirmed that Maunder 'being a baker and living thereby, is now so feared of her neighbours for that disease that nobody will almost buy any bread of her'.[611] Three other instances show the humiliation that taunting could bring. While two Cornish women were washing their clothes in St Germans, one said of the other 'she makes batches twice a week to wash her arse to keep the pox from it. There is no honest woman will do it.' It was said of an Exeter woman that she was cured of the pox by being in 'Fowler's tub', an apothecary's sweating tub which was used to treat venereal disease.[612] A Sandford woman was accused in 1614 of having had treatment on her 'uncomely' and 'nether' parts to cure her of a 'filthy disease'.[613]

Several men protested about intimate rumours about them. The unfortunately named Augustine Badcock was said in South Molton to have had the pox on his penis while a Crediton man was said to have the pox in his 'tail'[614] which could have meant either his posterior or his penis. However, it clearly was his backside that an Exeter man referred to as being diseased in 1617: he was told 'thou art a drunkard and a drunken rogue and a poxy rogue and the pox hangeth to thy arse'. In Tiverton William Dodge heard that he had been 'laid for the pox meaning the French pox and the old currier brought an oil to anoint thy bollocks'.[615] William Trickey of Exeter complained that Alice Endicott had said 'thou has had the pox and thou hast been laid for the pox by Budd the surgeon and thou was burned by a kinswoman of Elizabeth Wills and thou hath now no prick left by reason of the pox and burning'. Likewise, it was said in Brampford Speke that William Kewe 'is a horned cuckold & a cuckold knave and his wife so bad as a bored sow for she burned half an inch of William Myste's member'.[616]

An Okehampton man heard that a woman said of him that he was 'a rogue, a poxy rogue, a poxy knave and a poxy whoremonger and thy *verdigris* or pox comes out of thy arse.' *Verdigris*, the green pigment obtained from copper, was used as a treatment for syphilis through to the early 1800s.[617] Robert Avery, accused of being sexually wayward, was said in 1583 to have purchased a lateen spoon for the substantial sum of 3s 4d. The spoon, made partly of copper, was for 'use in the curing of diseased yards'. The most detailed description concerns the curate of Sheldon in about 1631. William Facey, a surgeon, was treating George Palfrey, the newly arrived curate. He said in a private house in nearby Churchstanton 'Mr Palfrey had a bad disease and that he was wont to say Burn Beds and Have Beds, but now (he meaning and speaking of the said Mr Palfrey) hath burnt his great bed and said also that he (the said Mr Palfrey) was swollen in the yard as big as a tinning pot of three pints. And he did think that he should lose part of his yard and said that he did make water at three or four places and was as black as the bottom of a pot'.[618]

It may have been syphilis that Thomas Adams of Exeter was referring to in 1621 when he called his master a cuckold and said that better women than his mistress had been whipped as prostitutes. Adams also said that he hoped one day to see his master's 'eyes fall out of his head'. Damaged eyesight was one of the well-known symptoms of syphilis. Syphillis might also have been the reason for Alice Rowland of Shebbear being called a copper-nosed drab in 1575. Nose deformities could result from the disease and replacements were made of various materials.[619]

Some insults provide minimal details such as when in 1567 a Great Torrington woman was told she was 'unclean' and it was said of Mary Hole of South Tawton by Nathaniel Arscot 1640 'thou art a whore and a maggot-arsed whore'. Wilmot Pind of Exeter had more justification to feel aggrieved. A neighbour said 'her guts doth rot in her body, that the worms crawleth from her, that she is not fit to lie with any man'.[620] Other women were said to be rotted or rotten by disease such as Alice Drake of Exeter ('old rotten whore') or Margaret Tailor of Witheridge ('old rotted pocky whore'). In Chulmleigh two women exchanged insults until one said to the other 'thou hast one of thy breasts rotted already and thy other shall shortly I warrant thee'.[621]

Both men and women were called scabs, a late sixteenth-century word which could indicate a low scoundrel. These insults often were part of a longer string of abuse such as 'a beggarly scab and drunkard', 'a whoremaster scab', and 'a rascal, a scab, a rascal scab, a scurvy knave'.[622] A second meaning for scabs were the pustules or scales which were a consequence of infection. Hence in Milton Dameral a man was called a 'scurvy, ragged, scabbed, pocky constable'. A Totnes woman was called Mistress Scabbed Arse as well as a scabbed-arse whore. She was also said to have blabber-lips, which meant they were larger than normal. A contemporary ballad noted 'the blackamores are blabber-lipped'.[623]

Scurvy was a popular adjective to use in relation to women and when called a whore. Symptoms include spots on the skin and it may be these that were referred to as part of general abuse implying unhealthiness. There is also one use of the word 'scabbard' which implies it had two meanings: in Blisland in Cornwall a blacksmith was called a scabbard (a medieval word for a scabbed person) but his accuser also claimed he had scabbards for which she treated with plasters.[624] In contrast a Chudleigh shoemaker claimed that after have sex with a married woman 'she hath filled me full of the scabs'. The implication is that these scabs were parasites and it this use which was meant in Exeter when a constable was called a blood-seeking scab.[625] A sense of the word is given in *There's nothing to be had without money*, a contemporary ballad.[626]

> 'One evening as I passed along,
>   A lass with borrowed hair
> Was singing of a tempting song –
>   *Kind Sir*, quoth she, *draw near.*
> But he that bites this rotten crab
>   May after chance to catch the scab;
> No pander, bawd nor painted drab
>   Shall gull me of a penny.'

Two women, in Welcombe and Exeter, were called full-of-lice whores and the curate of Chagford was told he was a full-of-lice rogue and that he would soon 'pick lice under a hedge again'.[627] In 1583 a Totnes man was called a cormorant and a villain scab but also a 'pricklouse'. This might have implied he had parasites but a secondary meaning was that he was a tailor. A 'cormorant' was an early sixteenth-century word for an insatiably greedy person.[628]

Three slander cases of the late 1560s all involved rumours of leprosy. A Great Torrington woman was said to be a leper and unclean while a Broadhembury man was called a white leper. His wife was urged to avoid contact with him. Both had lazar hospitals near them, at Little Torrington and Honiton, but there were others across Devon, and the slander cases indicate apprehension in being associated with this disease. The vicar of Broadclyst would have known the impact of declaring from the pulpit that a parishioner was a witch who had 'scabbed scurvy and pocky hands and full of leprosy'.[629]

Others simply objected to being called diseased. For instance, in 1565 Katherine Vawter, also of Broadclyst, was called an arrant whore who 'had a dozen knaves taking from her tail and . . . that [only] a whore had physic on her clothes since that she was 16 years of old'. Finally, one woman was called a wry-mouthed jade, by which it meant she had a facial distortion.[630]

FIVE

Lecherous Men: Whoremongers, Cuckolds and Wittols

Men had a number of sexual insults, most of which were exclusive to them, with various terms used to describe their genitals including member, yard, tarse, nippy, prick, bollocks and stones. Ridicule alleged illicit actions and sometimes involved wives and other family members. For example, at Stoke Canon in 1615 a man was asked if he was the son of Martin Owen, 'the cuckold'. Likewise, the term 'whoreson' was given to a number of men and while it meant that the mother was a whore, it had evolved into a general term of contempt; in some instances it is difficult to ascertain which sense was intended. Bastard was similar in having two meanings.[631] Sexual insults exclusive to men comprised allegations they had been wayward, that their wives were sexually uncontrollable or that the men had conspired with their wives in illicit sex.

> ▶ 42. *'But Cuckold! Wittol! Cuckold! The devil himself hath not such a name,'* The Merry Wives of Windsor *by William Shakespeare, c1600, Act II, Scene ii.*

Fornicators, harlots, whoremongers, whoremaker and whoremasters

There was a choice of words to suggest men were sexually wayward. Only men had the specific term of fornicator although women were also described as committing acts of fornication including a Winkleigh couple in 1618: a villager called her neighbour a 'thong-cutting rogue' who 'did commit fornication with the old woman Duke against the door'. One man named as a fornicator was Richard Benner of Kingsteignton who was said to be an old fornicator and not worthy to live in a commonwealth.[632] John Pope of North Petherwin was also called an old fornicator while a Bishopsteignton man was named as both a fornicator and adulterer[633] and these two terms were often used together in abusive slander.

A similar term was 'harlot' although in this period it was used to describe both men and women.[634] This included men who lived in Crediton in 1581, Thorverton in 1603 and Stokeinteignhead in 1637.[635] In comparison a man of Christow was called a harlot and

a rascal harlot in 1619 and a man of Talaton was named a harlot knave in 1612 as was another of Zeal Monachorum in 1571.[636] Two Moretonhampstead men explained its meaning in the early 1580s. One testified he 'thinketh this word harlot signifieth a man that liveth an incontinent life' while a second said 'if a man be named to be a harlot with any woman he taketh it to signify an adulterer'. From the 1200s onwards it could also define a vagabond or disreputable man.[637] These meanings can be seen in other slander such as at Crediton in 1540 when a local man was told 'thou art a harlot and thy wife a whore'. Likewise, an Ugborough man was called old harlot several times and then urged 'forsake thou Thomas Jefferie's house and his wife for she is an unhonest woman. No man can say good of her and what doest thou there so often unless thou play the harlot with her?'[638] The alleged behaviour of John Blackaller and his employer in Littlehempston in 1575 provides a clear context for the term's meaning. One parishioner called him a harlot to whom Blackaller asked 'With whom did I play the harlot?' 'With thy dame, Cicely Sumpter' he was told and Blackaller responded 'Thou lies'. But his witness said 'Nay, thou hast, for I saw it.' Another neighbour testified 'I saw them in the chimney corner together and her clothes up above her navel and Blackaller standing up right against her' and yet one more said he 'did see John Blackaller and Cicely Sumpter by the chimney corner in her house together and the said Cicely to take up her clothes and John Blackaller to take her about the middle and kiss her and hug her to him'.[639]

In 1599 an argument broke out between two men in Crediton in which one said to the other 'What art thou? Thou art but a harlot, all the county knoweth it that thou hast a bastard, for it is even there at thy nose and it is thine own picture and thine own body'. Another witness thought that the slander included a comment on their noses being the same and that the child was 'the very picture of him'.[640] The use of the word harlot was accompanied with the suggestion of illegitimate children in other instances: a King's Nympton man was even called a bastard maker in 1641 as were other men who lived in Bishop's Nympton, North Molton,

Ottery St Mary, Pilton, Stokeinteignhead, Tiverton, Loxhore and Exeter.[641]

Three other terms identified men with whores by adding 'monger', 'maker' and 'master'. 'Whoremonger' was one of the most widely insults used against men. It signified men who were closely associated with whores. The word was seldom used on its own but with a string of other insults. Women were more likely to utter the word. In some instances it accompanied allegations of illegitimate children such as when told to an Exeter man in 1623 ('thou art a base whoremongering rogue and it is long since thou hadest a bastard') or to a man of Roseash in 1600 ('thou art a whoremonger, thou hast begotten a bastard, begotten Agnes Ward with child').[642]

Whoremongers' intrinsic connection with whores can be seen at Chagford ('thou wilt not come to my mother's house because there is never a whore for thee, if there had been a whore there, thou wouldst have come . . . it is well known what thou are, thou art a whoremonger and all the country knows it') and particularly at Staverton ('thou art an arrant whoremonger and thou hast a hundred whores').[643] In Exeter's meal market in 1584 a woman told John Triggs 'thou art a whore hunter, thou huntest [with] hounds but thou huntest whores too'. Another man, John Whitfield of Crediton, was told in 1637 'thou art a whoremonger and I will take it to my death that thou art a whoremonger and thou hadst Palmer's maid behind the door in a new year's day in the morning and thou didst give her lace and pins'.[644]

In Drewsteignton a local man used a slightly different term: he accused John Potter of being a whoremaker. Not only did he specify that Potter had kept a woman for seven years he also said that he was 'as arrant a whoremaker knave as any in Devonshire'.[645]

Nearly every other string of slander alleging whoremongering includes another word, whoremaster. The term's meaning was clarified by a witness who heard John Moggeridge being called a whoremaster and then was told he had 'run away with a whore' which the witness thought meant 'that he was a man of an incontinent life'.[646] To some extent it indicated a man who procured women for their sexual services, in effect a male bawd or pimp. Some extravagant claims were made. An Exeter man was told he was 'as arrant a whoremaster as any in Exeter' but a man of Ilsington was informed 'there was not such an old whoremaster more in the country'.[647] However, it was a Kenton man who had the greater accolade: in 1620 he was 'the veriest whoremonger or whoremaster as on the earth'. Many insults named sexual partners or allude to their number. A West Buckland man was told in 1622 'thou are an old whoremaster and rideth up and down and keepeth a whore in every town' whereas an Upottery man allegedly kept one 'in every bush'.[648]

Cuckolds: bull heads, cucumbers, hardheads, hornabus, horners

The term 'cuckold' was as widely used as whoremonger or whoremaster but it was not illicit behaviour on the behalf of the man that was being criticized.

Several Devonians clarified its meaning. A Stoke Canon parishioner thought in 1615 'the word cuckold is generally accounted and reputed and held to be a scandalous and an opprobrious word, by which his wife is meant to be a whore and a woman of incontinent or adulterous life'.[649] A few years later a Bradninch man explained it meant a man's wife was a whore which was identical to a Cornish explanation that it 'signify a man that hath a whore to his wife'.[650] Another Cornishman reflected that cuckold 'in common construction amongst all the inhabitants of Liskeard as elsewhere within the realm of England is a word of infamy, reproach, slander and disgrace and intimates thereby the said John Every's wife to be a whore and a woman of incontinent life'. Yet another Cornishman, Andrew Mark of Lostwithiel, explained it in personal terms when he said to Walter Gobble 'thou art the veriest cuckold in Cornwall and thy wife is as notable a whore as any in England & I meaning himself will abide by it for I have occupied her myself divers times as have there made thee a cuckold'.[651]

Cuckoldry insulted the husband by alleging that his wife was unfaithful through his inability to control her actions suggesting weakness of will or possibly unsatisfactory sexual performance. Much of the slander simply addressed the man as a cuckold ('thou art a cuckold') or also directly commented on his wife ('thou art a whore and thy husband is a cuckold').[652] It was possible to do this in a less direct manner. By 1540 horns had been associated with cuckolds for several centuries and much of the slander makes references to them.

In 1615 a Sandford man held out two fingers to another which, in one observer's understanding, indicated he was a cuckold 'as far as this deponent ever heard when one man points to another in such sort with his fingers that is a married man'. Exeter's mayoral court recorded instances of showing fingers to represent horns and imply cuckoldry.[653] Along with pointing figures other physical ways of implying a cuckold was the physical placing of horns. In 1561 a great broil broke out near St Petrock's Church in Exeter after children were told to throw bones into Eustace Oliver's shop. He subsequently argued with their mother, Alice Ward, and both Ward's husband and Oliver were called cuckolds. 'I will beat the horns from his head' said Oliver and Ward told him he was a hornmaker.[654] A generation before, in 1582, horns had been set up in a Swimbridge garden and even earlier, in the parish church of St Clether in Cornwall, sheep and bullock horns were placed over the pulpit.[655] These all indicated cuckoldry. It was with this intent that an Exeter man was mocked by a woman telling him in 1638 that his wife had made him horns which she hung 'upon the Blue Bell'.[656]

It was threatened to place horns above a man's door in Bovey Tracey in 1616 and ram's horns were put on an Exeter door in 1623.[657] Doors were particularly relevant to cuckolds' horns. In 1558 a Tavistock man was called a cuckold and told to build his door higher because his 'head was so high that he might not go into it'. A similar comment was made in Cullompton when another man was told 'thou art a cuckold, go in and look in a glass and see how thine horns do grow, heap thy door higher with thy horns'. Exeter's medieval North Gate was said to be too low to allow a cuckold's head to pass through in 1583.[658] In Bishop's Nympton another man was told that his horns would grow through his hat and a husband heard that while he was at Torrington Fair his wife had made him a cuckold. He was laughed at by being told his horns were so large that 'if thou didest fall forwards thy horns would keep or defend thee from harm'.[659] The suggestion being made in these cases was that the wives had been active with a number of men. This must have been the implication when in East Budleigh a woman offered to give a silver spoon in order that a man's horns could be gilded.[660]

In two South Devon parishes the slos, the porous bone inside the horns, were mentioned. In Dartmouth Cicely Hawkins was slandered when it was said in 1593 she had traded sex for a sheep's head and haunch. A neighbour said 'the horns groweth out in her husband Hawkins' head and I will beat away the slos of them with my staff'. This was similar to the belief expressed at Chudleigh in 1573 when one parishioner said of another 'I stood at his gate and had a stone in my hand and if he had come out to me I would have slocken [drawn] out the slos from his head, meaning as this deponent believeth, that he would strike the horns from his head in that horned beasts had slos growing upon their heads'.[661]

Horns could be alluded to without using the term 'cuckold' as in Exeter in 1587 when Roger Chardon told Richard Weeks 'I would have beaten the horns out of thy head'. It was because of the horns that Cornish cuckolds were also called horn beasts and hardheads. Instead of being called a hardhead, John Rolston was called a stone-headed cuckold in Netherexe.[662] Another word altogether was used at Tavistock in 1626 when Thomas Fleshman complained that William Burne said 'thou art a cucumber and a hornabus, and thou lieth like a cucumber or hornabus, a cuckold'. The term 'cucumber' was also said at Exeter in 1620 and that was also used alongside cuckold and bull head. It has not been recorded in this sense elsewhere in England nor apparently has 'hornabus'.[663] The association with a cucumber is suggested in contemporary printed verses which was headed 'a catalogue of young wenches, which will be exposed to sale by inch of candle, at the cuckold's

43. *A nude, by Francesco Salviati, of about 1550, which may not have accurately represented Philip Harper but Thomas Bartlet.*

coffee house in Cucumber Lane'. Also at Tavistock in 1624 a parishioner was called a cuckold, hardhead and a ninnyhammer which, as was discussed, meant a fool. An Exeter man had an even more unusual insult thrown at him in 1624. He was told he was a cuckold, a cuckoldly knave and a cuckoldly 'roastmeat'.[664] In Crediton a man was told he was a cuckold and a horner, the man that makes another a cuckold.[665]

Wittols

Far worse than being called a cuckold was being named a wittol. In Devon it was determined that it was exactly nine times worse. In 1605 Nicholas Breton wrote *An old man's lesson and a young man's love* in which the elder man asks his son to name the most monstrous beast. His lad answers 'a wittol, because he hath a world of horns'. Alexander Skirret of Tavistock, noted earlier as being called a cuckold, ninnyhammer and hardhead in 1624, was also named as a wittol. He was one of a number of men to have both epithets such as Edward Richards of Bradninch in 1629.[666] Various witnesses explained the meaning as it was understood in Devon. In 1625 an Exeter man said it was commonly interpreted as 'a man nine times worse than a cuckold' and that was how it was 'commonly interpreted and understood in the city of Exeter and in all or most parts of this kingdom of England'.[667] The phrase 'nine times worse' had been used in 1617 by a Churchstow man in explaining the term as being in the 'common understanding of the country people'.[668] That phrase was first in print as late as 1616. It was also used in Launceston in 1624 and when spoken in Crediton a few years earlier it was also explained that wittol was 'in common construction is taken to signify a man that should be a bawd to his own wife'.[669] The reason why a wittol was worse than a cuckold was that the husband was complicit in his wife's sexual behaviour. A witness in Exeter explained in 1622 'that the wife of the man of whom the said word wittol is spoken was and is an incontinent woman and a whore and that her husband hath and doth consent to her incontinency and whoredom'. Thus, in 1629 an Exeter man excused his making Simon Norris a cuckold because it had been done with Norris' consent.[670] The term had been in use since at least the 1400s.[671]

Braggers

Other name-calling arose from men boasting about their sexual conquests such as in 1567 at Northlew when William Herrel told his neighbour that 'Margaret Asheton was an unhonest woman for he himself had japed her two times in one forenoon'. A Woodbury Salterton man also bragged in 1586 when he claimed 'that he did take up the clothes of Mary Jennings and had to do with her against the Witch, being a tree in the village.'[672] Likewise, a Dawlish man boasted to a group of men that he had 'carnal knowledge of the bodies of Issot Tapley and one Lucombe's wife within a hedge near the highway and that the said Ewell showed them the very place where he had committed adultery with them'. Later he also crowed about having sex with yet another man's wife.[673] Robert Avery of Marsh Barton in Newton St Cyres bragged of his recent sexual adventures while having a meal with his neighbours. A witness recalled Avery said 'he had to do with a woman upon Pullenton hill and if his cloak had not been [on] he had been utterly spoiled, *For by God's blood*, said he, *I think she was asleep while I was in doing with her, I bid her watch her side and I*, said he, *will watch my side. Sure enough and yet if my cloak had not been we had been taken then by one that come there while.*'[674] Thomas Letheren of King's Nympton was more complimentary: while working in a field he told his co-workers that Ann Ditchet 'had a very good stroke'. In contrast, an Exeter man boasted about his own skills in lovemaking: he allegedly required a woman to 'hold up her clothes almost an hour'.[675]

A man of Upton Pyne was candid about why a married woman preferred him to her husband: Philip Harper said 'I have a better prick than he'. After an Exeter man had sex with a woman in a porch he bragged that he could 'hold up his finger and have the use of twenty women's bodies at his command.' It must have been with an air of boastfulness that another Exeter man, standing below Rougemont Castle where he had just 'made water', 'held his yard in his hand' and called out to two passing women 'Wenches, be your hands clean? See what here is for you'.[676]

Boasting brought a number of men to the church court. In 1559 a Launceston man crowed that after Anstice Tooker had her first child she 'doth fuck the better' but even more explicit is a conversation attributed to Robert Knight in Stokenham. Richard Wakeham spoke to Richard Philip on the way to church during Whitsun 1583. Philip said 'Robert Knight doth report by Margaret Spratt that he hath been so far in her as he may go for his bollocks' to which Wakeham replied 'Fie! for shame that you will say so, if he say so it is a pity of his life.'[677] He would have been advised by Robert Furse, a Dean Prior gentleman, to 'have no delight in filthy talk, for surely those things are not honest to be spoken that are vicious and filthy to be done'.[678]

Perhaps the most explicit of the boasts was that attributed to Thomas Follet in Ottery St Mary. He 'played' with Margaret

Stephens in a private house in the town and put his hand upon her French bodice. Upon which she asked if he was not abashed to do so. He then 'put his hand a little further' and 'catched her by the wren's nest and plucked away some of the hair and wrapped it up in a paper and showed it in one George Lane's house in Luppit' which caused a scandal.[679]

It was not just a man who boasted about sex in Beaford in 1580. When Harry Acland was asked why he was late coming to work he answered that he had overslept. His excuse was that 'the maids there will not suffer me to sleep in the evening'. Another witness later overheard Agnes Burrage, one of these female servants, say 'Harry has forgotten how he was drawn out by the members last night but I will handle him better the next night if he be so lusty'. She later said it was 'but a merry jest'. It was another North Devon man, John Hatherleigh, who dismissed the engagement of William Escott with Thomasine Bennet. He said 'it is no matter lest Escott shall ride in mine old boots – for I have occupied her already'.[680]

Some slanderous comments may have partly originated in jealousy or even admiration. A married woman was told in 1635 to remember her trip to Exeter and sudden return to Dartmouth. John Tailor told her 'Oh Joan, Joan, remember the butcher that dressed four quarters with one prick?' In 1616 an Exeter man seems to have acquired very personal details from two men: he accused Alice Parsons of having had sex with John Endicott twice and with Edmund Newcombe on seven occasions. It was also with a boastful air that Marian Southwood was given the alleged details of the not so private life of Christian Trick of Witheridge. Southwood had said in 1637 'thou art a whore and George Cruss alias Mogford did occupy thee four times in a night and once was in the morning about break of day'.[681]

In 1568 John Pope of Otterton was responsible for spreading a salacious story about his own wife which originated with his mother in law. He told several friends that he had come across his mother in law by chance one day who urged him 'Make haste, it is more than time that you were at home. For that villainy is at home at thy house'. He arrived in time to see a man escaping by the back

44. *'Impudent Strumpet'*, Othello *by William Shakespeare, c.1603,*
Act IV, Scene ii.

garden. In the entry, Pope said, he found 'their nature on a saddle'. More graphic were the words of Joan Dowdall of the North Devon parish of Shirwell. She said in 1624 'did you hear anything of John Bussacott? He lay with a wench in [North] Molton and drawn so much in her tail as if he had thrown a bucket of water after it would have been a horse colt'.[682] Given he complained of her words, it is unlikely that he thought this was boastful.

What is likely to be the least boastful account for a man concerns Lanlivery in Cornwall at Midsummer in 1572. John Huitt later testified that he:

'came to the house of the said Thomas Bartlett and enquired of the said Agnes Bartlett his wife for him, and she made answer that he was not at home and this respondent said that he was. Then said she if you will not believe me go in and see. So this respondent went up into a chamber thinking that the said Thomas had been there asleep and when he could not find him he this respondent laid him down upon the bed in the said chamber. And within a half quarter of an hour after there came into the said chamber one John Hamlyn and laid himself down upon the said bed by this respondent. And immediately after him came up into the said Chamber the said Agnes and a maid of hers and willed them to come down and did strike them upon the legs with a stick. And then this respondent and the said Hamlyn took her and did cast her upon the bed, but she stayed not there any time at all but went down with her maid again, the said Thomas Bartlett being then from home, and further sayeth that he hath divers times resorted to the said Agnes her house in the absence of her husband but there hath been some of her servants present always and his resorting thither was to no evil intent'.[683]

The reason behind this incident may have originated with a rumour spread by John Carlyan. He later admitted 'that he heard one John Huitt to say Thomas Bartlett was too short and could not get a child without the help of his neighbours and upon his report this respondent hath told the same to divers persons'.[684] It was not Bartlett's height that was allegedly deficient.

SIX

Lascivious Women: From Strumpets To Whores

Sex dominated insults given to women and the name-calling, which in Devon ran to at least twenty different terms, all suggested that women had been sexually wayward.

Some ridicule alleged prior convictions for sexual crimes such as at Totnes where in 1617 a woman was reminded that her nose had been slit (a punishment given to prostitutes).[685] In two instances women were said to have worn ray hoods, a garment which identified medieval prostitutes. There were other 'badges of infamy' across Europe and the ray (or striped) hood was used in Bristol[686] and Exeter. One such woman was Joan Luter, later described as 'a well-favoured woman and sweet fair and standing much in her own liking', who was punished in Exeter in 1524 for her misrule in being 'a very strumpet and harlot'. Hooker also called her 'a lewd, naughty and misliving woman'. Part of her punishment was being forced to wear a ray hood.[687]

This hood's significance was referred to in 1559 when two women argued on their way home from Honiton market. One called the other a whore who 'had been driven through the country in a ray hood'. Her husband recalled the actual word used was that she had been 'veased', that is rushed, through the country.[688] Nearly twenty years later, in Rattery, another woman told two men that they had spoken like fools in telling her 'thou art an arrant whore and hast worn a ray hood and shall have a cockscomb to set up thy ray hood, Mistress Scabbed Arse and scabbed-arse whore and blabber-lipped whore and that she had 2 lips to make a groat [4d] 12d withal and that they would proclaim it at the pillory at Totnes in the market place and there pronounce it three times with one breath that she is an arrant whore'.[689] The reference to a cockscomb may have in itself been sexual but it also meant a fool's cap and a conceited fool. It may also have been a ray hood which was meant in Bishop's Nympton in 1597 when a woman was told she had two bastards and had come home in a 'French hood' (which had been a popular form of headgear for several generations).[690]

Many women who were reminded of alleged punishments were told that they had been 'carted,' that is humiliated by being placed in a cart and either driven through the streets or whipped as they walked at the cart's end. Many such women were called 'carted whores' including Judith Gibbs who denied it by telling her opponent 'I am no carted whore'. It was another Exeter woman who said to another 'thou art a carted whore and a molsen whore and I Joan Drewe was never carted in the high street of Tavistock and never had piss pots cast onto me nor basins beaten before me'.[691] One woman was said to have been brought from Crediton to Exeter in a cart and was subsequently reminded she was a whore and called a carted whore. Only larger urban areas, such as Plymouth and Exeter, had carts as a form of punishment. All women were banished from Exeter once they were carted or otherwise punished for leading lewd and 'misliving' lives.[692]

Terms

A variety of terms suggested sexual immorality. Three words also applied to men including, as noted earlier, the term 'harlot' which had several meanings. More men than women were recorded as having been named as harlots in the Exeter diocesan church records but it was also used about a Tavistock woman in 1558: Agnes Saunder was called a whore and it was also said that 'her husband came the whiles she played the harlot'. The same phrase was used in the North Devon parish of Alverdiscott in 1579 and of another woman in Broadhempston in 1575.[693] Two Exeter women each called the other harlot in 1541 and the year before it was said of Richard Drake in Otterton that he kept a woman in his house 'like a harlot'. Several generations later a South Molton woman was called a quean, whore and a harlot. The term harlot became restricted to women in the eighteenth century.[694]

Another term which was not gender specific was 'minion'. This was used in a heated argument in 1594 to describe a Georgeham woman: she was called a rogue, strumpet and a minion who told tales and lied. One early sixteenth-century meaning for minion was that it indicated a woman kept for sexual favours.[695] It was also said in 1621 to castigate a married woman of Exeter as being a constable's minion.[696]

'Baggage' was used mostly for women and only occasionally for men. It indicated a 'worthless good for nothing woman, a woman of disreputable or immoral life, a strumpet'. Baggage was one of the most commonly used insults in Devon. At Chawleigh in 1577 one parishioner thought that in the 'accustomed speech of the country' that 'a baggage is accounted for a woman of ill life', another interpreted it as 'a misliving woman of her body' and a third explained it was 'such persons as be unhonest and incontinent of life *that is* in adultery or fornication or such like and doth signify an unhonest woman in that kind of offence'.[697] The meaning given at Topsham in 1581 ('a common whore') and in Totnes two years later ('she is a whore') is similar to that a few years later 'in Kenton and in the country there about and do signify a woman of an ill and incontinent life'.[698] These definitions fit the national use of the word which was first recorded in 1603, much later than in Devon. Amongst the angry words spoken in South Tawton in 1617 about Joyce Battishall were that 'I was never found as thy wife was playing the baggage with a knave at Holland Gate'. One witness simply equated it with the word whore: it 'doth signify and import as much in effect as the word whore doth in this deponent's judgement and is so commonly taken within the parish of South Tawton and elsewhere'. The Cornish had the same meaning.[699]

The essence of the insult was that these women exchanged sex for money. Thus, in Northam Christian Lange was told in 1626 'thou art a whore and a baggage whore and thou art maintained by other men' and in Stoke Canon a woman was told in 1615 'thou art a whore and a baggage to ten men'.[700] The words baggage and whore were nearly always used together including in such places as Bideford, Dodbrooke, East Budleigh, Exeter, Okehampton, Ottery St Mary, Plymouth and Tawstock.[701] In 1597 a Bideford woman was called a green baggage by which it may have been meant that she recently had a baby, was young or that she was naïve.[702]

There were another seventeen terms that were exclusively reserved for women. Four were only recorded in one instance each. In 1627 Joan Stapledon of Woolfardisworthy was called a 'hobby' as well as a scurvy trash and an arrant baggage.[703] The term 'trull', which from the early 1500s also denoted a female prostitute, was used in Dartmouth in 1626 when Agnes Wood was told 'thou art a drunkard, a whore, a drunken whore and a trull baggage'.[704] In Burrington the word 'polecat' was used. In 1593 Sidwell Callard was called a polecat whore and the slanderer said she would prove her to be a polecat. An Exeter woman was called a 'rumbelow' in 1619, this too meant a wanton woman.[705] The remaining thirteen terms for sexually wayward women were bitch, curtal, drab, hackney, jade, mare, minx, pack, punk, quean, slut, strumpet and whore. Each was used by William Shakespeare.

Strumpets

In 1618 'Away thy strumpet' was said to a woman on the Fosse in Dartmouth and by the word strumpet one witness thought it meant 'so much in effect as the word whore doth in common understanding'. Mary Hart was called a strumpet in Axminster and was told that she did not live 'honestly'. In Cheriton Fitzpaine a woman suspected of having illicit sex was noted in 1584 as being 'a very lewd strumpet' while a Cornish woman that same year, who had also been seen having illicit sex, was called 'a very light woman and a common whore and notorious strumpet'. 'Light' signified a wanton or unchaste woman.[706]

The word 'strumpet' had by 1500 been commonly used in England for several centuries and was deployed as an insult across Devon through the sixteenth century. In 1662 Thomas Fuller used it to describe two women who he noted as the mothers of the Gubbings, the wild race of heathens who lived near Brent Tor. These two, both pregnant, took up with lewd fellows and lived 'in caves (rather holes than houses) like swine, having all in common, multiplied without marriage into many hundreds, their language is the dross of the dregs of the vulgar Devonian'.[707] 'Strumpet' was often used concurrently with 'whore' such as at Tawstock where Jane Pointer was called a whore, an arrant whore and a strumpet, Elizabeth Butt of Ottery St May was a whore and a strumpet whore, and Dorothy Porter was a whore, a common whore and a filthy strumpet.[708] John Hooker also chose to pair it with another term to describe previously noted Joan Luter. In 1524 she was, as mentioned, a 'very strumpet and a harlot'.[709] Another context for this term can be found in evidence regarding Joan Hole, an Exeter servant suspected of having an illegitimate child born in Taunton. She was supposedly taken to Somerset by a woman described as 'a very baggage and common strumpet'.[710] The terms baggage, strumpet and whore were not only commonly said but were interchangeable. Other terms were only occasionally used.

Minx

In 1618 an Exeter woman, accused of keeping a bawdy house, was called a 'minx'.[711] The term could imply a lewd woman and appears to have been used from the late sixteenth-century but only sparingly.[712] There are only a handful of recorded instances for Devon. When two women argued in a Cullompton street in 1616 one said 'thou art a whore and I had never a midwife fetched before marriage as thou hast' and added 'thou art a proud minx'.[713] It was also used when two Exeter women disputed the possession of a church pew in 1634. Widow Basely not only called rival a minx but also instructed her to go home and learn more manners. In this instance minx probably meant she was impudent given she was also called a 'giglet' and 'young thing'.[714] It was also in Exeter that it was used while women washed clothes by a mill leat in 1621. Sheets were repeatedly thrown out of a washing tub as the women brawled. At one point one woman asked another 'How now Mistress Minx? Are you she that threw the sheets into the water? I shall pull your nose from your face, you cuckold minx'.[715]

Punks

In *All's Well That Ends Well* William Shakespeare wrote that a finely dressed 'punk' charged three shillings and six pence for sex.[716] The term had been in use in England since the 1570s[717] but in Devon it was recorded only in Exeter. It may not have been in common use. The word was cited in *Cuckold's Haven*, a ballad of the early 1600s.

> 'A woman that will be drunk,
>   will easily play the punk;
> For when her wits are sunk
>   all keys will fit her trunk'

In 1622 Elizabeth Berry of Exeter complained in the church court that Elizabeth Bradshell had called her not only a whore but also a punk, a common punk, a base punk and an over-ridden punk. Her accuser added that Berry had an illegitimate child 'begotten by a gentleman in a green satin suit'.[718] That same year these two women also appeared before the mayor's court. One witness explained that Mrs Berry was lying in bed and in the midst of giving birth, with a midwife in attendance, when bailiffs arrived to arrest her. Others suggested that she was merely ill. Ignatius Jurdain, the city's crusading justice, sent constables to the house and he himself

45. 'Sir, give him head, I know he'll prove a jade', The Taming of the Shrew *by William Shakespeare, c1590, Act I, Scene i.*

later came to inspect the proceedings. In the midst of a great brawl Mrs Bradshall demanded that Mrs Berry, whom she called not only a base punk but a counterfeit whore, hangman's whore and three halfpenny whore, should be forcibly removed from her bed and imprisoned. That same year another woman complained that Mrs Bradshall had said that she was a whore and had 'laid behind the church with a strange man'. She also mentioned Mrs Berry in connection with being a bawd.[719] Only a few years before another Exeter woman was also ridiculed as a punk: William Northcott called Edward Dight's wife a punk and 'afterwards made horns unto her with his fingers turning himself about crying Bow and saying all the neighbours were also punks putting his finger in his backside.'[720]

Mares

A slightly more commonly used word appears to be 'mare' which had been in national use since at least the 1300s. In 1623 it was deployed to describe Mary Bussell of Ottery St Mary ('thou art a whore, a base whore, a bitcherly whore and a mare')[721] while an Exeter woman three years before called another woman her husband's mare.[722] In Southleigh a woman was called a stray mare while in Lympstone another was termed a muscle mare.[723] Much more insulting was Agnes Payne telling Mary Melhuish of Combe Martin in 1629 that 'thou art a mare and thou hast hath a cunt like a mare and go thou and ask of Abraham Pincombe and he can tell.' According to the witness Payne meant by using the word mare that she was a whore, led an incontinent life and that Pincombe had illicit sex with her. A Cruwys Morchard parishioner noted ten years earlier that a mare was a whore.[724]

The term 'skinning a mare' was recorded in Kenton and Tamerton Foliot as well as in Cornwall. It was explained in Tamerton Foliot that when it had been said that Anne Luxmoore and John Parker had skinned a mare together it was meant that they had 'committed adultery or fornication and lived incontinently together'.[725] In the Cornish parish of St Cleer there was also 'a mare skinned'. In 1638 a husband and wife told several neighbours that William Webber and Sibley Kittoe were seen in a milk house and in a field with Webber's 'breeches down'. Several witnesses testified that they understood the phrase to mean that the couple had been either incontinent together or had committed adultery or fornication.[726] In Plymouth several men were standing at Fisher's Nose and called out to another in a boat to 'bring home the skin of the mare that he skinned at Cargreen'. When asked what was meant by the phrase it was explained that a woman had purchased wood with sex.[727] A Kenton use of the phrase concerned a rumour that a couple had illicit sex in a field of brooms: it was said 'the news was full in the town that a mare was skinned down in Mr Hobbs his broom close'.[728] The phrase appears to indicate isolated incidents.

Sluts

In a contemporary ballad a man describes his wife:

'My wife if such a beastly slut,
Unless it be an egg or a nut,
I in the house dare nothing eat,
For fear there's poison in the meat;
The dogs do lick both dish and pan.'

There were several meanings to the word 'slut' including from the early 1400s that it described a dirty woman. It may have been with this sense that Joan Penny of Dartmouth was described in 1634 as a dunghill slut. A 'moving dunghill' then meant a dirty man or woman. Penny's morals were also questioned as she was said to have been carted[729] and it may have been this fifteenth-

46. *A jade or a strumpet? From a contemporary engraving.*

century meaning that was intended. Certainly this was intended in 1626 when a Sandford woman was called 'a slut no better than a whore'.[730] Equally, ten years later a Plymouth woman was called 'a whore, a soldier's whore and a soldier's slut' but less certain is the meaning when it was applied to a Tiverton woman in 1635 who was called 'a brazen-faced slut, a cripple, a fat arse, a fat breech and a hagabout jade'. Also uncertain is the abuse given to an Exeter woman who was called a beggarly slut in 1638 as well as a runabout which was used to describe a wandering beggar.[731]

The term slut was used in several instances alongside allegations of excessive drinking. In 1634 a Tiverton woman was called a drunk, a drunken woman, a drunkard and a drunken slut.[732] A Broadclyst woman was told in the late 1620s that she was 'a whore and a very drunkard and drunk slut & why did'st thou ride to Exeter and thy husband thought that thou had'st ridden to Ottery & thou did'st go to Exeter and lie with Richard Tayler at Exeter when thou toldest thy husband that thou wert at Ottery and I will not go to Exeter to lie with such a man'.[733] Both being unclean and a drunkard were suggested in Cornwall in 1634 when Dorothy Copplestone was called a 'drunken, filthy, idle slut'.[734] In the early 1600s a female servant, who allegedly had refused to clean shoes or the house, took exception at being called a base slut. Her Payhembury employer, however, concluded that she 'loves to fare well, lie well and do little'.[735] Finally, there is also related term, a 'slut bone' but this was only applied in one instance to a man in Exeter in 1565. A shouting match between Mrs Hose and Richard Gervis took place in a lane in St Mary Major parish. She was called a whore and amongst the string of abuse against him, including princock, bull head knave and cuckold, was the term slut bone. No meaning has yet been found for this term.[736]

Curtals

There are a handful of instances in which the sixteenth-century term 'curtal' was recorded. The word has been in print in England since 1545.[737] The longest recorded strand of abuse which included it was said in Totnes. In 1586 a woman, who was suspected of stealing apples, was told 'thou art an arrant bulled whore, a bowl-eyed whore, a common whore, a curtal whore and every servingman's whore'.[738] A few years earlier another Totnes woman had also been called a curtal and 'worse than a curtal . . . but a baggage'. The witness explained that 'the common people do take it that if a woman be called a curtal or baggage it is meant that she is a whore'.[739] A fuller context for the meaning was provided when Jane Hutchin was called in Exeter 'a jade and a base jade and a curtal and thou art a whore and a base whore and thou didst lie three nights with a tinker at the Magdalen meaning that she lay with another man than her husband and committed adultery or fornication with him'.[740] The Devon examples show a clear association with whoredom and there are other instances such as a Cornish woman who was called in 1592 'a whore and an arrant whore and a scurvy whore and a curtal whore'.[741]

Drabs and packs

A high number of recorded instances of the word 'drab' indicates it was a fairly popular choice of insult. It was in print in 1526 and possibly earlier.[742] In 1567 two women in Great Torrington fell out in an alehouse late at night.

Barbara Frost said to Agnes Hewitt 'Get thou home drab'.

Hewitt then asked 'Does thou call me drab?'

Frost responded 'Yea, thou art a beggarly drab and a drunken drab'.

Hewitt then told her 'Thou art a whore to call me beggarly drab or drunken drab.'[743]

When it was said of one woman in Kenton in 1585, along with jade and baggage, it was explained that all three terms 'in Kenton and in the country there about do signify a woman of an ill and incontinent life'. This sense was used at Marldon and Yealmpton[744] as well as Shebbear (an arrant whore and a copper-nosed drab), Dodbrooke (a whore, baggage and drab) and Exeter (slut, quean and drab).[745] More imaginatively, two Exeter women were called scolding drabs, at Tawstock another was called a lying drab and a Littlehempston woman was called a dribble-tail drab.[746] Sexual activity was suggested when in 1596 Maude Browning of Cheriton Bishop was told to remember 'thou arrant whore drab when the candle was turned at thy tail and remember when the slippers were left behind'.[747]

The village of Halwill near Okehampton has the only recorded instance of the term 'pack'. In 1569 Joan Colborne was called a drab and a 'naughty pack'. Joan Adam also told her to return to Okehampton to 'try thy honesty'.[748] The term is obscure but it appears to have had a sexual connotation.

Jades

Jade became a common term of criticism which, as was shown, indicated a woman with a dishonest life but earlier, in the 1300s, Chaucer used the term ('thou ride upon a jade') to mean a worn-out

47. *A leering man and woman carved on a bench end, Church of St Peter, Thornbury.*

horse.[749] In 1635 a Plymouth woman was called a very whore, trash, baggage and jade and told that while her husband was honest she deserved the cart more than those who had been punished in it.[750] Both Judith Horn of Exeter and Agnes Wyott were called jades but this was unusual in that the word was nearly always used as part of a longer strand of insults. A few women were called thievish jades and other variants were said in Huxham ('an ill-favoured drooling jade), Honiton ('a filthy jade), Lympstone ('an arrant jade), Totnes ('a scurvy trashing jade' and another 'a drunken jade'), Stoke Gabriel ('a bottle-arsed jade and a burnt-arsed jade'), Exeter ('an over-ridden jade' and 'a runagate jade') and Chagford ('rigby jade').[751] The earliest reference is 1565, only five years after its first appearance in print, when Joan Bowden at North Petherwin was called an old whore, old bawd and jade[752] but most of the recorded instances of the word were made in the early 1600s.

Queans

It is tempting to associate the derogatory meaning of the term 'quean' with the degrading of the position of a queen under Henry VIII with the rapid turnover of his six wives. However, quean had that meaning many years before and had been in print as such since at least 1518.[753] More than a century later, in 1623, when Thomas Dobbins was allegedly found in Barnstaple's churchyard at midnight, it was said that his companion was a woman of loose and uncivil behaviour. The term chosen to describe her was quean. She was later described more fully as being of a light and dissolute life.[754] A contemporary ballad advised readers to 'hate cards, dice, whores and queans'. The curate of Ottery St Mary described a woman there in 1625 as being 'a very idle and misliving wench' and a quean 'as it is thought'.[755] A South Molton woman had her character fully described when she was called not only a harlot and whore but also Richard Pyke's quean.[756] In contrast the word was objectionable enough in itself for an Exeter woman to be called in 1622 a quean, an arrant quean and a drunken quean.[757] In 1635 when Joan Banks of Exeter objected to being called a whore, quean and a parson's quean, the slanderer tried to explain that the words were spoken in merriment.[758]

Hackneys

Women were occasionally called hackneys, named after the horse, later a carriage, which was for hire. The term was recorded as early as the thirteenth century. Most Devon uses were as 'hackney whores' such as in Colebrooke, Cornworthy, Crediton, East Budleigh, Heavitree and Totnes.[759] This meaning was confirmed in slander at Crediton where a man was said to have had the carriage of a woman and in Buckfastleigh where a woman was told 'thou art a whore, old whore, arrant whore & Mr Collins his whore, his hackney to ride to assizes & sessions so long as thou were able to serve his turn'. Alice Combe, of an unknown parish, was told she was a common hackney and whore and that she was' taken on the highway'.[760]

Bitches

From the fifteenth century onwards the term 'bitch' has described lewd women. In 1637 Margaret Hardy was called either a bottle-nosed bitch or whore. Witnesses could not agree on which words were used but it would appear that these terms were interchangeable.[761] The two words were often used together and indicated a lewd woman. Thus, a Plymouth woman was called both a whore and a bitch in 1624[762] as was another at Launceston in 1636.[763] Another Cornish woman was not only called a whore and a bitch but also told she was as common as the highway.[764] Women were also compared to dogs: in Honiton a woman was told that 'thou hast as many hang about thee as a sot bitch hath dogs' whereas another of Dean Prior was told she was 'as common as a dog and bitch'.[765] The term 'sot bitch' was in print as early as 1528. The term 'bitch' does not appear to have been as popular as it is today but it was also extended in its form of bitchery, that is lewdness. Hence Mary Bussell of Ottery St Mary was told she was a 'bitcherly whore' and a woman of Ugborough was told she was a 'bitchery'.[766]

Whores

In 1614 the unfortunately named Ann Clapp heard the 'whore' shouted at her across Beer churchyard. Women were often recorded as calling one another whore and occasionally disputed which one was greater. For example, in Hemyock in 1596 one woman 'marvelled' at being called a whore and said 'if any of us be a whore she is a whore, for I have held the door while a man was in the chamber with her'.[767]

Whore was the most pervasive insult given to women and today remains just as common, and powerful, as it was then. In Devon at least 200 adjectives were teamed with the word. Old, common and drunken were among the most popularly used but arrant was the most prevalent. Other terms alleged illicit sexual activity including notable, notorious and over-ridden and other combinations of words also suggested whoredom such as baggage, bitcherly, curtal, hackney, polecat and strumpet. When a Chudleigh woman was called a stewed whore in 1568 it meant that she had come from a brothel; disgust or contempt was registered by calling a woman an abomination or bobtailed-whore and impudence was suggested in being named a brazen-faced whore.[768]

Many adjectives implied poor health or hygiene such as bulged, burned, burned-arse, burned-skinned, burned-tailed, dirty, filthy, foggy (bloated), foul, full-of-lice, gout-legged, maggot-arsed, pale, pocky, poxy, rotted, rotten, scabbed-arse, scale-faced, scurvy, sickly, squirt-arse and stinking (whores). Poor health may have been suggested by calling Agnes Toole of Exeter a black-mouthed whore[769] but less certain is why women from Crediton, Exeter, Ottery St Mary and Totnes were called black whores in the early 1600s.[770] Equally puzzling is the string of abuse hurled at Joan Bennet in Kentisbeare in 1634. She was called a whore, a broad-faced whore, a black-faced whore, a black-browed whore and a flat-footed whore. The word black was then also used in various connotations including black art (the art of picking a lock), black box (a lawyer), black fly (the parson who collects tithes) and black arse as in the phrase 'the pot calls the kettle black arse'.[771]

Physical descriptions were common such as beetle-browed, blabber-legged, blabber-lipped, black-browed, bottle-nosed, bowl-eyed, broad-faced, copper-nosed, crook-legged, crooked-nose, fat-arsed, flat-footed, gerbil-tailed, great arse, haggle-toothed, hollow-mouthed, long-nosed, long-sided, open-arsed, platter-faced, tallow-faced, tallow-sided, totter-legged, ugly and ugly-faced. So too were descriptions of their characters such as abominable, base, idle, lazy and savage. Dishonesty was suggested in being either a cozening, cunning, cut purse, cutting, false, lying, pick purse, rascal, rascally, thievish or villainous whore. Helen Hooper of Exminster was called a slocking whore in 1621.[772] Slocking was either enticing or taking by deceit. Thus one Christian Lake was said to have slocked a married man's feather bed. His wife said 'Lake did never pay but my husband John Gove being slocked by her the said Christian Lake into her house did throw her the said Lake upon the bed and kissed out the money which was to be paid for the said bed'.[773] Being called a meeching whore was one of a number of insults Joan Clarke of Kingsbridge had from her husband.[774] Meeching then meant sneaking. Poverty was suggested by beggarly, ragged, ram beggar, ranging and runagate. Having a criminal record was indicated by such adjectives as bridewell, carted and whipped.

The naming of a woman as a broom close, close, culver house, ditch, furse, hedge, mill, sedge or summerhouse whore are indications of where assignations took place. When Joan Hawking of Cardinham in Cornwall was called a hedge whore her accuser also said 'a man was seen with thee in the hedge'. This may be why other women were called either an alehouse or barley [?field] whore.[775] Hedge whore was an occasional term, used in Exeter, Southleigh and Lansallos in Cornwall, and was later defined as a low beggarly prostitute as well as 'an itinerant harlot, who bilks the bagnios and bawdy houses, by disposing of her favours by the way side under a hedge'.[776]

Other terms identified the man, or men, with whom women had sex including Flemish, French, Frenchman's, Irish and Welsh whores. In 1563 a Dartmouth woman was slandered when it was said 'the Spaniards had more to do with her than Walter Weke' and in Salcombe a woman was said to have had sex with a Frenchman forty times. A similar association was made with a West Worlington woman a few years before.[777] Other relevant descriptions include any husband's, brief man's, captain's, coachman's, every-servingman's, everyman's, gentleman's, hangman's, her husband's, horseman's, man-of-war, my husband's, ostler's, priest's, shoemaker's, soldier's, stranger's, tailor's, tinker's and warden's whores. Some topographical adjectives may have related to ancestry or residence including Anne Moreton of Exeter who was described as a Taunton whore but she had also been said to have 'run about the country' with a man who was not her husband. Less certain is why a woman was called a Coombland whore in Newton St Cyres. It may be that she had had illicit sex in Coombland Wood or she may have lived near there.[778] Another woman was called a Cadleigh Park whore which probably referred to that place near Ivybridge.[779]

At Lapford in 1632 Jane Gater called Anne Rennet 'a base whore, chamber pot whore and that thou didst hold the chamber pot to Philip Crispen and George Bellamy'. This may have referred to the practice in some brothels where prostitutes held a special chamber pot for their client while he urinated. Another woman was called a piss pot whore. Even more insulting was the abuse hurled in Topsham at a woman who was told that she had 'piss pots' cast on her and basins beaten while she was punished for whoredom by being carted in Tavistock.[780] In 1617 a man allegedly held a horn into which a Chittlehampton woman was said to have urinated. It would appear that the intimacy involved was scandalous.[781]

Some descriptions are puzzling because meanings for words have altered. Several women were called strong whores by which it meant that they had acted flagrantly and not that they had any noteworthy strength.[782] Elizabeth Gold was called a 'base, black, muddy whore' in Crediton in 1640. It may have been intended that muddy meant muddled but it also had the meanings of sullen or corrupt. In 1572 a Cornish woman was called a fine whore and a subtle privy whore who was also a 'grany' whore. The Exeter woman called a sheepish whore may have had low intelligence and not been meek.[783] Grace Verder of Marldon was called a spoiling whore in 1623 and this may have meant that she was destructive. Agnes Bartlett of Lostwithiel was called a stiff whore in 1572 which probably was intended to claim that she was obstinate.[784] In 1600 Christian Dever, a Salcombe woman, was called not only a pale whore but also a rigged one. This may have been derived from 'rigg', which meant an impudent and wanton young woman. Dever was also said to have ridden on Owen Bebel's back and one later definition for riggelting was 'riding upon men's backs'.[785]

Some slanderers did not accuse a single woman of being a whore but a number of them at once. In 1619 one Exeter woman insulted her neighbours in saying 'there was not one honest woman in all Paris Street and that the men were as bad too'.[786] It was also in Exeter that a group of women were collectively slandered by being called 'a company of whores' and a Crediton man said to a roomful of his neighbours 'you are all whores from the youngest to the eldest'. Meanwhile, an entire village outside was insulted when it was said there was not one virgin in Chevithorne. One of those who heard the slander objected and said that little Besse Crosse was an honest woman as was Eleanor Prouse amongst others.[787]

Upon being called a whore many women denied it by claiming their behaviour was as exemplary as their accusers including in Nymet Rowland where one said 'I am as honest a woman as thou art'. She was then told she had had so much sex that she should have had 100 bastards. In Plympton a woman replied 'I am as honest a woman and have as many clothes as thou that hadst a bastard up Roborough Down'. In Axminster the slanderer responded by merely spitting. A Dunsford woman was modest: she replied 'I am almost as honest as thy dame.'[788]

Some women called whores had specific allegations of their behaviour from their absent husbands. In Broadclyst Helen Rutleigh allegedly had told her husband she was at Ottery St Mary when she had actually travelled to Exeter where she was with another man. Sidwell Barber of Ashbury was told she was a whore when she kept a man all night in her home while her husband was away. In the Cornish village of Poundstock Joan Webb complained that she was told 'John Bray had to do with thee and I myself had to do with thee and thy servant Eleanor St John said that when thy husband Thomas Webb the elder is lacking or absent thou doe'st send away her servants that John Bray and thee may work their wills.'[789]

Some women were told that men other than their husbands knew their bodies. In Totnes one woman was told Thomas Cole 'did know what she bare under her apron as well as her the said Elizabeth Hansom's husband'. In contrast, at Pilton Philip Hodge admitted 'I have had to do with Elizabeth Hill and have known her body as well as ever I did know mine own wife's body and I have occupied her and if she be with child then the child is mine'.[790]

Married women across Devon used streams of insults against women they accused of having had sex with their husbands. Each was called a whore and the language could be much more vitriolic. This included such places as Bradninch ('thou art a whore and any husband's whore and my husband keepeth thee'), South Tawton ('a whore, and thou are my husband's whore and he doth keep thee as common as the highway, thou art a drunkard and thou fellest from thine horse in Okehampton market'), Alphington ('thou art a base whore, a sot bitch, a brazen faced whore and thou art my husband's whore'), Berry Pomeroy ('thou art a whore, a common whore both of thy body and tongue, a burnt-arse whore, my husband's whore & my husband keepeth thee a burned-bastard whore') and Broadclyst ('thou art a whore, a base whore and thou didst lie by a hedge with a rogue or with my husband').[791] Two Crediton women objected ('thou art a whore and an arrant whore and thou hath lain with my husband all night', 'thou art a whore and my husband's whore and I came & found my husband dealing with thee & thou heldest up thy smock with thine teeth')[792] as did three wives in Cullompton of different women ('thou are a whore, a base whore and my husband doth keep thee, a scum whore and a runagate whore', 'thou are a whore, a base whore and a stinking whore and thou has been my husband's whore these three or four years', 'thou art a whore and a base whore and my husband meaning Robert Salter her husband had a bout with thee upon St Andrew's day in the morning and I will pull the kerchief from thy head and the band from the neck of thee where so ever I meet with thee.').[793]

A common expression was 'playing the whore'. Thus in Honiton in 1635 it was said of Ann Abbot that 'thou didst play the whore when thy husband was asleep by the fire'. Similarly, in Cullompton a woman 'played the whore homeward', in Tiverton it was said to have been in the entry to a house, in Dartmouth under a bay bush, with two men in a field in Belstone, and in Exeter with Captain Parker in the gaol garden at Rougemont Castle.[794] Finally, it was a Cornish woman that was said to have played the whore with another woman's husband in her house and then came to his home where she again 'played the whore'.[795]

Some women were pilloried as not just being whores but being despicably active with it. A Barnstaple woman was thus described as being 'as hot as all the ovens in the town'.[796] Women who were investigated in charges of fornication had to explain their behaviour such as Thomasine Flood of Farway who admitted she had sex with William Cox in a wheat field and then with his nephew who had been waiting by the gate until his uncle finished. Joan Allen complained her reputation in Tavistock had been soiled by a neighbour claiming that she 'lay in every hedge and bush with every knave'. A Silverton woman was called 'as very a whore as any in England'. Margaret Randle, an East Ogwell woman, was said to travel to Newton Abbot six or seven times a week to sell her sexual services. She was also alleged to go to Newton Abbot twice or thrice in a day for 'mankind'.[797] However, the most irrevocable insult was that given to Eleanor Patrick. Her vicar, Reverend John Trender of Barnstaple, recorded her name amongst the burials for 28 April 1599 and added alongside it 'a whore of fame'.[798]

Conclusion

Insults tell us much about society. In the years from 1540 to 1640 they reflected behaviour which the ruling elite discouraged such as thievery, drunkenness and witchcraft. Other ridicule was about being poor or diseased. In addition, men were mocked for being unintelligent and dishonest whereas for women the insults concerned crimes of the tongue or ears; they were called scolds and gossips as well as eavesdroppers. Above all, sexual licentiousness dominated insults for both men and women. Those who were affronted by such accusations denied their validity and some took their opponents to court. It may have been that the resulting witness statements were inaccurate or even false. Nevertheless, the testimonies remain significant in that these particular insults were considered objectionable enough to warrant action in court.

Many insults were exchanged during bickering between friends, family or neighbours but one particular element of society was insulted to a greater extent than any other. Those in positions of authority were challenged and insulted as they undertook their duties. Often they were told that their stations were lower than those they represented. Court officials, local government officers and clerics and their families were subject to an extraordinary range of abuse.

Although blasphemy has been noted (as insults to God), much of the invective in this study is concerned with ordinary people who were verbally abused whilst they were engaged in their daily lives. Society was then largely illiterate and verbal communication provided the main means of disseminating not just national news but of events in Devon's hamlets, villages and towns. Like now, scandal was of particular interest.

Insults were given by word and also through actions. A considerable number of physical gestures were deployed which were intended to demean and humiliate. There was inventiveness in these postures and some were humorous. The most common physical insult was a pair of animal horns but two fingers were also used to great effect. These were both used to identify a man as a cuckold and his wife as unfaithful. Some verbal insults also suggested physical action and the most popular of these was 'Kiss my arse' but references to farting were also common.

Some court cases suggest that prosecutions were initiated in order to refute associations with conduct which could bring subsequent prosecutions. Claimants did not object in court to having been told that they were selfish, tight-fisted or did not have a sense of humour but they protested in regard to associations with theft, dishonesty, illicit sexual behaviour, witchcraft or murder. This must have been one of the driving forces in maintaining a good reputation.

Reputations were important in other ways. They affected not just an individual's standing in a community but had implications for marriage, employment and housing. A poor reputation, as has been shown, could ruin lives.

The witness statements tell us much about other aspects of society including of the sex lives of ordinary people. These details are otherwise unrecorded and in some cases outline permissive behaviour which runs counter to popular notions of mores in Elizabethan society. It is clear that in some households a shortage of space provided a greater degree of intimacy, and thus observation, than we have today.

It cannot be determined how truthful witnesses were and thus if statements were reliable accounts of arguments. Some cases were clearly part of a longer history of enmity. The decision by Exeter's council to reward informers with half of any miscreant's fine must bring into question the impartiality of their statements. But the terminology used must have had a high degree of believability. It is unfortunate that so little comparative evidence has survived amongst Devon's other borough records and that some church court manuscripts were destroyed when the Luftwaffe bombed Exeter in 1942. More records would no doubt broaden the language and thus our understanding of the nature of insults. Nevertheless, 'whore' was the most common insult for women and it is significant that more than 200 adjectives were teamed with it. No doubt others were unrecorded. 'Knave' and 'Rogue' were among the most popular insulting terms to give men. The cases prove there were dozens of others for men and women.

Terminology can be seen to change through the period. 'Mell' and 'sard' were recorded in use only in the sixteenth century whereas 'jape' continued into the early 1600s. The language recorded for many witnesses suggests local pronunciations and highlights archaic words and phrases. 'Nippy' may have been used primarily in Exeter and 'skinning a mare' might be a West Country or even Devon phrase. The word 'ninnyhammer' was limited to Tavistock but this may be reflective of the paucity of evidence for West Devon. 'Cucumber' or 'hornabus' may have been Devon words for a cuckold, but this may be better understood once there is another county study. Until then it could be assumed that insults in Devon were representative of those uttered across England.

It is clear that new insults appeared over the course of these 150 years. A new wave of disease ridicule followed the arrival of syphilis in the early 1500s. The term 'puritan whore' was conceived only because of the Reformation and indeed religious changes were responsible for a great number of insults. A woman married to a cleric could most easily be called a priest's whore when that marriage was legally invalid. The use of the term heretic was also caught up with national religious policy and the civil war muddied the definition of a traitor.

Insults first featured in a Devon publication a century after this period. It was probably Andrew Brice, the Exeter newspaper proprietor, who wrote *The Exmoor Courtship* and *The Exmoor Scolding* in 1746. He showed the development of local insults, amongst less reliable ones, in heated, and fictional, quarrels between two Exmoor women.[799] The language written by Brice was intended to amuse his middle class readership; the slanderous words of the earlier period had a very different purpose.

ILLUSTRATIONS

The images which head each chapter are details taken from 'The Musicians' Brawl', by Georges de La Tour, c1625. (J. Paul Getty Museum, 72.PA.28) Frontispiece. Yale Center for British Art, B1988.14.592; **1, 6, 10, 14, 15, 17, 22, 26, 27, 29-30, 33, 36-9, 47**. The author; **2**. J. Paul Getty Museum, 91.GB.67; **3**. J. Paul Getty Museum, 85.GC.439; **4, 46**. William Chappell, *The Roxburghe Ballads* (Hertford, 1879), 349, 353; **5**. Yale Center for British Art, B1975.3.919; **8**. J. Paul Getty Museum, 90.GG.7; **9, 16, 35**. Charles Hindley, *The Roxburghe Ballads* (Hertford, 1874), Vol. 2, 73, 99 & 182; **11**. Yale University Art Gallery, 1954.58.5; **12**. J. Paul Getty Museum, 84.GA.647; **13**. Rijksmuseum, RP-P-1885-A-9288; **7**. Yale Center for British Art, B1975.4.703; **18**. Yale University Art Gallery, 1990.57.1; **19-20**. Yale Center for British Art, B1977.14.12115 & B1975.4.247; **21**. *The Western Antiquary* (1881), 150; **23**. Yale Center for British Art, B1977.14.1490(15); **24**. Yale Center for British Art, B1975.3.1184; **25**. Charles Hindley, *The Roxburghe Ballads* (Hertford, 1873), Vol. I, 256; **28**. Yale Center for British Art, B1977.14.1490 (23); **31**. Yale Center for British Art, B1977/14/1490(75); **32**. William Chappell, *The Roxburghe Ballads* (Hertford, 1870), 344; **34**. Yale Center for British Art, B1977.14.1490(76); **40**. Wellcome Library EPB 5953/B; **41**. Wellcome Library ICV No 10790; **42**. Yale Center for British Art, B1976.1.496; **43**. Getty 86.GB.574; **44**. Yale Center for British Art, B1976.1.38; **45**. Yale Center for British Art, B1976.1.169

REFERENCES

1   J. A. Vage, 'The Records of the Bishop of Exeter's Consistory Court, c.1500–c.1660', *Transactions of the Devonshire Association*, Vol. 114, 1982, 79-85.

2   A haunting phrase used by Professor Christopher Brooke in *The Medieval Idea of Marriage* (Oxford, 1989), 4.

3   For one such example see Devon Heritage Centre (hereafter DHC), ECA/EQS/OB61/334.

4   Andrew Clark (ed.), *The Shirburn Ballads, 1585–1616* (Oxford, 1907), 48, 52.

5   Louis B. Wright (ed.), *Advice to a Son* (Ithaca, 1962), 24-6; Anita Travers (ed.), *Robert Furse, a Devon Family Memoir of 1593* (Devon & Cornwall Record Society, NS 53, 2010), 14, 16.

6   Todd Gray (ed.), *Devon Household Accounts, 1627–59, Part II* (Devon & Cornwall Record Society, NS 39, 1996), xxvi ; Tom Cain and Ruth Connolly, *The Complete Poetry of Robert Herrick* (Oxford, 2013), I, xlix.

7   "Cotton, William (*d.* 1621)," Mary Wolffe in *Oxford Dictionary of National Biography*, eee ed. H. C. G. Matthew and Brian Harrison (Oxford: OUP, 2004); online ed., ed. David Cannadine, January 2008, http://0-www.oxforddnb.com.lib.exeter.ac.uk/view/article/6431 (accessed August 9, 2016).

8   Frank Barlow, Foreword, xix, in Todd Gray, Margery Rowe and Audrey Erskine (eds), *Tudor and Stuart Devon* (Exeter, 1992); John Chynoweth, Nicholas Orme and Alexandra Walsham (eds), *The Survey of Cornwall by Richard Carew*, (Devon & Cornwall Record Society, NS 47, 2004), 55-7; DHC, Chanter 855B/162.

9   Carole Levin, *The Heart and Stomach of a King* (Philadelphia, 1994), 66-90; Willard Mosher Wallace, *Sir Walter Raleigh* (Princeton, 1959), 76; John Sugden, *Sir Francis Drake* (1990), xiii; Harry Kelsey, *Sir John Hawkins* (Yale, 2003), 114, 267-81.

REFERENCES

10   Todd Gray (ed.), *The Chronicle of Exeter, 1205–1722* (Exeter, 2005), 20-21.

11   DHC, ECA/EQS/OB61/302-303; Georges Edelen (ed.), *The Description of England by William Harrison* (1994 edn), 187; Francis Grose, *A Classical Dictionary of the Vulgar Tongue* (1796), no page number.

12   DHC, CC6/400; "incontinence, n.". OED Online. June 2016. Oxford University Press. http://www.oed.com/view/Entry/93905?redirected From =incontinence (accessed August 08, 2016).

13   "nigger, n. and adj.". OED Online. June 2016. Oxford University Press. http://www.oed.com/view/Entry/126934?rskey=rlORnd&result= 1&isAdvanced=false (accessed July 26, 2016).Todd Gray, *Devon and the Slave Trade* (Exeter, 2007), 26-8.

14   See, for example, the burial entry for Thomas 'the son of a Blackmore' in February 1631/1632 in the parish of Exeter St Mary Major, held at the Devon Heritage Centre.

15   DHC, CC179B/13-14, CC179A/II/61-3, CC179A/IV/71-3, CC179B/10-12, Chanter 855/152-3, Chanter 859/211-214, Chanter 856/79-81.

16   DHC, Chanter 855A/92, Chanter 855B/2, 385-6, 200-201, Chanter 860/451, Chanter 856/90 & 74-5, Chanter 866/502-504, Chanter 860/410, Chanter 859/37, Chanter 856/19, Chanter 861/45-6, Chanter 855B/378.

17   For instance, see DHC, Chanter 859/376.

18   DHC, Chanter 867/659-66.

19   DHC, CC217/214, 229; CC87; Chanter 867/640-1 & 651.

20   DHC, Chanter 867/790-3; CC17/21.

21   DHC, Chanter 855/54.

22   Mark Stoyle, *From Deliverance to Destruction* (Exeter, 1996), 54-5; DHC, ECA/EQS/OB63/385.

23   DHC, ECA/EQS/Act Book IV/153.

24   DHC, Chanter 856/72-4.

25   Laura Gowing, 'Gender and the language of insult in Early Modern London', *History Workshop*, No. 35 (Spring, 1993), 2-3.

26   Chappell, *Roxburghe*, II, 303. He also wrote:

'Her legs are like the elephant's,
     the calf and small all one;
Her ankles they together meet,
     And still knock bone to bone;
Her pretty foot not above the eighteens,
     So splayed as never was,
An excellent usher for a man
     That walks the dewy grass.'

27   DHC, Chanter 855/183.

28 DHC, ECA/EQS/OB61/377 & 486-7. See also DHC, ECA/EQS/ OB62/123 for a third occasion in which the words were spoken.

29 DHC, Chanter CC3A/45.

30 Harrison, *Description of England*, 189.

31 DHC, CC4B/99.

32 Christopher Hill, *Society & Puritanism in Pre-Revolutionary England* (1966), 298-353.

33 John McCafferty, 'Defamation and the Church Courts in Sixteenth-Century Armagh', *Archivium Hibericum*, Vol. 48 (1994), 90.

34 DHC, CC134/188.

35 Peter Christie, *Of Church Reves and of Testamentes* (Devon Family History Society, no place of publication, 1994), 32-4.

36 DHC, Chanter 861/165-70.

37 DHC, Chanter 861/341-44.

38 DHC, Chanter 864/264-6.

39 DHC, Chanter 859/26-8, Chanter 856/270, CC21/39.

40 DHC, Chanter 861/67.

41 DHC, CC17/173 & 179.

42 DHC, CC20/114-115.

43 DHC, Chanter 866/45-9 & 171-2, CC25/149.

44 DHC, Chanter CC25/124 & 156.

45 DHC, CC152 & Chanter 867/197.

46 DHC, Chanter 867/527-9 & 658.

47 DHC, CC20/42.

48 DHC, Chanter 41/51; Wallace T. MacCaffrey, *Exeter, 1540–1640* (Boston, 1978 edn), 98.

49 DHC, Chanter 855/275.

50 DHC, ECA/EQS/OB63/305. See for example, Muriel E. Curtis, *Some Disputes Between the City and Cathedral Authorities of Exeter* (Exeter, 1932).

51 DHC, CC19B/153.

52 DHC, CC134/181.

53 DHC, ECA/EQS/OB62/125.

54 DHC, ECA/EQS/OB61/418 & 422; CC19B/114.

55 DHC, ECA/EQS/OB61/44; CC20/49 & CC134/367.

56 DHC, CC5/343 & CC20B/34.

57 DHC, CC5/449 & 392.

58 DHC, CC20/76-7, 81-2 & ECA/EQS OB62/400.

59 Gordon Williams, *Shakespeare's Sexual Language* (1997).

60 Charles Hindley, *The Roxburghe Ballads* (1874), II, 25, 465.

61 L. R. Poos, 'Sex, lies, and the Church Courts of Pre-reformation England', *The Journal of Interdisciplinary History*, 25.4 (1995), 590.

62   DHC, Chanter 867/855-6; Plymouth & West 'Devon Record Office [hereafter PWDRO], 1/361/10; DHC, ECA/EQS/OB61/197-8 & OB62/81. See also Chanter 854B/41-2 & Chanter 857/376.

63   DHC, Chanter 859/192; Todd Gray (ed.), *Devon Household Accounts, 1627–59, Part I* (Devon & Cornwall Record Society, NS 38, 1995), xxvii; DHC, 406A-2/PF 14.

64   DHC, Chanter 857/111; Chanter 859/211-214.

65   DHC, Chanter 854B/269 & 285-6.

66   DHC, Chanter 862/228; Chanter 862/276.

67   DHC, Chanter 867/464.

68   DHC, ECA/EQS/OB61/431-2.

69   DHC, Chanter 855/342-4.

70   DHC, Chanter 855/290-1; Chanter 855A/23; Chanter 859/392.

71   Todd Gray and John Draisey (eds), Witchcraft in the Diocese of Exeter: Part II', *Devon & Cornwall Notes & Queries,* Vol. XXXVI – Part VIII (Autumn, 1990), 283-5.

72   R. N. Worth, *History of Plymouth* (Plymouth, 1890), 85; James Phinney Baxter, *The Trelawny Papers* (Portland, 1884), 225-34, 166-7.

73   DHC, CC5/48.

74   DHC, CC19B/280.

75   DHC, CC23/130.

76   DHC, CC7/96.

77   DHC, Chanter 861/461 & Chanter 857/62.

78   DHC, CC4/104.

79   DHC, CC179/75-80, 92-5.

80   DHC, CC6/160.

81   DHC, Chanter 860/410; Chanter 867/734-5.

82   DHC, Chanter 866/380-3 & CC25/46.

83   DHC, Chanter 854C/447.

84   DHC, Chanter 856/326-9.

85   DHC, Chanter 855/450.

86   DHC, Chanter 855/514.

87   DHC, Chanter 861/145.

88   DHC, Chanter 854B/87; Chanter 861/485.

89   DHC, Chanter 867/477-80 & 712, CC170A/II/37-8.

90   DHC, Chanter 859/50, Chanter 855A/123, Chanter 855B/362-3, CC3A/50, Chanter 855/528, Chanter 866/551.

91   DHC, Chanter 865/36.

92   DHC, Chanter 855B/11; CC6/236.

93   Thomas Westcote, *View of Devonshire* (Exeter, 1845), 260; Robert Whiting, *The Blind Devotion of the People* (Cambridge, 1989), 228; DHC, CC18/29.

94   Ronald A. Marchant, *The Church Under the Law* (Cambridge, 1969), 137-8; David H. Pill, 'Exeter diocesan courts in the early sixteenth century', *Transactions of the Devonshire Association*, Vol. 100 (1968), 51.

95   DHC, CC3B/91; Grose, *A Classical Dictionary*, no page number.

96   DHC, ECA/EQS/OB61/372; DHC, Chanter 57/3, CC4B/128, Chanter 864/332-4 & CC3B/82.

97   DHC, ECA/EQS/OB61/520-521.

98   DHC, Chanter 855B/306-7; C. Anne Wilson, *Food and Drink in Britain* (1973), 168-9.

99   DHC, ECA/EQS/OB61/269.

100   DHC, ECA/EQS/OB61/405.

101   DHC, ECA/EQS/OB61/29.

102   DHC, ECA/EQS/OB61/237.

103   DHC, ECA/EQS/OB62/103.

104   DHC, CC19B/173 & CC4B/219.

105   Martin Ingram, 'Ridings, Rough Music and the Reform of Popular Culture in Early Modern England', *Past & Present*, No. 105 (Nov. 1984), 80-82.

106   DHC, Chanter 865/78-82. For Plymouth, see R. N. Worth, *Calendar of the Plymouth Municipal Records* (Plymouth, 1893), 129 & 137.

107   DHC, Chanter 854B/250-1; Williams, *Shakespeare*, 138; Chappell, *Roxburghe*, I, 171-2.

108   DHC, ECA/EQS/OB61/302-303.

109   DHC, Z19/18/9, folio 290.

110   Westcote, *View of Devonshire*, 291.

111   *Carew*, 108.

112   Richard W. Cotton, *Barnstaple and the Northern Part of Devonshire during the Great Civil War* (1889), 66-9; Todd Gray (ed), *Devon Household Accounts, 1627–59, Part II* (Devon & Cornwall Record Society, NS 39, 1996), xlviii-xlix.

113   R. Pearse Chope (ed.), *Early Tours in Devon and Cornwall* (Newton Abbot, 1967 edn), 92.

114   DHC, CC6A/125; CC179A/IV/5-7.

115   DHC, CC3B/69; CC3/75, CC152 & CC3B/69 & 76; CC3B/53; CC4B/99; CC179A/IV/59.

116   DHC, Chanter 866/584, Chanter 866/93-107, Chanter 855/420, Chanter 855/287, Chanter 57/3, CC180, CC179B/13-14, CC6/10-11 & CC17/57.

117   DHC, Chanter 867/708, Chanter 864/422, CC179A/I/5-8 & 24-6, CC179A/IV/5-7, Chanter 861/40.

118   DHC, CC6/10-11, Chanter 864/294, CC4/24, CC91/4.

119   DHC, CC4B/167 & CC3B/84.

120   DHC, CC3/75; Chanter 864/332-4; CC91/4; CC179A/IV/76-9; CC179B/
       13-14; Chanter 856/412.
121   DHC, Chanter 864/332-4.
122   DHC, CC86 & Chanter 864/422.
123   DHC, Chanter 855/360. It could also mean asthmatic: *An Exmoor Scolding*
       (Exeter, 1788), 44.
124   DHC, CC152.
125   DHC, Chanter 867/895, Chanter 865/47-50.
126   DHC, Chanter 864/19-21.
127   DHC, CC17/95; Edward Hyde Clarendon, *The miscellaneous works of the
       Right Honourable Edward Earl of Clarendon, Lord High Chancellor, author of
       the history of the rebellion and civil wars in England* (1751), 411.
128   DHC, Chanter 855/385.
129   DHC, Chanter 866/126-8.
130   DHC, Chanter 855b/318-22.
131   DHC, CC170.
132   DHC, Chanter 861/271-2.
133   DHC, Chanter 867/1103.
134   DHC, CC152, loose item; Grose, *A Classical Dictionary*, no page number.
135   DHC, Chanter 861/1.
136   DHC, Chanter 854B/63. I am grateful to Professor Richard Hitchcock
       for this translation.
137   DHC, Chanter 857/344. A second copy of the statement does not refer to
       the Cornish language.
138   DHC, CC3/112.
139   DHC, CC3B/126. "† scorp, v.". OED Online. June 2016. Oxford University
       Press. http://www.oed.com/view/Entry/173069?rskey=ckA6nz&result=
       2&isAdvanced=false (accessed August 06, 2016).
140   DHC, CC3A/1; "luxurious, adj.". OED Online. June 2016. Oxford
       University Press. http://www.oed.com/view/Entry/111510?redirected
       From=luxurious (accessed July 25, 2016).
141   "naughty, adj. (and int.)". OED Online. June 2016. Oxford University
       Press. http://www.oed.com/view/Entry/125392?rskey=gUr8Q3&result=
       2&isAdvanced=false (accessed August 08, 2016).
142   DHC, CC7/209.
143   DHC, Chanter 856/56.
144   DHC, EQS OB62/373 & 378 & OB61/377.
145   G. J. Davies (ed.), *Touchyng Witchcrafte and Sorcerye* (Dorset Record Society,
       IX, 1995), 65-7.
146   DHC, Chanter 855/349.
147   DHC, Chanter 855B/444.

148   DHC, ECA/EQS/OB61/356; Grose, *A Classical Dictionary*, no page number.

149   DHC, Chanter 867/459 & 485; *The Western Antiquary*, Vol. I (1882), 23, 30; Grose, *A Classical Dictionary*, no page number.

150   DHC, ECA/EQS/OB61/12-14.

151   Rosemary C. Dunhill, '17th century invective: defamation cases as a source for word study', *DCNQ*, xxxiii (part ii), 49.

152   DHC, CC84 & Chanter 866/359-60.

153   DHC, CC5/466.

154   DHC, Chanter 856/412.

155   DHC, CC6A/275.

156   DHC, Chanter 856/19.

157   DHC, ECA/EQS/OB62/232.

158   DHC, CC5/177; Joseph Wright, *The English Dialect Dictionary* (Oxford, 1898), IV, 679.

159   Richard Smith, *A brief treatise setting forth divers truths* (1547); DHC, Chanter 859/195.

160   DHC, CC4B/9.

161   DHC, Chanter 856/200.

162   DHC, ECA/EQS/OB61/280.

163   DHC, Chanter 855A, after page 153.

164   "mell, v.2". OED Online. June 2016. Oxford University Press. http://www.oed.com/view/Entry/116153?rskey=uSDdWt&result=6&isAdvanced=false (accessed July 25, 2016); DHC, Chanter 854B/I/229, 80, 103, 131 & 137-41; Chanter 855/317-22, 531; Chanter 855B/393-5.

165   "† sard, v.". OED Online. June 2016. Oxford University Press. http://www.oed.com/view/Entry/171008?rskey=Qfvcqk&result=3&isAdvanced=false (accessed July 25, 2016); DHC, Chanter 857/473; Chanter 859/113; Chanter 855/183; Chanter 864/243-4, 448.

166   J. E. Neale, *Queen Elizabeth 1* (1988 edn), 87; S. R. Scargill-Bird (ed.), *Calendar of the Manuscripts of the Most Hon. the Marquis of Salisbury* (1883), I, 257; "swive, v.". OED Online. June 2016. Oxford University Press. http://www.oed.com/view/Entry/195994?rskey=vK3DZa&result=1&isAdvanced=false (accessed July 25, 2016).

167   DHC, Chanter 866/500-501, CC3/75, CC5/196 & 428, CC6B/166, CC20B/9, CC20B/110, CC25/76, Chanter 855/49, Chanter 855/1; "jape, v.". OED Online. June 2016. Oxford University Press. http://www.oed.com/view/Entry/100776?rskey=6wtSBf&result=2&isAdvanced=false (accessed July 25, 2016).

168   DHC, Chanter 855B/253-5.

169   DHC, CC20A/110; "occupy, v.". OED Online. June 2016. Oxford

University Press. http://www.oed.com/view/Entry/130189?redirected From=occupy (accessed July 25, 2016); "bag, v.1". OED Online. June 2016. Oxford University Press. http://www.oed.com/view/ Entry/14612?rskey=oO1MXY&result=2&isAdvanced=false (accessed July 25, 2016).

170 DHC, CC3B/83.

171 DHC, CC25/93; Chappell, *Roxburghe*, I, 453.

172 sot, n.1 and adj.". OED Online. June 2016. Oxford University Press. http://www.oed.com/view/Entry/185012?rskey=jMLASR&result= 1&isAdvanced=false (accessed July 25, 2016); DHC, CC5/166 & CC6B/145.

173 DHC, CC19B/75.

174 DHC, CC179A/IV/69-71.

175 DHC, CC179A/I/24-6.

176 DHC, CC6/123, 195, 207 & 218; "stinking, adj.". OED Online. June 2016. Oxford University Press. http://www.oed.com/view/ Entry/190416?rskey=dnBBtZ&result=2&isAdvanced=false (accessed July 25, 2016).

177 DHC, CC23/48; "savage, adj. and n.1". OED Online. June 2016. Oxford University Press. http://www.oed.com/view/Entry/171433?rskey= xZeeDu&result=2&isAdvanced=false (accessed July 25, 2016); DHC, Chanter 861/204.

178 DHC, CC6A/87; "show, n.1". OED Online. June 2016. Oxford University Press. http://www.oed.com/view/Entry/178735?rskey= LpGDdX&result=1&isAdvanced=false (accessed July 25, 2016).

179 DHC, CC6/175; "breech, n.". OED Online. June 2016. Oxford University Press. http://www.oed.com/view/Entry/23009?rskey= ShNyQ5&result=1&isAdvanced=false (accessed July 25, 2016).

180 DHC, ECA Act Book 2/316; Wright, *Dialect Dictionary*, IV, 279.

181 DHC, CC4B/25.

182 DHC, ECA/EQS/OB63/401; "shaft, n.2". OED Online. June 2016. Oxford University Press. http://www.oed.com/view/Entry/ 177239?rskey=ok4Hdm&result=2&isAdvanced=false (accessed July 25, 2016).

183 DHC, Chanter 861/356.

184 DHC, CC20A/111 & CC5/183.

185 DHC, Chanter 861/230.

186 DHC, CC17/43, CC22/75, CC25/125.

187 DHC, CC25/125.

188 DHC, CC16/5; "vagina, n.". OED Online. June 2016. Oxford University Press. http://www.oed.com/view/Entry/221017?redirectedFrom=vagina

(accessed August 19, 2016).; DHC, CC17/43; CC22/75; Chanter 867/207-210.

189 DHC, Chanter 867/259-62; CC6B/131.

190 DHC, CC19A/109.

191 DHC, Chanter 855/183 & CC5/244.

192 DHC, CC5/558.

193 DHC, CC22/65.

194 DHC, Chanter 867/259-62.

195 Whiting, *Blind Devotion*, 129; Mark Stoyle, *Loyalty and Locality* (Exeter, 1994), 97-8.

196 Tristram Risdon, *The Chorographical Description or Survey of the County of Devon* (Barnstaple, 1970 edn), 52.

197 "scum, n.". OED Online. June 2016. Oxford University Press. http://www.oed.com/view/Entry/173887?rskey=xPXrmc&result=1&isAdvanced=false (accessed July 24, 2016); DHC, CC17/66 & 79, CC3A/52, CC6B/14.

198 DHC, CC17/235 & CC20B/163.

199 DHC, Chanter 861/3701; ECA/EQS/OB62/142; Wainright, *Registers*, 17; Cornwall Record Office, AP/E/134.

200 "baggage, n. and adj.". OED Online. June 2016. Oxford University Press. http://www.oed.com/view/Entry/14622?redirectedFrom=baggage (accessed July 24, 2016); DHC, CC3A/84, CC20A/2, & CC3B/82.

201 DHC, CC3/116, CC5/436, & Chanter 864/360. These were Marhamchurch and St Tudy.

202 "princock, n.". OED Online. June 2016. Oxford University Press. http://www.oed.com/view/Entry/151462?redirectedFrom=princock (accessed July 24, 2016); DHC, Chanter 859/211-214.

203 DHC, Chanter 855B/162 & CC86.

204 DHC, CC6/136; CC19B/120; CC20A/129.

205 "carrion, n. and adj.". OED Online. June 2016. Oxford University Press. http://www.oed.com/view/Entry/28233?redirectedFrom=carrion (accessed July 24, 2016); DHC, ECA/EQS/OB62/21.

206 DHC, CC89/244; CC180; Robert Younge, *The Drunkard's Character* (1638), title page, 38.

207 DHC, CC5/189; CC6/307.

208 DHC, CC5/141; CC5/188; CC5/219; CC6/329; CC6B/106; CC25/57; CC17/141; CC17/204; CC5/133.

209 DHC, CC6/293-4.

210 Chappell, *Roxburghe*, II, 146.

211 DHC, CC4B/219; CC6/329.

212 DHC, CC7/50; CC3B/86-7; CC7/58.

213 DHC, Chanter 866/397-402.
214 DHC, CC25/23; CC23/266.
215 DHC, CC19A/10; CC20/90 & CC5/128.
216 DHC, CC5/98; Chanter 861/45-6; CC23/278 & 280.
217 J. Venn, 'Richard Venn, Vicar of Otterton', *The Western Antiquary*, Vol. 5 (1886), 17.
218 DHC, CC24/184; CC15/93.
219 DHC, Chanter 862/21; CC18/21; CC7/103.
220 DHC, CC6A/284-8.
221 DHC, Chanter 860/425; Grose, *A Classical Dictionary*, no page number; Chappell, *Roxburghe*, III, 319.
222 DHC, CC170.
223 DHC, CC6/273; Chanter 861/208; CC5/211 & CC20/77.
224 DHC, Chanter 861/40; CC4B/5; CC22/57.
225 DHC, CC5/500; CC170.
226 DHC, CC6/128; CC19B/277; CC20/60.
227 DHC, CC20B/122; CC6/127; Chanter 764.
228 DHC, CC7/64, CC17/202 & Chanter 867/666 & 692-4.
229 A. L. Beier, *Masterless Men* (1985).
230 DHC, CC23/180 & CC5/429, Chanter 866/174-7, CC19/113.
231 DHC, ECA/EQS/OB61/217 & 17.
232 DHC, Chanter 860/389; CC180, 21 June & 9 July 1641; "ram, n.1". OED Online. June 2016. Oxford University Press. http://www.oed.com/view/Entry/157719?rskey=WjgmNP&result=2&isAdvanced=false (accessed July 24, 2016); DHC, ECA/OB62/277.
233 "runagate, n. and adj.". OED Online. June 2016. Oxford University Press. http://www.oed.com/view/Entry/168879?redirectedFrom=runagate (accessed July 24, 2016); DHC, ECA/EQS/OB61/17 & OB62/196; Chanter 855/369-70; CC19/113.
234 DHC, CC5/48.
235 DHC, ECA/Act Book IV/3; Chanter 860/71.
236 DHC, CC25/45 & 187; CC5/188; CC20B/163; ECA/EQS/OB61/280 & 377.
237 DHC, CC6/236 & ECA/OB61/1; CC6/400 & 236.
238 DHC, CC20A/184; "runabout, n. and adj.". OED Online. June 2016. Oxford University Press. http://www.oed.com/view/Entry/168876?redirectedFrom=runabout (accessed July 24, 2016)DHC, Chanter 867/61-2.
239 DHC, Chanter 867/191; CC5/581.
240 "Jack, n.1". OED Online. June 2016. Oxford University Press. http://www.oed.com/view/Entry/100485?rskey=Q8m5Ua&result=

1&isAdvanced=false (accessed July 24, 2016); DHC, CC23/180 & CC5/436.

241 Keith Thomas, *Religion and the Decline of Magic* (1971); James Sharpe, *Instruments of Darkness* (1996).

242 Gray, *Chronicle of Exeter*, 74.

243 Todd Gray & John Draisey, 'Witchcraft in the Diocese of Exeter: Part VI. Topsham (1595 & 1596) & Georgeham (1597)', *Devon & Cornwall Notes & Queries*, Vol. XXXVII – Part II, Autumn, 1992, 70.

244 DHC, Chanter 861/142-3; Chanter 864/221; Chanter 867/995-8.

245 DHC, Chanter 855/71-2 & ECA/EQS/OB/62/2.

246 DHC, Chanter 855/407-408 & Chanter 855B/63-5, 102 & 122.

247 Todd Gray & John Draisey, 'Witchcraft in the Diocese of Exeter: Part II. East Worlington (1558), Townstal (1558) & Moretonhampstead (1559)', *Devon & Cornwall Notes & Queries*, Vol. XXXVI – Part VIII, Autumn, 1990, 282-5.

248 Todd Gray & John Draisey, 'Witchcraft in the Diocese of Exeter: Part III. St Thomas by Exeter (1561) & St Marychurch (1565)', *Devon & Cornwall Notes & Queries*, Vol. XXXVI – Part IX, Spring, 1991, 310-314.

249 Todd Gray & John Draisey, 'Witchcraft in the Diocese of Exeter: Part IV. Whimple (1565), Chawleigh (1571) & Morwenstow (1575)', *Devon & Cornwall Notes & Queries*, Vol. XXXVI – Part X, Autumn, 1991, 367.

250 Todd Gray & John Draisey, 'Witchcraft in the Diocese of Exeter: Part III. St Thomas by Exeter (1561) & St Marychurch (1565)', *Devon & Cornwall Notes & Queries*, Vol. XXXVI – Part IX, Spring, 1991, 306-308.

251 DHC, CC3A/20.

252 DHC, CC3/no reference number.

253 DHC, CC3B; CC6; CC18/21; Chanter 864/294.

254 DHC, ECA/EQS/OB 62/52, 151, 341, 393, 400.

255 DHC, ECA/EQS/OB 61/12-14, 661.

256 Todd Gray, 'Witchcraft in the Diocese of Exeter: Dartmouth, 1601–1602, *Devon & Cornwall Notes & Queries*, Vol. XXXVII – Part VII, Spring, 1990, 230-8.

257 Todd Gray & John Draisey, 'Witchcraft in the Diocese of Exeter: Part IV. Crediton (1584) & Sidbury (1588)', *Devon & Cornwall Notes & Queries*, Vol. XXXVII – Part I, Spring, 1992, 30.

258 DHC, Chanter 866/630-3; DHC, ECA/EQS/OB61/372 & OB62/16.

259 DHC, CC6B/92, CC20A/68 & ECA/EQS/OB61/527-8.

260 "paddock, n.1". OED Online. June 2016. Oxford University Press. http://www.oed.com/view/Entry/135920?rskey=oEKzbQ&result=1&isAdvanced=false (accessed July 24, 2016).DHC, Chanter 866/359-60 & Chanter 855/365.

261 "pickthank, n. and adj.". OED Online. June 2016. Oxford University Press. http://www.oed.com/view/Entry/143441?rskey=desall&result=1&isAdvanced=false (accessed July 24, 2016); "'beef,eater, n.". OED Online. June 2016. Oxford University Press. http://www.oed.com/view/Entry/16956?redirectedFrom=beefeater (accessed July 24, 2016); DHC, ECA/EQS/OB61/308 & OB62/342.

262 DHC, CC5/343; Grose, *A Classical Dictionary*, no page number; DHC, ECA/EQS/OB61/520-1.

263 DHC, CC5/167; PWDRO, 1/355/53.

264 DHC, C89/122; For example, see DHC, Chanter 855B/444, Chanter 859/312-313 & Chanter 867/362-3.

265 DHC, Chanter 856.

266 "knave, n.". OED Online. June 2016. Oxford University Press. http://www.oed.com/view/Entry/103934?rskey=WZM67J&result=1&isAdvanced=false (accessed July 25, 2016); DHC, CC86, no document number; CC179/75-80; CC89/266.

267 DHC, CC19A/29.

268 DHC, CC20A/148.

269 DHC, CC1/bundle I, ii & CC19B/34.

270 DHC, CC179A/5-8.

271 DHC, Chanter 855/337D; ECA/EQS/OB61/276.

272 DHC, CC17/201 & CC20B/137.

273 DHC, Chanter 857, 103.

274 DHC, CC6/145.

275 DHC, CC19/68 & CC19A/67.

276 DHC, CC19B/219.

277 DHC, CC20A/2; CC23/225; Chanter 867/732; CC21/53.

278 DHC, Chanter 865/74B; Chanter 867/521; Chanter 866/440-444.

279 DHC, Chanter 855/411.

280 "rogue, n. and adj.". OED Online. June 2016. Oxford University Press. http://www.oed.com/view/Entry/166894?rskey=Iq3wQz&result=1&isAdvanced=false (accessed July 25, 2016).

281 "rascal, n. and adj.". OED Online. June 2016. Oxford University Press. http://www.oed.com/view/Entry/158280?rskey=yskU7e&result=1&isAdvanced=false (accessed July 25, 2016); DHC, CC20/21.

282 DHC, CC3A/69 & 82; CC3B; CC4B/19; CC6/391; CC6A/15 & 214; CC15/110; CC18/24; CC20/21; CC89/172; Chanter 856/309; Chanter 864/12 & 53; Chanter 866/525-6.

283 DHC, CC4B/219 & CC6A/214; CC20A/2.

284 "slave, n.1 (and adj.)". OED Online. June 2016. Oxford University Press. http://www.oed.com/view/Entry/181477?rskey=6JKWhb&result=

1&isAdvanced=false (accessed July 25, 2016); DHC, Chanter 857/208-210.

285 DHC, Chanter 861/136-8.

286 DHC, CC20/101 & CC6B/116.

287 DHC, CC17/12 & Chanter 867/500-501.

288 DHC, Chanter 856/449-50.

289 DHC, CC20B/110 & CC174.

290 "varlet, n.". OED Online. June 2016. Oxford University Press. http://www.oed.com/view/Entry/221596?redirectedFrom=varlet (accessed July 25, 2016); DHC, Chanter 855A/no reference number & Chanter 856/307.

291 Gray, *Chronicle of Exeter*, 88.

292 "sucker, n.". OED Online. June 2016. Oxford University Press. http://www.oed.com/view/Entry/193420?rskey=JhGG52&result=1&isAdvanced=false (accessed July 25, 2016); DHC, Chanter 857/363-5.

293 DHC, Chanter 867/1061 & 1083-90.

294 DHC, CC134/161; Chanter 859/211-214; Thomas Wainwright (ed), *Barnstaple Parish Register* (Exeter, 1903), 3.

295 DHC, Chanter 867/690-2 & CC17/57.

296 DHC, Chanter 861/121-6, 142-3.

297 DHC, CC15/123.

298 DHC, CC19B/304 & Chanter 864/465.

299 DHC, Chanter 860/185; CC134/161; Chanter 860/200.

300 DHC, Chanter 867/842-3; "cock's-comb | cockscomb, n.". OED Online. June 2016. Oxford University Press. http://www.oed.com/view/Entry/35483?redirectedFrom=cockscomb (accessed July 25, 2016); DHC, Chanter 866/540-3.

301 Gray, *Chronicle of Exeter*, 75-6; "woodcock, n.". OED Online. June 2016. Oxford University Press. http://www.oed.com/view/Entry/230020?rskey=n8Q9lV&result=1&isAdvanced=false (accessed July 25, 2016).

302 "calf, n.1". OED Online. June 2016. Oxford University Press. http://www.oed.com/view/Entry/26330?rskey=qeyAEZ&result=1&isAdvanced=false (accessed July 25, 2016); DHC, Chanter 859, 371-5, 388.

303 DHC, Chanter 867/549-551;"mooncalf, n.". OED Online. June 2016. Oxford University Press. http://www.oed.com/view/Entry/121906?redirectedFrom=moon+calf (accessed July 25, 2016); DHC, Chanter 867/984.

304 "lubber, n.". OED Online. June 2016. Oxford University Press. http://www.oed.com/view/Entry/110780?rskey=3IvTq2&result=1&isAdvanced=false (accessed July 25, 2016).DHC, CC6B/68, Chanter 866/248-65, CC88,

305   W. Crossing, 'Local Expressions', *The Western Antiquary*, Vol. 3 (1884), 98.

306   "lob, n.2". OED Online. June 2016. Oxford University Press. http://
www.oed.com/view/Entry/109481?rskey=6uqDNC&result=
2&isAdvanced=false (accessed July 25, 2016); DHC, Chanter 860/349 &
355.

307   DHC, ECA/EQS/OB61/343 & Grose, *A Classical Dictionary*, no page
number.

308   DHC, ECA/EQS/OB62/618-619.

309   DHC, CC22/6; CC3, part of bundle 2, III, matrimonial and defamation
causes 16th century, no reference number; "puppy, n.". OED Online.
June 2016. Oxford University Press. http://www.oed.com/view/
Entry/154804?rskey=RfEiPi&result=1&isAdvanced=false (accessed July
25, 2016).

310   Herbert Reynolds, *A Short History of the Ancient Diocese of Exeter* (Exeter,
1895), 249-50; DHC, CC15/110; "mongrel, n. and adj.". OED Online.
June 2016. Oxford University Press. http://www.oed.com/view/
Entry/121222?rskey=1ebYDW&result=1&isAdvanced=false   (accessed
August 06, 2016).

311   DHC, CC6/302 & ECA/EQS/OB61/525; "jackanapes, n.". OED
Online. June 2016. Oxford University Press. http://www.oed.com/view/
Entry/100502?redirectedFrom=jackanapes (accessed July 25, 2016).

312   "ninny, n.1". OED Online. June 2016. Oxford University Press. http://www.
oed.com/view/Entry/127209?rskey=0H8YZB&result=1&isAdvanced=
false (accessed July 25, 2016); 'Dick of Devonshire', *Devon & Cornwall
Notes & Queries*, 1905, 34.

313   "ninnyhammer, n.". OED Online. June 2016. Oxford University Press.
http://www.oed.com/view/Entry/127211?redirectedFrom=ninny+
hammer (accessed July 25, 2016). Also see Thomas Middleton, *The family
of love acted by the children of his Majesty's revels* (1608).

314   DHC, CC19B/161; CC20A/149; CC22/6.

315   DHC, CC5/276.

316   Thomas Larkham, *A Strange Metamorphosis in Tavistock* (1658), pages 5, 6
& 8; *The Tavistock Nabol* (1658), 6-7; Thomas Larkeham (CCEd Person
ID 71334), The Clergy of the Church of England Database 1540–1835
Database http://www.theclergydatabase.org.uk>, accessed, 12 July 2016;
DHC, CC5/544.

317   DHC, CC15/169-171; Thomas Shadwell, *Epsom-Wells, a comedy* (1673);
"nincompoop, n.". OED Online. June 2016. Oxford University Press.
http://www.oed.com/view/Entry/127179?redirectedFrom=nincompoop
(accessed July 25, 2016).

318   "'bull,head, n.". OED Online. June 2016. Oxford University Press.

http://www.oed.com/view/Entry/24559?redirectedFrom=bullhead (accessed July 25, 2016); DHC, CC25/45.

319 DHC, CC18/16; Chanter 855B/162.

320 "hardhead, n.2". OED Online. June 2016. Oxford University Press. http://www.oed.com/view/Entry/84153?rskey=ftFyuB&result=2&isAdvanced=false (accessed July 25, 2016); DHC, CC4B/188.

321 "blockhead, n. and adj.". OED Online. June 2016. Oxford University Press. http://www.oed.com/view/Entry/20358?redirectedFrom=blockhead (accessed July 25, 2016); DHC, CC4/25; "slug, n.1". OED Online. June 2016. Oxford University Press. http://www.oed.com/view/Entry/182220?rskey=GF1rKR&result=1&isAdvanced=false (accessed July 25, 2016).

322 DHC, CC3/75; "pilled, adj.1". OED Online. June 2016. Oxford University Press. http://www.oed.com/view/Entry/143911?rskey=yA5de5&result=1&isAdvanced=false (accessed July 25, 2016).

323 DHC, Chanter 864/29.

324 "blinkard, n.". OED Online. June 2016. Oxford University Press. http://www.oed.com/view/Entry/20268?redirectedFrom=blinkard (accessed July 25, 2016); DHC, Chanter 855A/107.

325 DHC, Chanter 864/374; "'blinking, adj.". OED Online. June 2016. Oxford University Press. http://www.oed.com/view/Entry/20274?rskey=nplwpK&result=2&isAdvanced=false (accessed July 25, 2016); DHC, Chanter 11035, Loose folio.

326 DHC, Chanter 764/96 & CC6/175; Wainwright, *Barnstaple Parish Register*, 17.

327 "wench, n.". OED Online. June 2016. Oxford University Press. http://www.oed.com/view/Entry/227789?rskey=FD93JG&result=1&isAdvanced=false (accessed July 25, 2016).

328 DHC, Chanter 864/251 & Chanter 867/1,025-6.

329 DHC, Chanter 854B/143 & 157.

330 DHC, Chanter 862/276 & ECA/EQS/OB61/661; "goodwife, n.". OED Online. June 2016. Oxford University Press. http://www.oed.com/view/Entry/79987?redirectedFrom=goodwife (accessed July 25, 2016).

331 Gray, *Household Accounts*, I, 240-1; Jannine Crocker (ed.), *Elizabethan Inventories and Wills of the Exeter Orphans' Court* (Devon & Cornwall Record Society), NS 56-7 (2011 & 2014).

332 Christie, *Chirche-Reves*, 48.

333 Neale, *Queen Elizabeth I*, 68.

334 DHC, CC19B/120; "goose, n.". OED Online. June 2016. Oxford University Press. http://www.oed.com/view/Entry/80029?rskey=neRgsX&result=1&isAdvanced=false (accessed July 25, 2016).

335 DHC, CC174, Chanter 866/584 & Chanter 854B/34-8; "sow, n.1". OED Online. June 2016. Oxford University Press. http://www.oed.com/view/ Entry/185355?rskey=mG3AwB&result=1&isAdvanced=false (accessed July 25, 2016).

336 DHC, Chanter 855/447.

337 Todd Gray, *Devon's Ancient Bench Ends* (Exeter, 2012), 31-86; DHC, CC6/136, Chanter 866/93-107, CC5/356 & CC6/174; "giglet | giglot, n.". OED Online. June 2016. Oxford University Press. http://www.oed.com/ view/Entry/78243?redirectedFrom=giglet (accessed July 24, 2016).

338 DHC, CC17/66; Chanter 866/426-7 & 630-3; CC4/84 & 86; CC5/295; CC179A/76-9.

339 "jakes, n.". OED Online. June 2016. Oxford University Press. http:// www.oed.com/view/Entry/100668?redirectedFrom=jakes (accessed July 24, 2016); DHC, Chanter 857/75 & Chanter 856/56.

340 DHC, CC86 & Chanter 855/349.

341 For the earlier period see S. Bardsley, *Venomous Tongues* (Philadelphia, 2011), 137-9; Chappell, *Roxburghe*, II, 243.

342 Hugh R. Watkin, *Dartmouth Vol. 1 Pre-Reformation* (Exeter, 1935), 96, 213, 216.

343 Thomas Wainwright, *Reprint of the Barnstaple Records* (Barnstaple, 1900), I, 44.

344 Younge, *The Drunkard's Character*, 86; DHC, CC3/16, CC5/142 and Chanter 855A/292.

345 DHC, Chanter 867/623-5; Chanter 855/362-3; Chanter 856/99.

346 DHC, Chanter 855B/318-322; Chanter 855/344.

347 DHC, Chanter 855B/11.

348 DHC, Chanter 855/344.

349 DHC, CC5/48.

350 DHC, Chanter 855A.

351 DHC, Chanter 861/458.

352 Watkin, *Dartmouth*, 218, 220, 228, 233, 234, 238.

353 Bernard Capp, *When Gossips Meet: Women, Family and Neighbourhood in Early Modern England* (Oxford, 2003).

354 DHC, Chanter 866/101-107; Chanter 855/80; Chanter 855A/76.

355 DHC, Chanter 855A/118.

356 DHC, CC6/346.

357 DHC, CC179A/1/23-4.

358 DHC, CC179A/4/37-8.

359 "scold, n.". OED Online. June 2016. Oxford University Press. http://www.oed.com/view/Entry/172885?rskey=4nXWjT&result= 1&isAdvanced=false (accessed July 24, 2016).

360   W. H. H. Rogers, *West-Country Stories and Sketches* (Exeter, 1895), 68; Octogenaria, 'Plymouth Ducking Stool', *The Western Antiquary*, Vol. I (1881), 92.

361   Wainwright, *Reprint*, II, 49-51 & I, 44, 57. For the earlier period Maryanne Kowaleski has investigated fourteenth-century scolds particularly for Exeter: 'Words and Women out of Line: How Gossip Became a Crime in Medieval England', paper delivered at King's University College, February 2013.

362   J. R. Chanter, 'Cucking Stool', *The Western Antiquary*, Vol. I (1881–2), 89.

363   Watkin, *Dartmouth*, 199, 200, 201, 203, 211, 262. In 1522 two women and a man were fined for being common scolds and troublers of the peace.

364   Worth, *Plymouth Municipal Records*, 89, 98, 118, 141, 146.

365   DHC, ECA, Act Book IV, 170, 187; Kowaleski, 'Words', 14-15.

366   DHC, ECA/EQS/OB61, 1, 5-7, 43-5, 56, 187, 196-7, 197-8, 398, 400, 674; OB62, 16, 331, 353.

367   DHC, ECA/EQS/OB 61/680-1 & 196-7.

368   DHC, ECA/EQS/OB 61/661-2, 677.

369   DHC, Chanter 867/1029-31.

370   DHC, CC180/no reference number.

371   DHC, CC3B/40; Chanter 867/551-2.

372   DHC, Chanter 857/75.

373   DHC, CC6/236 & Chanter 866/598.

374   DHC, CC91/157 & Chanter 867/870-1.

375   DHC, CC179/75-80; CC179A/4/71-3.

376   DHC, Chanter 855/505.

377   DHC, Chanter 867/898-900. Cotton, William (*d*. 1621)," Mary Wolffe in *Oxford Dictionary of National Biography*, eee ed. H. C. G. Matthew and Brian Harrison (Oxford: OUP, 2004); online ed., ed. David Cannadine, January 2008, http://0-www.oxforddnb.com.lib.exeter.ac.uk/view/article/6431 (accessed August 9, 2016).

378   DHC, Chanter 864/448b.

379   DHC, Chanter 864/70-75.

380   DHC, CC4B/167; 3248A/4/16 & CC4B/52.

381   DHC, ECA/EQS/OB62/316.

382   DHC, DD62150.

383   DHC, DD62214, examination of Thomas Burges of Dartmouth, yeoman, 17 July 1626.

384   Beier, *Masterless Men*, 141.

385   Gray, *Chronicle of Exeter*, 85-6; John P. D. Cooper, *Propaganda and the Tudor State* (Oxford, 2003), 110, 95-6; NA, SP1/131/60.

386   Whiting, *Blind Devotion*, 144; R. N. Worth, *History of Plymouth*, 38; Mark

Stoyle, 'Fullye Bente to Fighte Oute the Matter; Reconsidering Cornwall's Role in the Western Rebellion of 1549', *English Historical Review*, CXXIX, No. 538, 549-77.

387   Neale, *Queen Elizabeth*, 87; S. R. Scargill-Bird (ed.), *Calendar of the Manuscripts of the Most Hon. the Marquis of Salisbury* (1883), I, 257.

388   DHC, Chanter 857/78.

389   Cooper, *Propaganda and the Tudor State*, 98-9; PWDRO, 1/361/2.

390   Paul Johnson, *Elizabeth I* (1988), 88.

391   H. Lloyd Parry, *The History of Exeter Guildhall* (Exeter, 1936), 52-3; MacCaffrey, *Exeter*, 38-9.

392   Parry, *Exeter Guildhall*, 52-5; DHC, ECA, Act Book 1/48a & Act Book 2/365.

393   DHC, ECA, Act Book 2/316; Wright, *Dialect Dictionary*, IV, 279.

394   Gray, *Chronicle of Exeter*, 96, 101.

395   Gray, *Chronicle of Exeter*, 99; Walter J. Harte, J. W. Schopp & H. Tapley-Soper (eds), *The Description of the City of Exeter* (Exeter, 1919), III, 931-5.

396   Percy Russell, *Dartmouth* (1950), 56-8.

397   DHC, DD61415.

398   DHC, 3248A/3/1.

399   DHC, 3248A/3/1 & 3248A/3/4.

400   DHC, 3248A/3/1.

401   DHC, CC166.

402   George Yerby and Paul Hunneyball, 'Ignatius Jourdain', in Andrew Thrush and John P. Ferris (eds), *The History of Parliament: the House of Commons 1604–1629* (Cambridge, 2010), IV, 929-33; Mark Stoyle, 'Ignatius Jurdain', *Oxford Dictionary of National Biography*, Oxford University Press, 2004, accessed 12 July 2016, http://www.oxforddnb.com/themes/theme.jsp?articleid=92747; Ferdinand Nicolls, *The Life and Death of Mr Ignatius Jurdain* (1654), foreword; F. Troup, 'An Exeter Worthy and his Biographer', *Transactions of the Devonshire Association*, Vol. XXIX (1897), 350-377; Stoyle, *Destruction*, 19-37.

403   Nicolls, *The Life and Death of Mr Ignatius Jurdain*, 10-12.

404   DHC, ECA/EQS/OB 61/237.

405   MacCaffrey, *Exeter*, 199-200; Troup, 'An Exeter Worthy', 360.

406   DHC, ECA/EQS/OB61/320.

407   DHC, ECA/EQS/OB61/365-7 & 529.

408   Stoyle, *Destruction*, 27, DHC, ECA/EQS/OB61/12-13, 29.

409   Stoyle, *Destruction*, 26; DHC, ECA/EQS/OB62/198.

410   DHC, ECA/EQS/OB61/90-1.

411   Grose, *A Classical Dictionary*, no page number.

412   Alan Brockett, *Nonconformity in Exeter, 1650-1875* (Manchester, 1962), 2.

413   Stoyle, *Destruction*, 26; DHC, ECA/EQS/OB 61/100, 416.
414   DHC, ECA/EQS/OB 63/267; Stoyle, *Destruction*, 39-42; Gray, *Chronicle of Exeter*, 124.
415   DHC, ECA/EQS/OB63/40.
416   DHC, ECA/EQS/OB 62/259; John Hayne (CCEd Person ID 70111), The Clergy of the Church of England Database 1540–1835 Database http://www.theclergydatabase.org.uk>, accessed, 12 July 2016.
417   Stoyle, *Destruction*, 26; DHC, ECA/EQS/OB 61/600.
418   A. H. A. Hamilton, *Quarter Sessions from Queen Elizabeth to Queen Anne* (1878), 84.
419   DHC, ECA/EQS/OB62/219.
420   MacCaffrey, *Exeter*, 91.
421   DHC, ECA/EQS/OB62/389.
422   DHC, ECA/EQS/OB62/88.
423   DHC, ECA/EQS/OB61/11 & 51.
424   DHC, ECA/EQS/OB62/4.
425   DHC, ECA/ECA/OB62/75; OB63/27 dorse; OB62/142, 174, 218, 354, 389.
426   DHC, 3248, 3/2.
427   DHC, C15/109; CC23/266.
428   DHC, Chanter 764/96.
429   DHC, CC3B.
430   Whiting, *Blind Devotion*, 115-116.
431   Maria Perry, *The Word of a Prince* (Woodbridge, 1990), 56.
432   Whiting, *Blind Devotion*, 122.
433   Joyce Youings, 'Early Tudor Exeter: the founders of the county of the city', Inaugural Lecture, University of Exeter (Exeter, 1974), 15; Gray, *Chronicle of Exeter*, 81-2.
434   Whiting, *Blind Devotion*, 126-7; Gray, *Chronicle of Exeter*, 39, 47, 81, 95, 97, 104, 80. Walter Staplehill may be 'W.S.' who informed on Thomas Bennet in 1531: John Foxe, *The Actes and Monuments* (1583), Book 8, 1036-8.
435   Gray, *Chronicle of Exeter*, 83.
436   DHC, Chanter 866/174-7.
437   Whiting, *Blind Devotion*, 255; DHC, ECA, Book 51/96-7.
438   Whiting, *Blind Devotion*, 126.
439   DHC, Chanter 860/425.
440   DHC, Chanter 861/34-6 & 40-3.
441   DHC, CC3B/76.
442   DHC, CC3B/69.
443   DHC, CC6/300; Chanter 764/81.

444   DHC, CC134.

445   DHC, CC89/85 & 50.

446   DHC, Chanter 867/727; Andrew Thrush, 'Barnaby Gooch', in Andrew Thrush and John P. Ferris (eds), *The History of Parliament: the House of Commons, 1604–1629* (2010), IV, 405-413.

447   Grose, *Classical Dictionary*, no page number.

448   DHC, ECA/EQS/OB61/17 & 55; CC3B/82; Keith Thomas, 'Bodily Control and Social Unease: The Fart in Seventeenth-Century England', in Angela McShane and Garthine Walker (eds), *The Extraordinary and the Everyday in Early Modern England* (New York, 2010), 18.

449   DHC, Chanter 867/727.

450   R. A. Roberts (ed), *Calendar of the Cecil Papers in Hatfield House*, Vol 10 (1904), 26-31; Viad, 'The diocese of Exeter in 1600', *Cornish Notes & Queries* (1906), 42-4; Susan Wiseman, *Writing Metamorphosis in the English Renaissance* (Cambridge, 2014), 65-6.

451   DHC, Chanter 764; Hamilton, *Quarter Sessions*, 84.

452   "forsworn | forswore, adj.". OED Online. June 2016. Oxford University Press.   http://www.oed.com/view/Entry/73635?redirectedFrom= forsworn (accessed July 25, 2016); DHC, CC3B/82, CC7/34, CC15/18, Chanter 855/157-8, Chanter 864/18-19, Chanter 864/53, Chanter 866/174-7, & CC24/8.

453   DHC, CC23/225; CC3A/13; CC6A/115.

454   DHC, CC19B/223; CC20B/78.

455   DHC, CC4B/52.

456   DHC, CC4B/167.

457   John Walters, 'Gesturing at authority: deciphering the gestural code of early modern England' in M. Braddick (ed.), *The Politics of Gesture: Historical Perspectives* (Past and Present, Supplement, 4, 2009), 96-127.

458   DHC, CC134/342.

459   DHC, Chanter 856/449-50.

460   DHC, CC25/240; Chanter 764/104.

461   DHC, CC170.

462   DHC, Chanter 855B/383-5; Audrey Erskine, 'Disturbances in Exeter Cathedral, 1599–1676', *Devon & Cornwall Notes & Queries*, Volume XXXVII, Part IV (Autumn, 1993), 119.

463   DHC, CC5/346.

464   DHC, CC6/10-11; Reynolds, *A Short History*, 227.

465   DHC, Chanter 864/18-19; CC6/302.

466   DHC, Chanter 855/49 & 70; CC3B/84.

467   DHC, CC6A/275; CC3B/52.

468 DHC, CC179A/57-61; CC19/113.

469 DHC, CC170; Chanter 864/53; Chanter 862/372; 3248A/3/2; CC6A/214; CC7/34.

470 DHC, Chanter 864/25-8.

471 DHC, CC25/235; Chanter 867/272-3; CC6A/21.

472 DHC, CC134/168 & 175; CC170.

473 DHC, CC3/75; CC11035.

474 Whiting, *Blind Devotion*, 128; Chanter 856/307-309, 318.

475 DHC, CC7/103; Chanter 867/842-3.

476 Yerby and Hunneyball, 'Ignatius Jourdain', IV, 930.

477 DHC, 3248A/3/1; Chanter 861/401-405.

478 DHC, Chanter 867/47-9, 51, 410-412.

479 DHC, CC24/6.

480 Whiting, *Blind Devotion*, 129; DHC, Chanter 854B/Part I/21-3 & Part II/219-220.

481 Richard M. Spielmann, 'The Beginning of Clerical Marriage In the English Reformation: The Reigns of Edward and Mary', *Anglican and Episcopal History* (Vol. 56, No. 3, September 1987), 251, 255; DHC, Chanter 855/37.

482 Exeter Cathedral Library & Archives, 4539/1-19; Whiting, *Blind Devotion*, 131 & 244; Gray, *Chronicle of Exeter*, 101; DHC, Chanter 856/272.

483 DHC, CC20B/11.

484 Whiting, *Blind Devotion*, 130; DHC, Chanter 855B/393-5 .

485 DHC, Chanter 855/184.

486 DHC, Chanter 857/513-514.

487 DHC, Chanter 855A/no number; CC19B/81; CC179A/12-14 & 34.

488 DHC, Chanter 855A/123.

489 DHC, Chanter 855A/234; Chanter 855/275 & 370.

490 Whiting, *Blind Devotion*, 128; DHC, Chanter 855/174.

491 DHC, CC3/75; CC91/87.

492 DHC, CC6/145-6; CC11035.

493 DHC, Chanter 864/108-110, 112-113.

494 DHC, Chanter 867/726.

495 DHC, Chanter 867/1100-1101, CC18/24 & CC18/27.

496 DHC, CC18/21 edited in Todd Gray & John Draisey, 'Witchcraft in the Diocese of Exeter, Part VII', *Devon & Cornwall Notes & Queries*, Vol. XXXVII – Part III (Spring, 1993), 100-101.

497 DHC, CC91/4.

498 DHC, CC23/303-304.

499 DHC, CC15/18.

500 John Frederick Chanter, *The Life and Times of Martin Blake* (1909), 34.

501   Todd Gray (ed.), *The Lost Chronicle of Barnstaple* (Exeter, 1998), 86-7.

502   Gray, *The Lost Chronicle of Barnstaple*, 79; DHC, CC3A/13.

503   Wainwright, *Barnstaple Parish Register*, 12, 18, 26, 40.

504   DHC, CC3A/20; CC3B/86-7.

505   DHC, CC3A/16; Chanter 867/237; Gray, *The Lost Chronicle of Barnstaple*, 79.

506   DHC, CC4/23.

507   DHC, Chanter 864/314.

508   DHC, CC21/39.

509   DHC, Chanter 860/410.

510   DHC, Chanter 856/312 & 360; Chanter 859/317.

511   DHC, CC3B/40; CC3B/53.

512   DHC, ECA/EQS/OB61/22-3, 44, 110-111, 176-7, 269, 331, 369 & OB62/142, 151, 180-1.

513   Patrick Collinson, *English Puritanism* (1983), 7-9.

514   Somerset Heritage Centre, DD WO 56/9/14.1.

515   DHC, CC90. The document is dated 22 October 1600 or possibly 1601.

516   Durham University Library Archives & Special Collections, Add. Ms. 1474, pages 7-8; Ruth Facer, *Mary Bacon's World* (Newbury, 2010), 170 which cites Hampshire Record Office, 28M82/F1. The Newcastle account was republished in about 1840: British Museum, 1994.0724.2 and DHC, Broadsides/045, 'The perpetual almanack', printed at Devonport.

517   Walter J. Harte, J. W. Schopp & H. Tapley-Soper (eds), *The Description of the City of Exeter* (Exeter, 1919), II, 340.

518   DHC, CC5/325; Chanter 854B/251; Chanter 857/208-210; Chanter 859/108; Chanter 864/448; Chanter 864/374; Chanter 859/2; Chanter 866/93-107; CC174; Chanter 867/826; Chanter 856/99.

519   Todd Gray (ed.), *Harvest Failure in Cornwall and Devon* (Camborne, 1992), xx-xxv.

520   DHC, Chanter 856/58-62.

521   DHC, Chanter 867/14-19; Chanter 861/1-7.

522   DHC, CC3A/1; CC179/II/117-123, 159-67.

523   DHC, Chanter 861/36.

524   DHC, Chanter 861/142-3.

525   DHC, Chanter 861/362.

526   DHC, Chanter 854D/528 & 531; Chanter 854B/I/138-9.

527   DHC, Chanter 859/55-9, 65; Chanter 857/105.

528   DHC, Chanter 861/371.

529   DHC, CC20B/125; CC15/175; Chanter 867/14-19, Chanter 861/344-7, & CC179B/10-12; Chanter 867/446-9; Chanter 867/449; Chanter 861/344-7; Chanter 864/272-3; Chanter 867/712; CC7/64.

530 DHC, CC3A/1; Chanter 861/121-6; CC16/17 & Chanter 859/48; CC152; Chanter 855A/361; Chanter 860/136; Chanter 862/45-50; Chanter 855/63; Chanter 857/367; Chanter 861/438-41, CC177A/157.

531 For instance, see DHC, Chanter 861/371; Chanter 857/388.

532 DHC, CC179A/24-6; Chanter 859/113.

533 DHC, Chanter 854B/i/102; Chanter 866, no reference number.

534 DHC, CC6/58; CC177A/154; CC19A/109.

535 DHC, Chanter 860/449 & Chanter 861/14.

536 DHC, Chanter 862/275.

537 DHC, CC3; Chanter 861/216.

538 DHC, Chanter 862/283.

539 DHC, Chanter 867/702-703.

540 DHC, Chanter 861/121-6.

541 DHC, Chanter 866/502-504.

542 DHC, Chanter 864/78-9; ECA/EQS/OB62/20.

543 DHC, *Church Reeves*, 27-8.

544 DHC, CC170.

545 DHC, Chanter 861/254.

546 DHC, Chanter 855B/295-6.

547 DHC, Chanter 855B/363-4.

548 DHC, ECA/Act Book IV/24 & 250.

549 DHC, ECA/EQS/OB61/305; ECA/EQS/OB62/60.

550 DHC, CC4/10.

551 DHC, Chanter 855/36.

552 DHC, CC15/55.

553 DHC, Chanter 862/444; CC6/113; CC17/171.

554 DHC, Chanter 867/700-702.

555 DHC, Chanter 867/59 & 336.

556 DHC, Chanter 862/45-50; Mrs Gwatkin, *A Devonshire Dialogue in four parts* (Plymouth, 1839), 75; CC3A/1.

557 Gray, *Household Accounts*, II, xxvi; "lusty, adj.". OED Online. June 2016. Oxford University Press. http://www.oed.com/view/Entry/111424?rskey=0seryr&result=1&isAdvanced=false (accessed July 25, 2016).

558 Clark, *Shirburn Ballads*, 270.

559 DHC, Chanter 861/24 & 451.

560 DHC, CC20A/24 & Chanter 865/74.

561 DHC, Chanter 867/509, Chanter 861/438-41, Chanter 862/176, Chanter 865/28 & 31-3, Chanter 866/171-2 & 384, Chanter 855A/463, CC179A/IV/71-3, CC86, CC179A/II/12-14.

562 DHC, Chanter 855B/363.

563 DHC, Chanter 857/14-18; ECA/EQS/OB62/108.

564 DHC, ECA/EQS/OB62/1; Chanter 862/436; Chanter 864/448.
565 DHC, Chanter 867/126-7; Chanter 864/108; Chanter 867/47-9.
566 DHC, CC6B/131.
567 DHC, Chanter 861/121-6.
568 DHC, Chanter 867/310-312, 14-19; Chanter 860/1-2.
569 DHC, Chanter 860/183-7.
570 DHC, Chanter 862/321; Chanter 867/391 & 427-8, CC23/202; CC6/161 & CC170.
571 DHC, CC86 & CC25/200.
572 DHC, Chanter 864/332-4; Chanter 861/214.
573 DHC, CC179A/II/55-6.
574 DHC, Chanter 867/452; Chanter 861/370.
575 DHC, Chanter 867/903.
576 For instance, see Chanter 857/208-210.
577 DHC, ECA/EQS/OB61/302; "pander, n.". OED Online. June 2016. Oxford University Press. http://www.oed.com/view/Entry/136752?rskey=0H4cGf&result=1&isAdvanced=false (accessed July 25, 2016).
578 DHC, Chanter 867/724-5; "bawd, n.1". OED Online. June 2016. Oxford University Press. http://www.oed.com/view/Entry/16346?rskey=KH87O7&result=1&isAdvanced=false (accessed July 25, 2016).
579 DHC, Chanter 867/901.
580 DHC, Chanter 855A/no reference number; Chanter 862/53-4.
581 DHC, CC20/98; Chanter 861/192-6.
582 DHC, ECA/EQS/OB62/93.
583 DHC, CC6B/106.
584 DHC, Chanter 854B/41-2.
585 DHC, CC20A/40.
586 DHC, Chanter 854B/34-8; Chanter 862/277-80; CC17/135.
587 DHC, CC4B/92.
588 DHC, ECA/EQS/OB62/81 & 276.
589 DHC, CC179B/13-14.
590 DHC, CC22/15; CC5/544.
591 DHC, CC6/132 & CC19B/48.
592 DHC, Chanter 867/391 & 427-32.
593 DHC, ECA/EQS/OB61/1.
594 DHC, Chanter 855/342.
595 DHC, Chanter 864/386.
596 DHC, CC92 & Chanter 867/732.
597 DHC, Chanter 864/318.
598 DHC, ECA/EQS/OB62/19.

599 Robert Hole, 'Incest, consanguinity and a monstrous birth in rural England, January 1600', *Social History*, Vol. 25, No. 2 (May, 2000), 186; DHC, Chanter 855/528.

600 Bruce M. Rothschild, 'History of Syphilis', *Clinical Infectious Diseases*, 2005: 40 (15 May), 1454; Claude Quétel, *History of Syphilis* (Baltimore, 1990), 9-16.

601 DHC, CC179/75-80 & 92-5.

602 DHC, Chanter 865/73; Chanter 855B/385-6.

603 DHC, Chanter 864/21-4.

604 DHC, CC3B/13.

605 ".burnt | burned, adj.". OED Online. June 2016. Oxford University Press. http://www.oed.com/view/Entry/25063?rskey=nvAtSs&result=1&isAdvanced=false (accessed July 25, 2016). DHC, Chanter 862/339 & CC3C; C4/104.

606 DHC, CC3/16; CC15/85, 75; CC4B/157.

607 DHC, CC22/11 & CC20A, no reference number.

608 DHC, CC5/240.

609 DHC, CC6B/166; Chanter 861/33.

610 DHC, Chanter 857/469; Chanter 854B/II/198.

611 DHC, Chanter 859/192. I am uncertain as to the transcription of the word 'greingoomber'.

612 DHC, Chanter 864/373; ECA/EQS/OB61/197-8; Lucinda McCray Beier, *Sufferers and Healers* (1987), 251.

613 DHC, Chanter 867/259-62.

614 DHC, CC19/14; CC17/133.

615 DHC, Chanter 867/658; CC5/183.

616 DHC, CC20/18.; Chanter 854B/34-8.

617 DHC, Chanter 854B/148; John Eberle, *A Treatise of the Materia Medica and Therapeutics* (Philadelphia, 1834), I, 330-1.

618 DHC, Chanter 861/160; Chanter 866/417.

619 DHC, ECA/EQS/OB62/21 & Chanter 859/37.

620 DHC, Chanter 856/99; CC7/42; ECA/EQS OB61/197-8.

621 DHC, CC4B/91; CC23/70; Chanter 862/431-2.

622 "scab, n.". OED Online. June 2016. Oxford University Press. http://www.oed.com/view/Entry/171622?redirectedFrom=scab-mite (accessed July 25, 2016). DHC, CC5/59, 200 & CC6A/15.

623 DHC, CC15/109 & Chanter 859/211-214; Chappell, *Roxburghe*, I, 60.

624 "† 'scabbard, n.2". OED Online. June 2016. Oxford University Press. http://www.oed.com/view/Entry/171626?rskey=TphVU6&result=2&isAdvanced=false (accessed July 25, 2016).DHC, Chanter 859/402.

625 DHC, Chanter 864/217; ECA/EQS/OB61/369.

626   Chappell, *Roxburghe*, II, 568.

627   DHC, Chanter 859/115-116, CC16/5, CC19/113.

628   "cormorant, n.". OED Online. June 2016. Oxford University Press. http://www.oed.com/view/Entry/41582?redirectedFrom=cormorant (accessed July 25, 2016); DHC, Chanter 861/204.

629   DHC, Chanter 856/99 & Chanter 856/368; R. L. Taverner, 'The administrative work of the Devon Justices', *Transactions of the Devonshire Association*, Vol. 100 (1968), 65; Nicholas Orme, *The Church in Devon: 400–1560* (Exeter, 2013); DHC, Chanter 855B/445.

630   DHC, Chanter 855B/11; ECA/EQS/OB61/343; "wry-mouthed, adj.". OED Online. June 2016. Oxford University Press. http://www.oed.com/view/Entry/230870?redirectedFrom=wry+mouthed (accessed July 25, 2016).

631   DHC, CC4A/9. For a discussion of sexual terms see Valerie Traub, *Thinking Sex with the Early Moderns* (Philadelphia, 2016), Chapter 6.

632   DHC, Chanter 867/855-6 & Chanter 859/26-8.

633   DHC, Chanter 864/29 & Chanter 856/313-318.

634   Poos, 'Sex, lies and the church courts', 591.

635   DHC, Chanter 860/349, CC3B/55 & Chanter 866/546-7.

636   DHC, Chanter 867/962-4, CC16/13 & Chanter 857/103.

637   DHC, Chanter 850/359-62; "harlot, n.". OED Online. June 2016. Oxford University Press. http://www.oed.com/view/Entry/84255?rskey=4r5QaJ&result=1&isAdvanced=false (accessed July 25, 2016).

638   DHC, Chanter 854B/II/185; Chanter 861/328.

639   DHC, Chanter 859/48.

640   DHC, Chanter 179A/55-6.

641   DHC, CC180, CC15/85, CC7/119 & 46, CC17/47, CC25/121-2, CC25/141, CC6/234.

642   DHC, CC20/81; "whoremonger, n.". OED Online. June 2016. Oxford University Press. http://www.oed.com/view/Entry/228785?redirectedFrom=whoremonger (accessed July 25, 2016); DHC, CC20B/61.

643   DHC, CC20B/31 & CC84.

644   DHC, Chanter 861/436-8 & CC25/199.

645   DHC, Chanter 867/521.

646   DHC, CC19B/152.

647   DHC, Chanter 866/440-444; "whoremaster, n.". OED Online. June 2016. Oxford University Press. http://www.oed.com/view/Entry/228784?redirectedFrom=whoremaster (accessed July 25, 2016).

648   DHC, CC20B/69; CC19/18; CC19B/38 & 205.

649   DHC, CC4A/9.

650   DHC, CC5/190; CC179A/IV/29-30.

651 DHC, CC17/172; CC5/452.

652 DHC, CC3B; CC24/24.

653 For instance, see DHC, ECA/EQS/OB61/196-7.

654 DHC, Chanter 855A/68, 81-4, 105-6.

655 DHC, Chanter 860/447 & Chanter 856/312.

656 DHC, CC6A/164.

657 DHC, Chanter 867/428; ECA/EQS/OB62/151.

658 DHC, Chanter 855/389; CC3B ; Chanter 861/160-1.

659 DHC, Chanter 861/127 & CC22/4.

660 DHC, Chanter 862/127.

661 DHC, Chanter 864/10-11 & CC179/Part II/157-9.

662 DHC, CC4B/188 & CC19B/234.

663 DHC, CC20B/2; Dunhill, '17th century invective', 49-51; DHC, ECA/EQS/OB61/372. The *Oxford English Dictionary* does not have this definition: "cucumber, n.". OED Online. June 2016. Oxford University Press. http://www.oed.com/view/Entry/45535?redirectedFrom=cucumber (accessed July 25, 2016).

664 DHC, CC5/276 & CC5/343; Magdalene College Archive, Pepys 5.418.

665 DHC, Chanter 859/201; "horner, n.1". OED Online. June 2016. Oxford University Press. http://www.oed.com/view/Entry/88488?rskey=h5jfRr&result=1&isAdvanced=false (accessed July 25, 2016).

666 DHC, CC5/276 & 190.

667 DHC, CC20B/22 & 34.

668 DHC, Chanter 867, 724-5.

669 Henry Farley, *The complaint of Paules* (Cambridge, 1616); DHC, CC20A/149 & Chanter 867/901.

670 DHC, CC19B/173; ECA/EQS/OB62/391.

671 "wittol, n.". OED Online. June 2016. Oxford University Press. http://www.oed.com/view/Entry/229753?rskey=aTXiUO&result=1&isAdvanced=false (accessed July 25, 2016).

672 DHC, Chanter 857/12; Chanter 862/145.

673 DHC, Chanter 862/45-52.

674 DHC, Chanter 861/160-2.

675 DHC, Chanter 867/631 & 642; ECA/EQS/OB62/21.

676 DHC, CC174; DHC, ECA/EQS/OB61/192-3 & OB62/6.

677 DHC, Chanter 855A/1 & Chanter 861/230.

678 Travers, *Furse*, 17.

679 DHC, Chanter 867/207-210.

680 Christie, *Church Reves*, 118-119.

681 DHC, Chanter 866/171-2; Chanter 867/515-516; DHC, CC25/120.

682 DHC, Chanter 856/347; CC20B/109.

683 DHC, Chanter 857/470.

684 DHC, Chanter 857/469.

685 DHC, CC17/66; Elizabeth A. Foyster, *Manhood in Early Modern England* (New York, 2014 edn), 182.

686 Jeffrey Richards, *Sex, Dissidence and Damnation* (1990), 119; Ruth Mazo Karras, 'The Regulation of Brothels in Later Medieval England', 122, in Judith M. Bennett, Elizabeth A. Clark, Jean F. O'Barr, B. Anne Vilen and Sarah Westphal-Wihl (eds), *Sisters and Workers in the Middle Ages* (1989 edn),

687 Gray, *Chronicle of Exeter*, 77-8; Harte, Schopp & Tapley-Soper (eds), *The Description of the City of Exeter*, III, 876.

688 DHC, Chanter 855/420.

689 DHC, Chanter 859/211-214.

690 DHC, Chanter 864/422.

691 DHC, CC20B/40; Chanter 865/78-82.

692 DHC, ECA/EQS/OB61/196-7; Harte, Schopp & Tapley-Soper (eds), *The Description of the City of Exeter*, III, 947.

693 DHC, Chanter 855/389; Christie, *Church Reves*, 93; Chanter 859/48.

694 DHC, Chanter 854B/II/41-2 & 273; DHC, CC17/255.

695 DHC, Chanter 864/70-75; "minion, n.1 and adj.". OED Online. June 2016. Oxford University Press. http://www.oed.com/view/ Entry/118859?rskey=EnfR19&result=1&isAdvanced=false (accessed July 25, 2016).

696 DHC, ECA/EQS/OB61/652-3.

697 DHC, Chanter 859, 370.

698 DHC, Chanter 860/358; Chanter 861/204; Chanter 862/60-63.

699 DHC, CC91/179; CC6B/128, in St Ives 'the word baggage doth in the common use of speaking signify . . . was or is a whore or a quean'; "baggage, n. and adj.". OED Online. June 2016. Oxford University Press. http://www.oed.com/view/Entry/14622?redirectedFrom=baggage (accessed July 25, 2016).

700 DHC, CC20B/127 & CC5/61; Chanter 867/408-9.

701 DHC, CC15/87, Chanter 862/396, Chanter 867/560, CC4B/11, CC4B/128, CC24/140, CC23/236, Chanter 864/69 & Chanter 867/14-19.

702 DHC, CC86.

703 DHC, CC5/295.

704 DHC, CC20B/24; "trull, n.". OED Online. June 2016. Oxford University Press. http://www.oed.com/view/Entry/206916?redirectedFrom=trull (accessed July 25, 2016).

705 DHC, Chanter 864/21-4 & ECA/EQS/OB61/263.

706 DHC, CC91/157; Chanter 867/870-1; Chanter 864/332-4; Chanter 861/362 & 371; "light, adj.1". OED Online. June 2016. Oxford

University Press. http://www.oed.com/view/Entry/108174?rskey=V8pATW&result=3&isAdvanced=false (accessed August 08, 2016).

707 Richard Barber (ed.), *Fuller's Worthies* (1987 edn), 108-109. See S. Bhanji, 'The Gubbings: Fact, Fiction and the Parish Registers', *The Devon Historian*, 54 (April 1997), 10-15; "strumpet, n.". OED Online. June 2016. Oxford University Press. http://www.oed.com/view/Entry/191949?rskey=NhNzrk&result=1&isAdvanced=false (accessed July 25, 2016).

708 DHC, CC16/47, CC17/173 & 245.

709 Gray, *Chronicle of Exeter*, 77-8.

710 DHC, Chanter 862/291.

711 DHC, ECA/EQS/OB61/50.

712 George Whetstone, *The Rocke of Regard* (1576); "minx, n.". OED Online. June 2016. Oxford University Press. http://www.oed.com/view/Entry/119017?rskey=naYjJq&result=1&isAdvanced=false (accessed July 25, 2016).

713 DHC, CC4A/89.

714 DHC, Chanter 866/93-107.

715 DHC, ECA/EQS/OB62/22.

716 William Shakespeare, *All's Well That Ends Well*, II.ii.21.

717 Thomas Lodge, *Wits Miserie* (1596); "punk, n.1 and adj.2". OED Online. June 2016. Oxford University Press. http://www.oed.com/view/Entry/154685?rskey=peBCxR&result=1&isAdvanced=false (accessed July 25, 2016).

718 W. Chappell (ed.), *The Roxburghe Ballads* (Hertford, 1869), I, 150; DHC, CC19B/79.

719 DHC, CC19B/204.

720 DHC, ECA/EQS/OB62/108 & OB61/343.

721 "mare, n.1". OED Online. June 2016. Oxford University Press. http://www.oed.com/view/Entry/113992?rskey=Bs16NT&result=1&isAdvanced=false (accessed July 25, 2016); DHC, CC20/55.

722 DHC, ECA/EQS/OB61/372.

723 DHC, CC5/403 & CC16/46.

724 DHC, CC22/75; CC5/499.

725 DHC, CC24/222.

726 DHC, CC6/380 & 382.

727 DHC, Chanter 861/274.

728 DHC, Chanter 867/712.

729 Chappell, *Roxburghe*, II, 186; "slut, n.". OED Online. June 2016. Oxford University Press. http://www.oed.com/view/Entry/182346?rskey=

iP6BFI&result=1&isAdvanced=false (accessed July 25, 2016); DHC, Chanter 866/45-9; Grose, *A Classical Dictionary*, no page number.
730 DHC, CC5/54.
731 DHC, CC25/126; CC6/175; Chanter 866/598.
732 DHC, CC6/129.
733 DHC, CC5/219.
734 DHC, CC6/133.
735 Gray, *Household Accounts*, I, xxi.
736 DHC, CC180, Chanter 855B/115-117, 162-3, 188 & CC180.
737 Another instance was in Exeter in about 1620 when a woman was called a curtal whore: DHC, ECA/EQS/OB61/356-8; John Bale, *A Mysterye of Inquyte* (Geneva, 1545). This is earlier than the examples cited by the *Oxford English Dictionary*.
738 DHC, Chanter 862/189.
739 DHC, Chanter 861/204.
740 DHC, CC6B/168.
741 DHC, Chanter 864/305.
742 Anon., *A, C, mery talys* (1526); "drab, n.1". OED Online. June 2016. Oxford University Press. http://www.oed.com/view/Entry/57356?rskey=NhnOGQ&result=1&isAdvanced=false (accessed July 25, 2016).
743 DHC, Chanter 856/99.
744 DHC, Chanter 862/60-63; Chanter 855A/92; Chanter 857/513-514.
745 DHC, Chanter 859/37; Chanter 862/396; Chanter 867/623-5.
746 DHC, Chanter 855/505 & 68; Christie, *Church Reves*, 48; DHC, Chanter 855A/340
747 DHC, CC86.
748 DHC, Chanter 857/35.
749 Geoffrey Chaucer, *Whan that Apprill with his shouris sote and the droughte of marche hath pcid be rote* (London, 1477).
750 DHC, Chanter 866/108-109.
751 DHC, CC152, CC5/46, CC6/256 & CC6A/177, Chanter 867/366, CC19A/49, CC23/179, CC17/66 & CC23/303, CC4/104, CC24/70, CC6/236, Chanter 867/551-2.
752 DHC, Chanter 855A/480.
753 Dominicus Mancinus, *Here begynneth a right frutefull treatyse* (London, 1518). There are other early examples: "quean, n.". OED Online. June 2016. Oxford University Press. http://www.oed.com/view/Entry/156192?redirectedFrom=quean (accessed July 25, 2016).
754 DHC, CC20/21.
755 DHC, CC170; Chappell, *Roxburghe*, III, 272.

756 DHC, CC17/255.
757 DHC, CC19B/232.
758 DHC, CC6/171 & Chanter 866/126-8.
759 DHC, CC22/1, CC88, CC17/151, CC23/264, Chanter 866/317-318, CC6B/174 & CC3/11; "hackney, n. and adj.". OED Online. June 2016. Oxford University Press. http://www.oed.com/view/Entry/83066?rskey=M3S2CL&result=1&isAdvanced=false (accessed July 25, 2016).
760 DHC, Chanter 867/700-702; DHC, CC15/215 & 78.
761 "bitch, n.1". OED Online. June 2016. Oxford University Press. http://www.oed.com/view/Entry/19524?rskey=jrEHft&result=1&isAdvanced=false (accessed July 25, 2016); DHC, Chanter 866/525-6.
762 DHC, CC20A/152.
763 DHC, Chanter 866/471 & CC6/222.
764 DHC, CC19B/164.
765 DHC, CC179A/III/69-71 & CC19B/75.
766 William Tyndale, *The obedience of a Christen man* (London, 1528); DHC, CC20/55 & Chanter 867/556.
767 DHC, Chanter 867/170-2 & Chanter 864/309.
768 DHC, Chanter 856/199; CC20/91; CC23/112; C5/166.
769 DHC, CC25/141.
770 DHC, CC7/88, Chanter 867/957, CC23/237, CC6/180.
771 DHC, Chanter 866/22-8; Grose, *A Classical Dictionary*, no page number.
772 DHC, CC19A/151.
773 DHC, CC5/414.
774 DHC, Chanter 867/534.
775 DHC, CC17/176; CC16/12; CC24/93.
776 DHC, CC16/5, CC5/403 & CC21/59; Grose, *A Classical Dictionary*, no page number.
777 DHC, Chanter 855A/344 & CC5/188, Chanter 855/301.
778 DHC, Chanter 866/1 & 409.
779 DHC, CC4A/84.
780 DHC, CC24/19; Gamini Salgado, The *Elizabethan Underworld* (1977), 55; DHC, CC19A/73; Chanter 865/74.
781 DHC, CC17/130.
782 DHC, Chanter 855A/344 & Chanter 855/339-41.
783 DHC, CC7/88; Chanter 857/473; CC6/287. "muddy, adj. and n.2". OED Online. June 2016. Oxford University Press. http://www.oed.com/view/Entry/123257?rskey=9Qebyb&result=3&isAdvanced=false (accessed August 22, 2016).
784 DHC, CC20/66; Chanter 857/473.

785 *An Exmoor Scolding*, 41.

786 DHC, ECA/EQS/OB61/196-7.

787 DHC, Chanter 866/240-2 & Chanter 867/472 & 673-4.

788 DHC, Chanter 867/452; CC25/77; Chanter 864/332-34; Chanter 862/228.

789 DHC, CC5/219; Chanter 864/117; CC23/46.

790 DHC, CC3; CC5/251.

791 DHC, CC4B/105, CC5/98, CC5/166, CC3/16, CC6/114.

792 DHC, CC19/35, CC5/160.

793 DHC, CC20B/163, CC6/207, CC23/98.

794 DHC, Chanter 866/190-2, CC6/97 & 323, CC20B/126, Chanter 855B/385-6, Chanter 867/427.

795 DHC, CC6/284.

796 DHC, CC6B/166.

797 DHC, Chanter 855/63 & 338, CC25/76, Chanter 859/312 & 315.

798 Gray, *The Lost Chronicle of Barnstaple*, 35.

799 John Bowring, 'Language, with special reference to the Devonian dialects', *Report and Transactions of the Devonshire Association*, Vol. 2, (1866), 28.

INDEX OF PERSONAL AND PLACE NAMES

Index of personal and place names, illustrations noted in **bold**

234